Anonymous

The Bristol Warren and Barrington Rhode Island

Anonymous

The Bristol Warren and Barrington Rhode Island

ISBN/EAN: 9783337380403

Printed in Europe, USA, Canada, Australia, Japan

Cover: Foto ©ninafisch / pixelio.de

More available books at **www.hansebooks.com**

PHOENIX MUTUAL LIFE INSURANCE CO.
WARREN Life Insurance. Albert E. Leach PROVIDENCE

Henry W. Cooke Co

—— ESTATE AGENTS ——

City and Country Property
Mortgages. Insurance

Hospital Trust Building, . . Providence, R. I.

EDWARD L. WATSON   E. M. MACDOUGALL

INSURANCE

Fire, Marine, Accident, Burglary,
Plate Glass and Liability
Reliable Mutual & Stock Companies

E. L. WATSON & CO.

ROOM 205

49 Westminster Street,   Providence, R. I.

Industrial Trust Co.

49 WESTMINSTER STREET
PROVIDENCE, R. I.

Largest Bank in Rhode Island

BRANCHES IN
Pawtucket, Newport, Woonsocket, Bristol, Wickford, Pas[coag],
Westerly and Warren

CAPITAL	. . .	$3,000,000.00
SURPLUS	. . .	$4,000,000.00

BANKING DEPARTMENT. Interest paid on deposits. Issues Certificates of Deposit at attractive rates. Loans and Discounts. Collections made on all points on favorable terms.

FOREIGN EXCHANGE DEPARTMENT. Foreign Drafts and Letters of Credit available in all parts of the world. Cable Transfers.

TRUST DEPARTMENT. Authorized to accept Trusts. Is a Legal depositary for trust funds. Acts as Trustee, Executor, Administrator, Guardian, and as Registrar and Transfer Agent of Corporations.

Bowen Construction Co.
CHIMNEY BUILDERS AND ALL KINDS OF MASON WORK

A. E. Browning, President.   F. D. Simmons, Treasurer

LOOSE LEAF MANUFACTURING CO.
Quality Printers and Binders

Loose Leaf Forms and Devices

257 WEST EXCHANGE STREET, PROVIDENCE, R. I.

LEWIS B. WALDRON, President   JOHN R. MAGEE, Treasurer

THE WALDRON COMPANY
Steam and Gas Fitters
Plumbers - Tinsmiths

Steam Heaters, Stoves, Furnaces, Grates and Linings. Hardware and Kitchen Furnishings

Dealers in Automobile and Bicycle Accessories

49 Bradford St., Bristol, R. I.

Telephone No. 116-J   Telephone No 1.

MAUSOLEUMS

MONUMENTS

CROSSES

HEADSTONES

Kimball & Combe Co.
96 Westminster Street
PROVIDENCE, R. I.

GRANITE   Works at
MARBLE WESTERLY
BRONZE   RHODE ISLAND

OLDEST ESTABLISHED LAUNDRY IN PROVIDENCE

QUALITY
IN PROVIDENCE at 140 PINE STREET
Telephones: UNION { 4016 / 4017

SERVICE
In Warren, R. I. at Main and Church Streets
TELEPHONE - - - WARREN 44-W
In Bristol, R. I. at 491 Hope Street
TELEPHONE - - - BRISTOL 134-W

FREDERIC S. NOCK
Naval Architect and Yacht Builder

Yachts and Vessels

Of all kinds Designed and Built

High Speed Power Boats a Specialty

Storage in Building for Yachts up to 80 ft. long

STORAGE in Basin or on Shore

All Kinds of **Boat Repair Work**

MARINE RAILWAYS

Member of Society of Naval Architects and Marine Engineers

Telephones { Shop, 10-W / Residence, 35-R } East Greenwich, R. I.

BROWNELL & HINMAN

Plumbing, Heating, Tinsmithing
Electric Water Supply Systems

17 Lincoln Ave., Riverside, R. I.

TALBOT & HOPKINS
Licensed Electrical Contractors

Electric Wiring and Electrical Apparatus Installed. Special attention given to Repair Work and Wiring of Finished Houses and New Houses

44 CONSTITUTION STREET   -   BRISTOL, R. I.

Telephone 151-W or 158-Y

Store, 58 BRADFORD STREET

WORK TAKEN ANYWHERE IN NEW ENGLAND

Grading and Excavating　　　Cellars Made Water-Tight
Heavy Teaming, Artesian Wells　　Stone and Sand, all Kinds and Grades
Macadam Road Building.　Steam Rollers, Drills and Crushing Plants to Let

L. H. CALLAN
General Contractor

Concrete, Roofing, Asphalt and Granolithic Walks and Driveways

All Work Strictly First Class

237 Franklin Street,　　Tel. Con.　　BRISTOL, R. I.

F. A. Geisler
Florist

Cut Flowers of all Descriptions
Floral Designs
Orders Promptly Attended To

122 Mount Hope Avenue

BRISTOL,　　　　RHODE ISLAND

Herreshoff Manufacturing Co. Inc.
Yacht Builders
Bristol, R. I.

TELEPHONE 300

Cranston Worsted Mills
BRISTOL, R. I.
Manufacturers of

Mohair and Worsted Yarns

On Skeins, Spools, Dressers, Cones or Bobbins

We are the only manufacturers in the United States who make Fancy Yarns of Mohair and Worsted from the raw material to the finished product

Genapped Mohair and Worsted Yarns, Harness Twine, Etc.

Yarns Genapped and Dyed

CHAS. B. ROCKWELL, President and Treasurer

O'BANNON CORPORATION

Manufacturers of

COATED FABRICS

West Barrington,   Rhode Island

STAPLES COAL CO. OF RHODE ISLAND

J. W. MARTIN, President

Anthracite and Bituminous
COAL

BRISTOL, R. I.   Tel.   **WARREN, R. I.**

NATIONAL
INDIA RUBBER COMPANY

KEDS

PARACORE

HERE WE MANUFACTURE KEDS
A NEW SHOE WITH A NEW CHARM
CANVAS RUBBER SOLED
ALSO WIRE OF HIGH QUALITY
FOR ALL ELECTRICAL PURPOSES

PARACORE
RUBBER COVERED

WEATHER PROOF
LEAD ENCASED
LAMP CORDS

BRISTOL   RHODE ISLAND

SAMUEL P. COLT, President
GEORGE SCHLOSSER, Vice President
MAURICE C. SMITH, Jr., Secretary-Treasurer

Warren Manufacturing Company

JOSEPH HUTCHESON, President
A. W. DIMICK, Treasurer
C. T. THOMPSON, Agent
H. J. GOURLEY, Superintendent

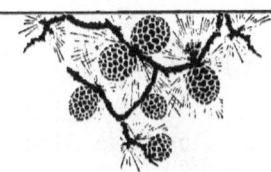

SATEENS, TWILLS
PLAIN AND FANCY GOODS
COMBED AND CARDED YARNS

Office and Mill,   Warren, R. I.

Capital	Surplus Earnings
$500,000.00	$250,000.00

THE MECHANICS NATIONAL BANK

34 Dorrance Street

Opposite City Hall and Railroad Station

Interest Paid on Checking Accounts

Certificates of Deposit issued at attractive rates

We have a Savings Department in which deposits made on or before the fifteenth day of January, April, July and October will draw interest from the first of said months. Dividends not paid on balance of less than $100.00.

We Respectfully Solicit Your Banking Business

CHARLES C. HARRINGTON,	H. EDWARD THURSTON,
PRESIDENT	CASHIER
ROWLAND G. HAZARD,	EDWARD A. HAVENS,
VICE-PRESIDENT	ASSISTANT CASHIER

PROVIDENCE, R. I.

Citizen's Savings Bank

846 Westminster Street

President - - JAMES B. PAINE
Vice President - ARTHUR E. AUSTIN
Vice President - CHARLES F. IRONS

TRUSTEES

JAMES B. PAINE	CHARLES W. BUBIER
ARTHUR E. AUSTIN	EDWIN O. CHASE
CHARLES F. IRONS	ARTHUR O. OSTBY
CHARLES C. DARLING	ARTHUR L. PECK
ARTHUR B. HATHAWAY	WILLIAM WILLIAMS
ARTHUR S. VAUGHN	

BOARD OF INVESTMENT

JAMES B. PAINE	EDWIN O. CHASE
ARTHUR E. AUSTIN	ARTHUR O. OSTBY
ELIJAH ALLEN	ARTHUR L. PECK
ARTHUR B. HATHAWAY	WILLIAM WILLIAMS
CHARLES W. BUBIER	ARTHUR S. VAUGHN

E. ALLEN, Treasurer

Providence Boiler Co.

F. T. SAXE, Proprietor

Builders of

BOILERS, TANKS, SMOKESTACKS

GENERAL PLATE IRON WORK

Boiler and General Repairs a Specialty

NEW AND SECOND HAND BOILERS
IN STOCK
MARINE AND STATIONARY

PLATE METAL WORK

For Breweries, Sugarhouses, Etc. Etc.

REPAIR ON IRON SHI

Telephone Union 2161-W.   Nights and Sundays, Telephone Union 2161-J

Cor. Dyer and Ship Streets

WHEATON'S EXPRESS, Riverside, R. I.
Anything-Anywhere-Anytime
H. E. WHEATON   Telephone East Providence 813-R

Grain, Feed, Fertilizers
POULTRY and ANIMAL REMEDIES

Long Distance Furniture Moving   Cushion Seats for Parties

HAWKINS LUMBER COMPANY

Everything in Wood

From

Sills to Shingles

Neponset Roofing and Shingles

RIVERSIDE - RHODE ISLAND

DYER TRANSPORTATION LINE

FREIGHT SERVICE
Between
Providence, Bristol and
Fall River
DOCK FOOT OF STATE STREET
Bristol

E. M. BOYCE, General Manager

RIVERSIDE WET WASH LAUNDRY

Charles K. Stewart, Proprietor

FIRST CLASS WORK
PROMPT ATTENTION

Telephone E. Prov. 963-W

16 First Street,   East Providence, R. I.

BROWN'S MOTOR EXPRESS

W. F. Brown, Proprietor

Trucking and Furniture Moving

Personal Attention   Long or Short Distance Work   Any Time Any where

Telephone Gaspee 279

65 Broad St., Providence, R. I.

Edward E. Arnold, Pres.   Henry A. Hoffman, Treas.   Wm. H. Hayward, Sec.

Established 1815

ARNOLD, HOFFMAN & CO. Inc.

Importers, Jobbers and Manufacturers of

Indigo, Dye Stuffs, Chemicals

PROVIDENCE, NEW YORK, BOSTON AND PHILADELPHIA

ALWAYS SATISFACTORY

PAINTS

Manufactured by

OLIVER JOHNSON & CO., INC.
PROVIDENCE, R. I.

PEOPLES SAVINGS BANK

IN PROVIDENCE

INCORPORATED 1851   SIXTY-SEVENTH YEAR

HOME OFFICE:

27 Market Square, Providence

Deposits Over $12,400,000.00

Protected by Securities of Market Value Exceeding $13,400,000.00

Money deposited on or before the 15th of any month draws interest from the 1st

---

WILLIS S. PINO

SEEDS

41 and 43 Washington Street
Providence, R. I.

FREDERICK L. PIERCE
GENERAL CONTRACTOR AND BUILDER

Office, 74 Weybosset Street

Telephone { Union 2781-W / Angell 1213-R

PROVIDENCE - R. I.

TITLE GUARANTEE COMPANY
Of Rhode Island
66 South Main St., Providence, R. I.

Examines and Insures Titles to Real Estate anywhere in Rhode Island

If you buy land or take mortgages on land you should insist on our Title Policy. It is the cheapest and most important form of insurance.

"The Laundry That Satisfies"
307 Broad Street, Providence, R. I.

B. B. READ, President   B. S. C. GIFFORD, Treasurer

ALLEN, SLADE & CO., Inc.
Wholesale Grocers
Tea and Coffee Importers. Coffee Roasters

Spice Grinders

18-30 Third St., Fall River, Mass.

SAM-O-SET LAUNDRY, Inc.

OUT DOOR DRYING
SHIRTS, COLLARS, CUFFS, BLOUSES

Telephone Angell 612

9 Pleasant St., Providence, R. I.

PUGH BROTHERS COMPANY
High Grade Automobiles
Distributers of the World's Most Popular Motor Cars,
Willys-Knight and Overlands

Don't fail to look over our used car bargains. We carry the largest assortment of used cars in New England.

49-53 Mathewson St., Providence, R. I.
Established 1894.   Tel. Union 7420—7421—7422

Fall River Branch, 532 South Main Street, Fall River, Mass.

LISABELLE'S COLLECTION AGENCY

Established 1890 by T. Lisabelle

Prompt and Persistent Attention to all Collections. Collections made in all parts of the world. Collections for Non-Residents a Specialty

76 Dorrance Street, Providence, R. I.
Union 4771-R
Branch Office, 36 Olneyville Square.   West 72-R

Rocco M. Famiglietti Co.
GENERAL CONTRACTORS

Licensed Drain Layer.   Personal Attention Given to All Work

Office, 539 Charles Street
PROVIDENCE, R. I.

Residence, 367 Branch Avenue   Telephone Connection

A. A. WHITE CO.
Rubber Stamps, Stencils, Seals
Of Every Description

BADGES, PLATES, CHECKS, NUMBERING MACHINES, ETC.

114 Westminster Street,   Providence, Rhode Island

Telephone Union 2253-W

WALTER B. CLARK
PICTURE FRAME MAKER AND GILDER
Mirrors, Carved Frames, Etc.
131 Washington Street, Providence, R. I.

TOPS, DUST AND SLIP COVERS
Also anything in Leather, Fabrics and Celluloid-Glass for Automobiles
Exclusive Agents for **U-SAV-YOUR**
Automobile, Piano, Furniture—Cleaner, Polish and Varnish Preservative
Guaranteed to satisfy or refund price paid.   By Mail 60c. prepaid

WEBSTER & CO.
270 Pearl St.   Phone U 3470-W   Providence, R. I.

Albert M. Vance Co.
PRINTERS
30 Warren Avenue, East Providence, R. I.
Phone 1008-R

The National Detective Agency
BERNARD M. GOLDOWSKY, Principal and General Manager
In Providence since 1901   Branch, 11 Clinton St., Newark, N. J.
Telephone Union 5550; Union 3924; Broad 1205; Broad 2682

Executive Offices, Industrial Trust Co. Building, Providence, R. I.

CARL W. BERNSTROM, 13 Chestnut Ave., Auburn, R. I. Telephone Broad 4502-W
EMIL BERNSTROM, Worcester, Mass.   **UNDERTAKERS**
BERNS COMPANY
BENJ. J. BERNSTROM, Manager.   Undertaker since 1888.   Tel. Union 5979-R
Notary Public.   Wills, Deeds, Mortgages Drawn and Legalized
301 Pearl Street, Providence, R. I.   (Between Broad and Pond Streets)

All public spirited business men should be represented in this their Local Directory

Grand View Farm

Best place in Rhode Island for Rest and Recreation
Beautiful Scenery.   Seashore and Country combined.
Fresh Vegetables, Milk, Eggs and Poultry.
FIRST CLASS BOARD.   REASONABLE RATES

Write for Further Particulars

C. H. Aldrich, Proprietor

NORTHUP BROS.

ICE CREAM and CONFECTIONERY

Light Lunches Served

539 Hope Street, Bristol, R. I.

The Bristol Phoenix

Established 1837.   J. F. FARRALLY, Editor and Manager

Published
Tuesday AND Friday Afternoons

FARRALLY BROS., Publishers.   Tel. Four Four Bristol

❦ ❦ ❦ ❦ ❦

The Phoenix is a Live Local Paper Read by Bristolians at Home and Abroad

❦ ❦ ❦ ❦ ❦

⇥ Semi-Weekly $2.00 a Year ⇤

❦ ❦ ❦ ❦ ❦

THE PHOENIX goes into more than 1000 homes of Bristol and enjoys a prestige and popularity peculiarly its own

FOR THAT REASON

Advertising in the Phoenix Brings Results

The Rates are Reasonable

FINE JOB PRINTING AT REASONABLE PRICES

Take a Trial Trip

547 HOPE STREET, BRISTOL, R. I.

HOTEL BELVEDERE

H. P. MORRISSEY, Prop.

European Plan

FIRST CLASS IN EVERY DEPARTMENT

Hope Street, Opp. Post Office

Telephone 20210   BRISTOL, R. I.

WILLIAM M. CONNERY
Clothing, Furnishings and Hats

491 HOPE STREET,   BRISTOL, R. I.

TELEPHONE CONNECTION

SAMUEL KINDER & BROTHER
Florists and Gardeners

317 HOPE STREET   Telephone Connection   BRISTOL, R. I.

ARTHUR DES LAURIER, Mgr.   Telephone 1041-R
233-J

THE FRANKLIN STREET GARAGE COMPANY

THAMES STREET, OPP. FRANKLIN ST. DEPOT

DEALERS IN

AUTOMOBILES AND SUPPLIES

Automobiles To Let by Day, Hour or Trip
Repairing, Renting and Tire Vulcanizing

BRISTOL, - R. I.

LUIGI MALAFRONTE
176 Bradford Street
Emigration Agent & Notary Public
Real Estate.   Fire Insurance

Telephone Connection

Residence, 270 Wood St., Bristol, R. I.

HAROLD G. SHERMAN, Ph. G.
Registered Pharmacist
Cameras and Supplies
Prescriptions Accurately Filled
399 WOOD ST., BRISTOL, R. I.

PIMENTEL & SOUSA
Dealers in
⟫ CHOICE MEATS ⟪
217 Wood Street,   Bristol, R. I.

PETER GIUSTIANY
Dealer in
Meats, Groceries, Fruits and Provisions, Etc.
Bills Payable Weekly.   Telephone 142-M Bristol, R. I.
247 Thames St., Bristol, R. I.

J. ROSA FURTADO
Fine Groceries
229 STATE STREET, BRISTOL, R. I.

A. C. PANZARELLA
Dealer in
BOOTS AND SHOES, DRY GOODS, LADIES' AND GENTS' FURNISHINGS
401 Wood Street,   Bristol, Rhode Island

LUSO-AMERICAN
Grocery and Meat Market
157 Bradford Street   -   Bristol, R. I.

Antony J. Sousa, Proprietor.   Telephone Connection

WILLIAM H. BELL
— DEALER IN —
FURNITURE, CARPETS AND CROCKERY
Nos. 361-365 HOPE STREET
Telephone 73　　　　　　　　　　　BRISTOL, R. I.

BUFFINGTON PHARMACY
Agent for WHITMAN'S Green Seal and Belle Mead Sweets
Best Soda in Town.　Prescriptions Carefully Compounded
458 HOPE STREET, BRISTOL, R. I.

J. H. YOUNG & CO.
Prescription Pharmacists
479 HOPE STREET, BRISTOL, R. I.

HENRY M. DARLING
Newsdealer
CONFECTIONERY, TOYS, POST CARDS, POPULAR MUSIC, COLUMBIA RECORDS AND GRAPHOPHONES, CIRCULATING LIBRARY, PERIODICALS, STATIONERY, TOBACCO, CIGARS, ALL THE SUNDAY PAPERS.
CENTURY EDITION 10 CENT MUSIC AND McKINLEY 10 CENT MUSIC A SPECIALTY

444 Hope Street, Y. M. C. A. Block, Bristol, R. I.

A WELL SELECTED STOCK OF
Jewelry, Cut Glass, Fine China, Colonial Mirrors, Souvenirs,
and NOVELTIES Carried in Stock at All Times
REGISTERED OPTOMETRIST.　　Lenses Furnished on Short Notice
EDWARD D. KUNZ, Jeweler AND Optician
Cor. of STATE and HOPE Sts., BRISTOL, R. I.

Telephone Bristol 20202　　　　　　　Rate $1.00 per day and upwards
Bristol Hotel
JAMES F. McLAUGHLIN, Prop.
——American and European Plan——
24 STATE ST.,　　　BRISTOL, R. I.

"DINE WITH ME"
George Brown
HOME LUNCH ROOM AND RESTAURANT
Pure Food——Quick Service
5 Bradford St., near Thames St., Bristol, R. I.

GOFF'S MARKET
ADA M. GOFF, Prop.
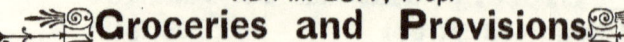
Groceries and Provisions
Cor. High St. and Lincoln Ave., Bristol, R. I.

WILLIAM W. PERRY, CIVIL ENGINEER AND SURVEYOR

THE PERRY COMPANY
Storage Warehouse
COMMISSARY AND SUPPLY COMPANY
WIRE FENCES

W. W. Perry, Manager. Tel. Con. BRISTOL, R. I.

RICHARD S. STUART
Blacksmith & Horse Shoer
OYSTER DREDGES MADE AND REPAIRED

Steamboat Wharf, Foot of State Street - Bristol, R. I.

SPENCER ROUNDS
Carpenter and Builder
Also Building Mover
60 Constitution St. (Residence 17 Pierce Ave.) BRISTOL, R. I.

PELEG CARD   **PELEG CARD & SON**   HARRY E. CARD
Masons, Contractors and Builders
10 Washington St., Bristol, R. I.

JOSEPH A. DAGENAIS
Blacksmith, Wheelwright and Horse Shoeing
Also Machine Forging and General Jobbing. Wagons Made and Repaired

Rear 281 Thames Street   BRISTOL, R. I.

O. L. WOOD
Hack, Boarding and Livery Stable
Also Expressing
23 Court St., - Bristol, R. I.
Telephone 20-W

CENTRAL GARAGE
James T. Haines, Proprietor
REPAIRS AND SUPPLIES
41 State Street,   Telephone 20-R   Bristol, R. I.

E. F. TORREY
Automobile, Carriage and House Painting
1039 Hope St.   Tel. Con.   Bristol, R. I.

LET US QUOTE YOU PRICES
ON
YOUR NEXT JOB OF PRINTING

HATEVER THE JOB MAY BE, WE THE TOTALLY DIFFERENT PRINTERS CAN DO IT. WE ARE EQUIPPED TO GET OUT AT SHORT NOTICE, ORDERS, NO MATTER HOW LARGE OR SMALL ∴ ∴ ∴ ∴ ∴ ∴ ∴ WE SPECIALIZE ON JOBS WHICH CALL FOR SPECIAL RULING, PUNCHING, PERFORATING, NUMBERING, DUPLICATE SHEETS, BLOCKING ∴ ∴ ∴ ∴ ∴ ∴ WE FURNISH ORIGINAL DESIGNS IN BILL HEADS, LETTER HEADS, STATEMENTS, NOTE HEADS, ENVELOPES, BUSINESS CARDS ∴ ∴ WE CAN FURNISH CLASSY POSTERS, TICKETS, DANCE ORDERS, PROGRAMS, MENUS ∴ ∴ ∴ ∴ ∴ ∴ ∴ ∴ ∴

Warren Printing & Publishing Company
Publishers of the "GAZETTE", State Street, Warren

C. R. BLACKMAR, Jr.
Electrical Contractor
All Kinds of Electrical Construction And Repairs Promptly Executed

Agent for Westinghouse Lamps

2 Church Street,   Warren, R. I.

George M. Wilbur
EMBALMER AND FUNERAL DIRECTOR
And Dealer in
BURIAL CASKETS and FUNERAL SUPPLIES

WARREN   RIVERSIDE   BRISTOL
209 South Main St.   38 Union Street

Telephone Connections

E. M. MARTIN LUMBER CO.

LUMBER
and
BUILDERS' MATERIALS
and
INSURANCE

Telephone 133

Church Street, - Warren, R. I.

C. H. SEYMOUR & CO.

C. H. SEYMOUR

Plumbing, Steam and Gas Fitting

Tin Plate, Sheet Iron and Copper Workers

Sewerage & Construction Work

Telephone 158-J

Main Street, - Warren, R. I.

GEORGE E. SHERMAN

Child Street Nursery

TREES, SHRUBS, EVERGREEN
and CALIFORNIA PRIVET

Ornamental and Fruit Trees

WARREN, R. I.

George R. Cole
DEALER IN

GROCERIES, MEATS AND FISH. PROVISIONS OF ALL KINDS

Terms Strictly Cash

BAKER STREET, WARREN, R. I.

George R. Cole
Garage.   **Ford Service**

BAKER STREET, WARREN, R. I.

OSCAR ROBERTS
Registered Pharmacist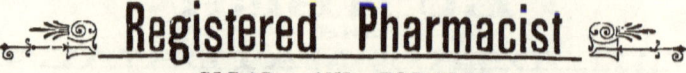
CIGAR AND TOBACCO
Prescription Work a Specialty
Telephone 20203

46 North Main Street, Warren, R. I.

ARTHUR J. MAKER
Optometrist & Jeweler
Watch and Clock Dealer and Repairer
163 SOUTH MAIN STREET,   -   WARREN, R. I.

WILFRED A. MONAST
BUILDING and JOBBING

Special Attention to
GRAVEL ROOFING
Telephone
193-X WARREN

63 Metacom Ave., Warren, R. I.

POTTER, COLLAMORE & CO., MACHINE SHOP
Automobiles and Power Boats Repaired. Model an Special Machinery Built to Order.   Lawn Mowers Sharpened
General Jobbing at Short Notice.   Automobilists Stop and Get Tires Inflated
Cor. of WHEATON and WATER Sts., WARREN, R. I.   Tel. 126-R

CHARLES ESTES
Land Surveyor and Civil Engineer
SEWERS AND DRAINS. All Field Notes of James S. Mason, C. E., of Warren, may be seen at this office. Also Field Notes of the whole town of Barrington, made in 1866
Telephone Connection   WARREN, RHODE ISLAND

FREDERICK I. JOHNSON
Licensed Electrical Contractor
Electric Wiring and Electrical Apparatus Installed.
Special Attention given to Repair Work and Wiring of Finished Houses
Tel. Con.   Office at Residence, 7 LYNDON ST., WARREN, R. I.

Standard Pharmacy

M. W. SAUGY, Proprietor

Corner Main and Miller Sts.,   Warren, R. I.

Charles C. Bliss
NEWSDEALER, STATIONERY AND POST CARDS
CONFECTIONERY and TOBACCO

GOFF'S BLOCK   Phone Connection   **WARREN, R. I.**

THE SANITARY MARKET and HOME BAKERY
J. H. MERCIER, Proprietor

Where you get More for Less

Cor. Main and Liberty Sts.,   Warren, R. I.

GO TO

HUGH HAWTHORNE
For the BEST GROCERIES at the LOWEST PRICES in Town
(Next Door to the Town Hall)

174 SOUTH MAIN ST., WARREN, R. I.

CHARLES DIONNE
Dealer in

Groceries, Meats and Provisions

140 CHILD ST.,   WARREN, R. I.

Louis F. Barker
CUT FLOWERS    FLORIST   FLORAL DESIGNS

Telephone Connection.   EAST WARREN, R. I.

JOHN M. SOCHA
Meats and Groceries
86 North Water Street, Warren, R. I.

MANUEL P. ROSA
Grocery   (Telephone Connection)   Market

CUNARD AMD FABRE STEAMSHIP AGENT

129 Child St., East Warren, R. I.

The Gables

Barrington, Rhode Island

Summer and Winter Home

Boating, Fishing, Beautiful Drives

For full information, Call, Write or Telephone

Telephone
Warren 202-13 M

THE GABLES
Post Office Box 42

L. P. BOSWORTH
DEALER IN

COAL	GRAIN	GROCERIES	PAINTS
WOOD	HAY	FLOUR	OILS
LUMBER	STRAW	FEED	ETC.

Masons' Materials

Broad Street, at R. R. Crossing

Telephone **BARRINGTON, R. I.**

Bay Spring Public Market
GROCERIES, MEATS and GENERAL MERCHANDISE
Cor. Bay Spring and Narragansett Aves., West Barrington, R. I.

M. A. PALMIERI, Prop.   Tel. Con.

MAYOTT & OGDEN
MEATS, GROCERIES and PROVISIONS

Bay Spring, West Barrington.   Tel. Warren 20206-M

JAMES F. GRANT
Barrington,   Rhode Island

Periodicals, Newspapers, Confectionery,
Cigars, Tobacco, Gasoline, Tires

WILLIAM H. ADAMS & SON
General Teaming
Stone, Gravel, Sand, Loam, Wood, Roofing, Lime, Hair, Cement, Sewer Pipe, Brick, Etc.

All Orders Given Prompt Attention

TELEPHONE CONNECTION

WEST BARRINGTON   -   -   **R. I.**

THOMAS A. LORD
Contractor and Builder
WEST BARRINGTON, R. I.

T. F. BOURASSA
Tin and Sheet Metal Work
Plumbing and Furnace Work, Cleaning and Repairing, Gutter and Pump Work, General Jobbing

West Barrington.   Rhode Island

GEORGE E. ALLEN CO.
Plumbing and Heating
FOURTH ST., Telephone   WEST BARRINGTON, R. I.

W. S. BENNETT & CO.
PRESCRIPTION DRUGGISTS
Cigars and Soda.   Confectionery

Cor. Joyce and Main Sts.,   Warren, R. I.

Support the Home
and the best way to do so, will be to learn Stenography and Office Work. Attend the CHILDS BUSINESS COLLEGE where Expert Teachers, Latest Methods and regular Office Equipment prepare you to become self supporting in the shortest time.

The Reason Why
most girls keep on the $9 level is because they have no $17 or $25 value for their employers.
Make yourself so efficient that you are WORTH $25.
Our methods and system will surely help you; and you can join either our Day or Night Classes.

You can begin your course any MONDAY
ENROLL NOW
THE CHILDS BUSINESS COLLEGE
290 Westminster Street, Providence, R. I.
"Over Woolworth's 5 & 10c. Store"

MANCHESTER & HUDSON CO.
DEALERS IN
Brick, Lime, Cement, Plaster

Portland Cement
White Cement
Sewer Pipe
Cistern Covers
Blue Stone

Well Pipe
Land Lime
Land Plaster
Lath Mortar
Plaster Board

55 POINT STREET, PROVIDENCE, R. I.

P. SKINNER Jr.
General Insurance Agent
Established 1868

Representing First Class Stock and Mutual Companies

259 Hope Street, Bristol, R. I.

THE BRISTOL WARREN AND BARRINGTON
RHODE ISLAND
DIRECTORY
1917-18

CONTAINING A
COMPLETE HOUSE, BUSINESS AND STREET
DIRECTORY FOR THE TOWNS OF BRISTOL, WARREN
AND BARRINGTON, ALSO TOWN GOVERN-
MENTS, POST OFFICES, CHURCHES, ETC.

PRICE $3.50

UNION PUBLISHING CO., PUBLISHERS
1013 Old South Bldg., Boston, Mass.

COPYRIGHT 1918, BY THE UNION PUBLISHING CO.

Warren Monumental Works
Cor. Railroad Avenue and Croade Street, Warren, R. I.

MISCELLANEOUS.

INDEX TO CONTENTS

Page

Advertisers:
  Bristol 31
  Warren 32
  Barrington 32
  Out-of-Town 33
Business Directory:
  Bristol County 207
  Out-of-Town 239
Cemeteries:
  Bristol 256
  Warren 259
  Barrington 260
Children's Home, Bristol 254
Churches:
  Bristol 254
  Warren 258
  Barrington 260
Fire Department, Warren 257
General Directory: Bristol 45
  Warren 109
  Barrington 175
Halls, Blocks and Buildings:
  Bristol 42
  Warren 43
Homes for Aged Men and Women, Bristol 254
Italian Names. Balance of names furnished subscribers later.
Libraries:
  George Hall Library, Warren 257
  Public Library, Barrington 260
  Rogers Free Library, Bristol 256
Newspapers:
  Bristol 254
  Warren 258
Post Offices 44
School, Barrington 260
Soldiers' Home, Bristol 254
Street Directory: Bristol 34
  Warren 37
  Barrington 40
Town Officers:
  Bristol 253
  Warren 256
  Barrington 259
Wharves:
  Bristol 43
  Warren 44
Woman's Exchange, Bristol 254

NATIONAL EXCHANGE BANK, 63 Westminster St., Providence
Stands First on "ROLL of HONOR" Among R. I. Banks. We respectfully ask for Your Account

MISCELLANEOUS. 31

INDEX TO BRISTOL ADVERTISERS.

Aldrich, Charles A.	16
Bell, William H.	20
Bristol Hotel	20
Bristol Phoenix (The)	17
Brown, George	20
Buffington, William H.	20
Callan, Col. L. H.	4
Card, Peleg & Son	21
Central Garage	21
Connery, William M.	18
Cranston Worsted Mills	5
Dagenais, Joseph A.	21
Darling, Henry M.	20
David, A.	opp. page 45
Farrally Bros.	17
Franklin Street Garage (The)	18
Furtado, J. Rosa	19
Geisler, Frederick A.	4
Giustiany, Peter	19
Goff's Market	20
Grand View House	16
Herreshoff Mfg. Co., Inc.	5
Hotel Belvedere	18
Industrial Trust Co.	front cover and insert between Bristol and Warren
Kinder, Samuel & Brother	18
Kunz, Edward D.	20
Luso-American	19
Malafronte Brothers	19
Malafronte, Luigi	19
National India Rubber Co.	6
Northup Bros.	16
Panzarella, A. C.	19
Perry Co. (The)	21
Perry, William W.	21
Pimentel & Sousa	19
Rounds, Spencer	21
Sherman, Harold G.	19
Skinner, P. Jr.	28
Staples Coal Co. of R. I.	5
Stuart, Richard S.	21

Merewether & Dunn
Plumbing and Heating Contractors
31 TURNER AVENUE, RIVERSIDE, R. I.

33 Canal St. — CHARLES J. JAGER CO. — Providence

ELECTRIC AND GASOLINE PUMPS AND PRESSURE SYSTEMS
We carry the largest stock of this kind in New England

MISCELLANEOUS.

Talbot & Hopkins	4
Torrey, E. F.	21
U. S. Rubber Co.	6
Waldron Co. (The)	2
Wardwell Lumber Co.	head lines
Wilbur, George M.	22
Wood, O. L.	21
Young, J. H. & Co.	20

INDEX TO WARREN ADVERTISERS.

Barker, Louis F.	25
Bennett, W. S. & Co.	27
Blackmar, C. R. Jr.	22
Bliss, Charles C.	25
Cole, George R.	23
Dionne, Charles	25
Estes, Charles	24
Hawthorne, Hugh	25
Industrial Trust Co.	front cover and insert between Bristol and Warren
Johnson, Frederick I.	24
Maker, Arthur J.	24
Martin, E. M. Lumber Co.	23
Mercier, J. H.	25
Monast, Wilfred A.	24
Potter, Collamore & Co.	24
Roberts, Oscar	24
Rosa, Manuel P.	25
Sanitary Market & Home Bakery	25
Seymour, C. H. & Co.	23
Sherman, George E.	23
Socha, John M.	25
Standard Pharmacy	25
Staples Coal Co. of R. I.	5
Warren and Barrington Gazette (The)	22
Warren Mfg. Co.	7
Warren Monumental Works	head lines
Warren Printing & Publishing Co.	22
Wilbur, George M.	22

INDEX TO BARRINGTON ADVERTISERS.

Adams, William H. & Son	27
Allen, George E. Co.	27
Bay Spring Public Market	26
Bosworth, L. P.	26
Bourassa, T. F.	27
Gables, The	26

LIVE WIRE collectors of BAD BILLS
"No Collection—No Charge"
WESTERN MERCANTILE CORPORATION
420-421 Grosvenor Building. Tel. Union 1526 Providence, R. I.

MISCELLANEOUS.	33

Grant, James F.	27
Lord, Thomas A.	27
Mayott & Ogden	26
O'Bannon Corporation	5

INDEX TO OUT-OF-TOWN ADVERTISERS.

Allen, Slade & Co., Inc.	13
Armington, Arthur A.	front cover
Arnold, Hoffman & Co., Inc.	12
Barrett Company (The)	back cover
Barrett, W. E. Co. (The)	opp. 77
Berns Co.	15
Blackstone Canal National Bank	foot lines
Bowen Construction Co. (The)	front cover
Brown, E. S. Co.	opp. 92
Brown's Motor Express.	11
Brownell & Hinman	page 4 and opp. 45
Butman & Tucker Co.	3
Childs Business College.	28
Citizens Savings Bank.	9
Clark, Walter B.	15
Cooke, Henry W. Co.	front cover
Dyer Transportation Line	11
Everett, C. J. Inc.	opp. 45
Famiglietti, Rocco M.	14
Goff, James C. Co.	head lines
Hawkins Lumber Co.	11
Hope Rubber Co.	insert opp. Barrington Dir.
Industrial Trust Co.	front cover and insert between Bristol and Warren
Jackson, Walter H. Co.	head lines
Jager, Charles J. Co.	head lines
Johnson, Oliver & Co., Inc.	12
Kimball & Combe Co.	2
Latham, Joseph A.	insert opp. Barrington Dir.
Leach, Albert E.	front cover
Lisabelle's Collecting Agency	14
Loose Leaf Manufacturing Co.	2
Louttit Home Hand Laundry.	13
Manchester & Hudson Co.	28
Mechanics National Bank of Providence (The)	8
Merewether & Dunn	foot lines
National Detective Agency (The)	15

R. I. RUG WORKS
Furniture Repaired and Repolished, Chairs Reseated
678 Westminster Street, Providence. Telephone Union 2202 and also Union 2204

WARDWELL LUMBER CO.
BRISTOL, R. I.

WINDOWS
WINDOW FRAMES
DOORS AND BLINDS
At Lowest Prices

MISCELLANEOUS.

National Exchange Bank..................head lines
Neilan Typewriter Exchange.................back cover
Nock, Frederic S....................................... 3
Penn Mutual Life Ins. Co......................opp. 44
Peoples Savings Bank in Providence................ 12
Pierce, Frederic L................................... 13
Pino, Willis S....................................... 12
Providence Boiler Co................................ 10
Providence Journal Co. (The)..................opp. 76
Pugh Brothers Co.................................... 14
Richards, John R.................opp. inside back cover
Riverside Hay & Grain Co............................ 10
Riverside Wet Wash Laundry.......................... 11
Rhode Island Rug Works.........................foot lines
Sam-O-Set Laundry, Inc.............................. 14
Title Guarantee Co. of R. I......................... 13
Vance, Albert M. Co................................. 15
Watrous, Ralph C. Co..........................head lines
Watson, E. L. & Co.............................front cover
Webster & Co.. 15
Western Mercantile Corp.......................head lines
What Cheer Laundry............................opp. 44
Wheaton's Express 10
White, A. A. Co..................................... 15
Ye Rose Studio................................opp. 93

BRISTOL STREET DIRECTORY.

Anthony av., from Woodlawn av. to Centre.
Arthur av., from Massasoit av., southerly to Spring av.
Asylum rd., from 1073 Hope, westerly to Colt's farm.

Bay View av., from 420 High, crossing Wood at 616, easterly to town line.
Beach rd., from Hope, westerly to R. R.
Beach Terrace, about 2 miles north Bristol, on R. R.
Borden av., continuation of Oliver from High easterly to 46 Munroe av.
Borden, from Reservoir av. to Centre.
Bourne av., from 149 Bradford, northerly.
Bourne, from 338 High to 507 Wood.
Bradford, from 326 Thames, easterly to Wood, opp. Rubber Works.
Bristol Highlands, about 2 miles north Bristol, on R. R.
Broad Common rd., from Metacom av., westerly and southerly to Gooding av.
Burnside, from 146 Hope to 64 High.

WALTER H. JACKSON CO. 435 Industrial Trust Building
PROVIDENCE, R. I.
"DELCO" ELECTRIC LIGHTING & PUMPING PLANTS
WINDMILLS, GASOLINE ENGINES AND TRACTORS

MISCELLANEOUS. 35

Burton, from 190 Hope, easterly to opp. 154 Wood.
Byfield, from 341 Hope to 201 High.

Catherine, from 252 Wood, easterly to 33 Prospect.
Central, north and south across 93 Bradford to Wardwell.
Centre, from Borden, northerly.
Charles, from 180 Wood, easterly.
Chestnut, from 1030 Hope, easterly to Metacom av.
Church, from 132 Thames to 289 Wood.
Church rd., from Hope to Bristol Highlands.
Coggeshall av., from 167 Franklin to Roma.
Cole, from 158 Wood, easterly.
Collins, from 154 Wood, easterly.
Congregational, from 282 High to 391 Wood.
Constitution, from 34 Thames, easterly to 247 Wood.
Cook, from 114 Constitution, southerly to 97 Union.
Cottage, from 118 High, easterly to 183 Wood.
Court, from 420 Hope to 235 High.

DeWolf av., from Mt. Hope av., southerly to Woodlawn av.
Dimond av., from 1051 Hope, westerly.
Doran av., from 119 Bay View av., northerly.
Dunbar av., from Garfield to Woodlawn av.

E street, from Collins, northerly across Cole to Catherine.
Easterbrooks av., from 241 State, northerly.
East State, from continuation of De Wolf av., easterly and westerly to Centre.

Fales av., from Hope near Bristol Highlands, westerly to R. R.
Ferry rd., from 1100 Hope, junc. of Wood, southerly to Bristol Ferry.
First, from 35 Mt. Hope av., northerly to 204 State.
Forest, from Highland, westerly to Bristol Highlands.
Fox Hill av., from 96 Mt. Hope av., southerly.
Franklin, from 460 Thames, opp. R. R. depot, easterly across Wood.

Garfield av., from 116 Wood, easterly.
Gibson rd., from 1218 Hope, westerly.
Gooding av., from Hope, near Warren line, easterly to Metacom av.
Gooding's lane, from opp. 182 Mt. Hope av., northerly.
Goulart av., from East State, near Gooding's lane, southerly.
Griswold av., from Ferry rd. to Metacom av.

WHITTEMORE & COLBURN
PRINTERS   15 Pine St., PROV.

King's Fibrous Plaster Board & Hard Plaster
JAMES C. GOFF CO.
81 to 49 Point St., Prov., R. I.

36   MISCELLANEOUS.

High, from Hope, beyond Walley, to 37 Washington.
Highland, from Gibson road, northerly, Bristol Highlands.
Hiland av., from Massasoit av., southerly to Spring av.
Hope, from Wood, junc. of Ferry rd., to Warren line.
Howe, from 68 Burton, southerly.

Jewett av., from 168 Mt. Hope av., southerly.
John, from 182 Thames to 417 Hope.
Jones, from Perry, northerly.
Juniper lane, from Chestnut, southerly to Sherry av.

Kickemuit av., from Metacom av., nr. Warren line, easterly.

Lincoln av., from 389 High, easterly to opp. 32 Munroe av.
Little's Narrows, from foot of Gooding av., near the shore.

Mason av., from 136 Mt. Hope av., southerly.
Metacom av., from Warren town line southerly to Griswold av.
Milk, from 48 Church, southerly across 30 Byfield.
Mt. Hope av., from opp. 289 Wood, easterly to Metacom av.
Munroe av., from 111 Franklin to 86 Washington.

Naoma, from Chestnut, northerly to Gooding.
Narragansett av., from 62 Court, southerly.
Noyes av., fom 48 Union to 29 Burton.

Oliver, from 562 Thames, easterly to opp. 46 Munroe av.
Orchard, from Borden, southerly to 136 Mt. Hope av.

Perry, from Wood, easterly and southerly to Juniper.
Pierce av., from 113 Constitution, northerly to 108 Church.
Plaza Plat, from foot of Church rd., about 1¾ miles north
    Bristol R. R. station.
Pleasant, from 234 Hope, easterly.
Poppasquash rd., from 843 Hope to Poppasquash Neck.
Prospect, from opp. 52 Mt. Hope av., southerly to 52 Catherine.

Reservoir av., from Borden, northerly.
Richmond, from 222 Wood, easterly.
Ridge rd., from Beach rd., northerly.
Rock, from 211 State, northerly to Shaw's lane.
Roma, from 593 Wood, easterly.
Russell av., from Massasoit av., southerly to Spring av.
Ryan av., from 229 State, northerly.

Sanitarium av., from Metacom av., above Bay View av.,
    easterly.
Second, from 49 Mt. Hope av., to 228 State.
Shaw's lane, from 410 Wood, easterly to Rock.
Sherry av., from 150 Bay View av. to Juniper av.

Ralph C. Watrous Co. FARMS and SUBURBAN PROPERTY For Sale
437 INDUSTRIAL TRUST BUILDING

MISCELLANEOUS.   37

Simmons, from 213 Mt. Hope av., northerly.
Smith, from 239 Hope, westerly to the water.
State, from 238 Thames to Third.
Summer, from 208 Hope, westerly.
Sunnyside av., from 1027 Hope, westerly.
Sunset av., from Church, northerly to Gibson rd., B. H.
Surf Drive, from Beach rd., northerly to the shore.

Thames, from the Ferry, northerly to Hope, opp. Washington.
Third, from 65 Mt. Hope av. to opp. 243 State.
Thompson av., from 103 Bay View av., northerly.

Union, from 224 Hope to opposite 200 Wood.
Usher, from 30 Mt. Hope av., southerly.
Usher av., from 574 Wood.
Usher Place, from 941 Hope, westerly to the railroad.

Varnum, from Perry, northerly.
Vernon av., from Massasoit av., southerly to Spring av.

Walley, from 132 Hope, bey. Burnside, easterly to Wood.
Walnut, changed to Gooding av.
Wardwell, from 544 Hope to Central.
Washington, from 754 Hope to Munroe av.
West, from Gooding, southerly to Centre.
Wheeler av., from Mt. Hope av., southerly.
William, from 160 High, easterly.
Wilson's lane, changed to Franklin.
Wood, from Hope, junc. Ferry rd., to 55 Bay View av.
Woodlawn av., from 102 Wood, to Metacom av.

WARREN STREET DIRECTORY.

Adams, from 36 Child, northerly to Market.
Arlington av., from Kickemuit rd., nr. Metacom av., southerly.
Asselin's Plat, from opp. 84 Market, southerly.
Asylum rd., from Child, bey. Kickemuit river, southerly to Town Asylum.
Avenue A, from Vernon, northerly.

Baker, from 125 South Main, westerly across South Water to the river.
Baltimore av., from Child, bey. Kickemuit river, northerly.
Barker av., from Child, opp. Pumping Station, southerly.
Barney, from 14 Wood to 20 Market.

Blackstone Canal Nat'l Bank | Established 1831
10 MARKET SQ. PROVIDENCE | STRONG AND CONSERVATIVE

WARREN MONUMENTAL WORKS
Cor. Railroad Avenue and Croade Streets, Warren, R. I.

MISCELLANEOUS.

Birch Swamp rd., from Kickemuit rd., north of Child to Swansea rd.
Bowen, from opp. 12 Union, across North Water to Westminster.
Bradford, from 343 South Main, westerly.
Bridge, from 303 South Main, to the water.
Broad, from 197 South Main, westerly to 168 South Water.
Brown, from 70 North Main, near Warren av., easterly.
Buffalo av., from Kickemuit av., near Child.
Buttonwoods av., from Kickemuit rd., bey. the river to State line.

Campbell, from 241 South Main, westerly.
Cherry, from opp. 237 South Main, easterly to Massasoit av.
Child, from 130 South Main to Touisset road.
Church, from 139 South Main, westerly across S. Water.
Cole, from Joyce, along the railroad, southerly across Croade.
Common, from 17 State to 8 Church.
Company, from 63 North Water to the water.
Coomer av., from 346 South Main, easterly.
Croade, from 180 South Main, easterly across the railroad to Cutler.
Cutler, from 37 Child, southerly by Cutler Mfg. Co.'s mill.

Eddy, from 16 State, southerly to 13 Washington.
Elm, from 145 Child.

Federal, from opp. 30 Wood to 32 Market.
Franklin, from 230 South Main, easterly to Park.

Green, from 194 South Main, opp. Broad, easterly.
Greene's Landing, from 311 South Main to the water.

Haile, from South Main at railroad crossing, westerly to the water.
Handy, from 59 Market, southerly to Child.
Handy's lane, from Swansea rd., easterly to Kickemuit rd.
Harris av., off Metacom av., near Bristol town line, easterly.
Hope, from 94 North Main, easterly to the railroad.

Jefferson, from 171 South Main, westerly to Eddy.
Johnson, from 69 North Water, westerly to the water.
Joyce, from 160 South Main, easterly to Cutler.

Kelley, from 36 North Main, easterly across the railroad.
Kickemuit rd., from 113 Market, easterly to town line.
King, from Franklin, next to Oil Works, to Taylor.
Kinnicutt av., from Child, bey. Kickemuit river, westerly.

National Exchange Bank Established 1801
If you think of changing your bank, there is
63 Westminster St., Prov. None better than this

MISCELLANEOUS. 39

Lewin, from 21 Baker to 16 Miller.
Liberty, from 103 North Main to 62 North Water.
Locust, from just beyond 260 South Main, easterly.
Luther, from 211 South Main, westerly to Lyndon.
Lyndon, from opp. 13 Washington, southerly to Luther.

Main, see North and South Main.
Manning, from opp. 9 Washington, southerly to Luther.
Maple, from opp. 360 South Main to the water.
Market, from 118 South Main to Swansea rd.
Martin, from 26 Wood, northerly.
Massasoit av., from 30 Franklin.
Meadow, from Kickemuit rd., opp. Arlington av., northerly.
Metacom av., passing through East Warren at R. R. crossing, southerly to Bristol.
Miller, from 115 North Main, westerly to the river.
Mulberry, from 57 Child, southerly.

Nobert, from North Main, above Hope, easterly.
North Main, from town line to Miller and Market streets.
North Water, from opp. 40 North Main to Miller.

Oak, from Franklin to the cemetery.

Park, from 76 North Main, easterly to the railroad, near Power Station.
Parker, from 41 Market to 32 Child.
Parker av., from Metacom av., bet. Franklin and Vernon, easterly.
Pleasant, from 23 North Main to the mill.

Railroad av., from Joyce, along the railroad, southerly to Croade.

Sanders, from 25 Market, southerly across Child.
School, from 11 Lyndon, westerly to 158 South Water.
Seymour, from South Main, ¾ mile south P. O., to Metacom av.
Sisson, from 53 North Water, westerly to Westminster.
South Main, from Miller and Market, southerly to town line.
South Water, from Miller, southerly across Wheaton.
Sowamsett av., from 246 South Main, easterly.
State, from 155 South Main to 124 South Water.
Summer, from 37 North Water, westerly to Westminster.
Swansea rd., continuation of Market street to Swansea.

Merewether & Dunn
Plumbing and Heating Contractors
31 TURNER AVENUE,   **RIVERSIDE, R. I.**

Taylor, from Avenue A to King.
Touisset rd., from Birch Swamp rd., across head of Child, to Warren Neck.
Turner, from 35 Market, southerly to Joyce.
Union, from 47 North Main to Miller.
Vernon, from opp. 267 South Main, easterly to Park.
Warren av., from 65 North Main, near the cemetery, to opp. 10 Liberty.
Washington, from 179 South Main, westerly across 145 South Water to the river.
Water, see North and South Water.
West, from Child, near Pumping Station, southerly.
Wheaton, from 207 South Main, westerly to South Water.
Windmill Hill rd., from Market to upper Kickemuit rd. bridge.
Wood, from 100 North Main, easterly to 1 Federal.

BARRINGTON STREET DIRECTORY.

Adams rd., B., from Ferry lane, southerly to Adams Point.
Alfred Drown rd., W. B., from Washington rd., crossing tracks at W. B. R. R. Station, southerly to the water.
Annawomscutt rd., W. B., from Washington rd. crossing Alfred Drown rd., to the water.
Ash, W. B., from Washington rd., near R. R. tracks, to Alfred Drown rd.
Bay rd., B., from Nayatt rd., southerly to the water.
Bay Spring av., W. B., from Washington rd., across R. R. tracks at O'Bannon Corp., westerly to the water.
Beach rd., B., from Rumstick rd., westerly and southerly to the water.
Bluff rd., B., from Nayatt rd., southerly to the water.
Bradford, Hampden Meadows, from Massasoit av., easterly to Walnut (east of R. R. tracks).

Cedar, W. B., from Washington rd., to Alfred Drown rd.
County rd., W. B. and B., from Peck's Corner, easterly to Barrington river, thence southerly, following the river and crossing R. R. tracks at B. R. R. Station, then easterly across river to Warren town line.
Crossways, Hampden Meadows, from New Meadow rd. to Sowams rd., nr. depot.

Elm, W. B., from Washington rd., near R. R. tracks, to Alfred Drown rd.

Federal av., from Middle Highway 1st north of Lincoln av., to the river, across bridge to Massasoit av.

A Scientific Collection Service Based On The Principle of
HONESTY.
Western Mercantile Corporation. 420-421 Grosvenor Building
Prov. R. I.   Tel. Union 1526

MISCELLANEOUS.   41

Ferry lane, B., from Rumstick rd., easterly to Mathewson av.
Fountain av., Hampden Meadows, from Washington av., easterly to Walnut.
Governor Bradford's Drive, B., from Rumstick rd., westerly to Bluff av.
Jenny's lane, from Rumstick rd 1st south of County rd., easterly to Mathewson rd.
Lake Drive, Nayatt, name given to the two roads, one going south and the other west, from Nayatt depot to Washington rd.
Lincoln av., W. B., from Washington rd. to W. B. Center, easterly to Upland Way.
Linden, W. B., from Washington rd. to Alfred Drown rd.
Lovers' lane, Hampden Meadows, from New Meadow rd. to Sowams rd.

Maple av., B., from County rd., opp. town hall, westerly to Middle Highway, nr. Nayatt R. R. Station.
Martin av., Hampden Meadows, from Massasoit av., near the bridge, northerly.
Massasoit av., Hampden Meadows, from New Meadow rd. westerly to the bridge, across to Federal av.
Mathewson rd., B., from County rd., south of R. R. Station, southerly along the shore to Martin Ferry.
Middle Highway, from County rd., 1st east Peck's Corner, southerly to Nayatt rd.

Narragansett rd., Bay Spring, from R. R. tracks at town line, southerly across Bay Spring av. to the water.
New Meadow rd., Hampden Meadows, from County rd., northerly across R. R. tracks to the state line.
Nayatt rd., from Rumstick rd., 1st on right, south County rd., westerly to Nayatt Point.

Oak, W. B., from Washington rd., near R. R. tracks, to Alfred Drown rd.
Old River rd., from County rd., northeasterly along river to E. Prov. town line.

Peck's Corner, ¾ mile north W. B. P. O., near E. Prov. town line.
Primrose Hill rd., from Old River rd., westerly.
Rumstick rd., B., from County rd., just south Barrington R. R. Station, southerly to Rumstick Point.

R. I. RUG WORKS Oriental Rugs Cleaned and Repaired.
Tels. Union 2203 and 2204
678 WESTMINSTER STREET, PROVIDENCE, R. I.

WARDWELL LUMBER CO. { Builders' Hardware, Paints, Glass, Masons & Carpenters' TOOLS
BRISTOL, R. I.

42   MISCELLANEOUS.

Shore rd., B., from Nayatt rd., southerly to the water.
Sowams rd., Hampden Meadows, from County rd., northerly across R. R. tracks at depot to New Meadow rd. at state line.
Upland Way, Nayatt, from Nayatt R. R. Station, northeasterly to Federal av.
Walnut, Hampden Meadows, from Bradford, northerly to Fountain av.
Washington rd., from Peck's Corner, southerly through W. B. to Nayatt rd. at the Point.
Water Way, B., from Nayatt rd., southerly to the water.
Watson av., B., from Nayatt rd., southerly to the water.
Willow, W. B., from Washington rd., near R. R. tracks, to Alfred Drown rd.

BUILDINGS, HALL, BLOCKS—BRISTOL.

Almshouse, Asylum rd., nr. R. R. track.
Armory Hall, 135 State.
Beach Terrace Casino, Beach Terrace.
Bell's Block, 363 Hope.
Benjamin Church Home for Aged Men, 1010 Hope.
Bradford's Block, 296-302 Hope.
Bristol Opera House, Bradford, near Hope.
Burnside Memorial Building, Hope, corner Court.
Byfield Hall, High, corner Church.
Colt Memorial Building, 550 Hope, corner Bradford.
Columbia Hall, 571 Wood, near Franklin.
Court House, High, opposite Court.
Custom House, Hope, near John.
Drury Block, 497 Hope.
Easterbrooks Block, 471 Hope.
G. A. R. Hall, 298 Hope.
Hasbrouck's Block, 537 Hope.
Holmes' Block, 3 State.
Knights of Columbus Hall, 487 Hope.
Kunze's Block, 53 State.
Odd Fellows Hall, 172 High, corner Constitution.
Pokanoket Hall, 537 Hope.
Portuguese Hall, 171 Franklin.
Post Office Building, Hope, near State.
Pythian Hall, 298 Hope.
Rogers Free Library Building, 525 Hope.
Santo Hall, A. P. B. D. E. Society, 171 Franklin.
State Armory, Thames, foot of Church.
Town Clerk's Office, Burnside Memorial Building.
Town Hall, Bradford, near Hope.
Trinity Parish House, Hope.
Y. M. C. A., 448 Hope.

Water Supply Outfits House Pumps	Walter H. Jackson Co. 435 Industrial Trust Building Providence, - R. I.	"Dodd" System Lightning PROTECTION

MISCELLANEOUS. 43

HALLS, BLOCKS, BUILDINGS—WARREN.

Armory Hall, Jefferson, near South Main.
Bank Building, 119 South Water, corner Church.
Bosworth's Block, 131 South Main.
Burke's Block, South Main, corner Child.
Conway's Block, South Main, opposite Joyce.
G. A. R. Hall, State, near South Water.
German Hall, North Main, corner Bowen.
Goff's Hotel Block, South Main, corner Joyce.
Grange Hall, Child, across Kickemuit River.
Hail Public Library, South Main, corner Croade.
Howland & Wheaton Block, 197 South Main.
Industrial Trust Building, Main, corner Market.
Institute Hall, South Main, near Luther.
Masonic Temple, 21 Baker, corner Lewin.
Odd Fellows Hall, 166 South Main.
Peabody's Building, 161 South Main, corner State.
Post Office, 136 and 138 South Main, corner Child.
Providence Telephone Building, Market, near Main.
Pumping Station, Child, side of Kickemuit river.
Town Hall, South Main, near Joyce.
Turner's Block, South Main, corner Church.
Twombley's Hall, North Main, near North Water.
Waterman's Blocks, between North Water and the river.

WHARVES IN BRISTOL.

Dyer Transportation Wharf, foot of State.
Herreshoff's Wharf, Hope, opp. Burnside.
Lawless' Pier, Hope, near Burton.
Namquit Worsted Mill Wharf, foot of Bradford.
Naval Reserve Torpedo Co., Thames, foot of Church.
Newport Ferry, foot of Constitution.
Paull's Wharf, 267 Thames.
Public Wharf, Thames, opp. Church.
Railroad Docks, Thames, opp. Franklin.
Staples Coal Co.'s Wharf, foot of State.
Steamboat Wharf, foot of State.
Sugar House Wharf, Thames, near Bradford.
Van Wickle's Pier, near Bristol Ferry.
Wardwell's Wharf, foot of Bradford.

WHITTEMORE & COLBURN
PRINTERS   15 Pine St., PROV.

JAMES C. GOFF CO. | **All kinds of**
31 to 49 POINT ST. | **Masons'**
Providence, R. I. | **Materials**

MISCELLANEOUS.

WHARVES IN WARREN.

Atwood's Wharf, South Water, foot of Washington.
Blount & Hunt's Wharf, South Water, south of Wheaton.
Buckingham's Wharf, South Water, foot of Miller.
Carr & Stubb's Wharf, rear 153 South Water.
Covo's Wharf, South Water, foot of State.
Greene's Wharf, Greene's Landing, South Warren.
Martin's Wharf, south Water, foot of Church.
Potter, Collamore & Co.'s Wharf, South Water, opp. Wheaton.
Rowe's Wharf, South Water, foot of Baker.
Smith's Wharf, North Water, foot of Miller.
Staples Coal Co.'s Wharf, rear 137 South Water.
Stubb's Wharf, opp. 155 South Water.
Warren Mfg. Co.'s Wharf, No. 1, foot of Sisson.
Warren Mfg. Co.'s Wharf, No. 2, rear of the mill.
Waterman's Wharf, South Water, foot of Bradford.

BRISTOL POST OFFICE.

Custom House Building, Hope street, near State. Postmaster, D. G. Coggeshall; Assistant Postmaster, William J. McShane. Mails arrive 7 and 8 A. M., 2, 4, 6 and 7 P. M. Mails leave 7.30 and 9 A. M. and 12 M.; 2, 6 and 7.30 P. M. Sundays, arrive 8 A. M. and leave 4.50 P. M.

WARREN POST OFFICE.

South Main street. Postmaster, John McPike; Clerks, Miss Sarah B. Brown, William Titmas, Miss Mary M. Stanton. Mails arrive 6, 7.45 and 10 A. M.; 1.20, 3, 5 and 7 P. M. Mails leave 6.30, 7, 8.05, 9.40 and 12.35 A. M.; 2.40, 4.45, 6.40 and 7.30 P. M. Sundays, arrive 7.45 A. M., leave 5 P. M.

POST OFFICES.

BARRINGTON POST OFFICE—County road and Rumstick road. James F. Grant, Postmaster; Miss Grace E. Cole, Assistant. Mails arrive 7.23 A. M., 12.52 and 4.52 P. M. Mails leave 9.52 A. M., 6.52, 2.52 and 12.57 P. M.

NAYATT POINT POST OFFICE—In Nayatt R. R. Station. Joseph J. Devlin, Postmaster. Mails arrive 7.20 A. M., 12.50 and 4.50 P. M. Mails leave 9.55 A. M., 2.55 and 6.50 P. M.

WEST BARRINGTON POST OFFICE—Washington, near Broadway. Reuben A. Gibbs, Postmaster; Assistant. Mails arrive 7.30 A. M., 1 and 5 P. M. Mails leave 9.30 A. M., 2.30 and 6.30 P. M.

A Policy with
THE PENN MUTUAL LIFE INSURANCE CO.

In addition to all the regular benefits of Life Insurance, contains a provision that in event of total and permanent disability pays to the insured a monthly income amounting to 10% of the face of the policy each year; besides the insured does not have to pay any more premiums. For further information, inquire of

Walter K. R. Holm, General Agent
17 Exchange St.,   Providence, R. I.

Floor Area 40,000 Sq. Ft.   Employees 250

Largest & Finest Laundry in New England
WHAT CHEER LAUNDRY
36 Burgess Street,   Providence, R. I.

IF YOU WANT TO SELL

Something to a man who wants to buy something that you want to sell,

CONSULT THE DIRECTORY

A. DAVID, the Tailor

Maker of

Ladies' and Men's Fine Clothes

Telephone 62-R and get our service at the door

Bristol, R. I.

C. J. EVERETT, Inc.

Expert Tree Work

SPRAYING

TRIMMING

REPAIRING

Mr. Everett gives his personal attention to all work

P. O. Box 333.   Telephone Connection

PROVIDENCE,   R. I.

BROWNELL & HINMAN

Plumbing, Heating, Tinsmithing

Electric Water Supply Systems

17 Lincoln Av., Riverside, R. I.

Ralph C. Watrous Co.
ESTATE MANAGERS. RENT COLLECTION A SPECIALTY
437 INDUSTRIAL TRUST BUILDING

BRISTOL
GENERAL DIRECTORY

COPYRIGHT 1918, BY UNION PUBLISHING CO.

ABBREVIATIONS.—Ab., above; agt., agent; av., avenue; bds., boards; bet., between; B. H., Bristol Highlands; bldg., building; blk., block; bey., beyond; cor., corner; ct., court; do., ditto; E., East; exp., express; f. n., factory number; fr., from; ft., foot; h., house; ins., insurance; manuf., manufacturer; mfg., manufacturing; N., North; N. I. R. Co., National India Rubber Company; nr., near; opp., opposite; pl., place; P. O., Post Office; pres., president; prop., proprietor; Prov., Providence; N. Y., N. H. & H. R. R., New York, New Haven and Hartford Railroad; r., rear; rd., road; rms., rooms; R. R., Railroad; S., South; sec., secretary; sq., square; st., street; supt., superintendent; treas., treasurer; U. S. A., United States Army; U. S. N., United States Navy; W., West. After the name of the street the word "street" is omitted.

For additional Italian names received too late to classify see Index to Contents

Abbott Fannie mill emp bds 148 High
Abenante Giovanni shoemaker 55 Bradford h do
Abenante John dry goods 53 Bradford h do
Abenante Luigi clerk Prospect
Abenante Pasquale at rubber works Prospect
Adams Annie A emp N I R Co bds 55 High
Adams Elizabeth DeW widow George W h Hope cor State
Adams Express Co 563 Hope
Adams Mary A h 55 High
Aiello Vincent tailor 374 Wood bds 3 Bedford
Alden Albertus A boat builder h 116 State
Alden Charles H salesman h 31 Noyes av
Alder Ernest E boat carpenter h 4 Howe
Aldrich Charles A prop Grand View House Prudence Island h 73 Constitution
Aldrich Lucius E pianist h 67 Burton
Alger Fred L rubber worker bds 42 Franklin

Blackstone Canal Nat'l Bank 20 Market Square PROVIDENCE, R. I.
Capital, $500,000.   Surplus Profits, over $500,000

Warren Monumental Works
Cor. Railroad Avenue and Croade Street, Warren, R. I.

Alger Julia A Miss h 19 Cole
Alger Margaret J widow George h 42 Franklin
Allan Emma E widow Robert bds 41 Union
Allen Clarence M brakeman h 55 Constitution
Allen Henry D W farmer h Poppasquash rd
Almeda August rubber worker h 1 Easterbrooks av
Almeida Jennie widow Manuel R rubber worker h 101 Union
Almeida Joseph rubber worker h 337 High
Almeida Joseph Jr U S A bds 22 Mt Hope av
Almeida Manuel rubber worker h 337 High
Almshouse (Philip A Manchester keeper) Asylum rd nr R R
Almy Alice B bds 11 Constitution
Almy Cornelia A widow Albert S h 11 Constitution
Alves Mary widow h 41 Gooding's lane
Anania Emanuel barber for Nicola Santulli h 8 Congregational
Anastas Luka shoe polishing parlor 489 Hope h over do
Anderson Angus C clerk bds Joseph Anderson
Anderson Clara A widow James h 616 Wood
Anderson John foreman N I R Co h 107 Franklin
Anderson Joseph gardener H L Clark h Hope nr Warren line
Anderson Robert H foreman (Prov) h 32 Cook
Anderson Robert J painter bds 616 Wood
Andrade Manuel inspector h 33 Bay View av
Andrade Manuel Jr rubber worker bds 33 Bay View av
Andrews Diantha E widow Perry bds 23 Burton
Andrews Thomas clerk bds 149 Mt Hope av
Androphy Julius machinist bds 20 Lincoln av
Anthony Andrew W (U S N) h 56 High
Anthony Edward farmer h Metacom av opp Griswold av
Armatage John B at boat shop h 26 Burton
Armstrong John fireman h 146 High
Arnold Charles A carpenter bds 48 Walley
Arnold Ernest W conductor N Y N H & H R R h 856 Hope
Arnold George U librarian Rogers Free Library h 707 Hope
Arnold Ray H Mrs h 48 Walley
Aruda Frank F salesman h 43 Oliver
Aseavor John rubber works h 163 Franklin
Ashton John T clerk N I R Co h 701 Hope
Ashton J Thomas foreman h 78 High
Ashton Martha widow James H Chestnut nr Juniper lane
Ashton Mary bds 78 High
Ashton William J rubber worker h 175 Wood
Atkinson Thomas local mgr The Great A & P Tea Co h 97½ Bradford
Auclair Ida emp N I R Co bds D'Wolf Inn Thames
August Anna housekeeper bds 901 Hope
August Elizabeth M school teacher bds 901 Hope
August Emanuel car inspector h 901 Hope

NATIONAL EXCHANGE BANK 63 WESTMINSTER ST.
PROVIDENCE
IF YOU ARE LOOKING FOR A STRONG BANK, WHERE A FRIENDLY
Welcome Always Awaits You, Open an Account With Us

August Emma V bookkeeper 30 Bradford bds 901 Hope
August Marguerite L clerk bds 901 Hope
August Theodora E bookkeeper 267 Thames bds 901 Hope

Babbitt Arselia M widow Edward S h 328 Hope
Bache Evelin prin Bache Private School r 86 State h 86 do
Bache Private School (Miss Evelin Bache prin) r 86 State
Bacon Caroline h 638 Wood
Bacon David L J carpenter bds 638 Wood
Bacon Edouard carpenter h 638 Wood
Bacon Ernest carpenter h 638 Wood
Bacon George A machinist h 640 Wood
Bacon Matilda M housekeeper bds 638 Wood
Bacon Osmer W (U S N) bds 829 Hope
Bacon William F carpenter h 829 Hope
Bailey John H Jr prin Byfield School h Hope nr Warren line
Bailey John W watchman Hogg Island
Bailey Mark H (U S A) bds J H Bailey Jr
Baker Beulah emp N I R Co bds D'Wolf Inn Thames
Baker Herbert W hairdresser 99 Bradford h 97 do
Baker Sadie A bds 290 Hope
Baker William I cutter h 32 Franklin
Balfour Elizabeth C Miss dressmaker h 409 Hope
Ball Sumner A carpenter and builder bds 63 Burton
Baptiste Manuel rubber worker h 7 Easterbrooks av
Barbera Pasquale bartender h 3 Orchard
Barbour Charles A carpenter 198 High h do
Barns Isolin and Hattie h 221 Hope cor Union
Baron Jacob binder h 104 Wood
Barrett Alton H (U S A) bds 744 Hope
Barrett Arthur W freight cashier Bristol Depot h 744 Hope
Barry James H night watchman h 122 Union
Bartlett Albert M fisherman h Little's Narrows
Barton Henry stable and teaming rear 45 State h 693 Hope
Bassing Jacob h 63 Church
Bassing Samuel I grocery and market 178 Thames h 63 Church
Bates Gilbert summer res h Little's Narrows
Battaglio Alfonso pool room 172 Bradford
Battcher Albert shipping clerk 182 High h 9 Charles
Battcher Henry h 190 Wood
Battcher Reinhard rubber worker bds 190 Wood
Beals Charles A h 1181 Hope
Beals Percy R oiler bds 1181 Hope
Beavis Thomas J carpenter 36 Mt Hope av

Merewether & Dunn
Plumbing and Heating Contractors
31 TURNER AVENUE, RIVERSIDE, R. I.

33 Canal St. CHARLES J. JAGER CO. Providence
ELECTRIC AND GASOLINE PUMPS AND PRESSURE SYSTEMS
We carry the largest stock of this kind in New England

48   BRISTOL DIRECTORY, 1917-18.

Belanger Albert machinist h rear 210 Thames
Bell Helen N teacher (N Y) bds 353 Hope
Bell Leroy D machinist bds 963 Hope
BELL WILLIAM H house furn goods 361 to 365 Hope h 353 do—see page 20
Belmore Edward at rubber works h 482 Thames
Belmore Eva mill emp bds 392 Thames
Belmore Medrick watchman h 392 Thames
Belmore M Louis electrician bds 392 Thames
Belmore Pamelia rubber worker bds 392 Thames
Belton Hilda emp N I R Co bds D'Wolf Inn Thames
Benard Albert E engineer h 728 Hope
Benard Henry C rubber worker h 720 Hope
Benavus Joseph rubber worker h 10 Selton
Bennett Emma S G widow Herbert F h 98 Bradford
Bense Aage H foreman h 31 Central
Bergeron Frank mill emp bds 39 Oliver
Bergeron Walter J (U S A) bds 39 Oliver
Bernard George F h Bay View av
Bernard Louis N rubber worker h Bay View av n Metacom av
Bertram Francis bds 4 State
Bertrand Aura rubber worker bds 17 Borden av
Bertrand Catherine Mrs bds 80 Bay View av
Bertrand Joseph L rubber worker bds 17 Borden av
Bertrand Leon h 17 Borden av
Best John W foreman h Ferry rd
Bickford Charles H boat builder h 65 Constitution
Bickford Sarah F widow Henry L bds 689 Hope
Bidon John driver h 3 Bradford
Billington Charles Mrs sum res Attleboro h Little's Narrows
Bingham Robert G at rubber works h 27 Byfield
Bingham Sarah A E widow Robert bds 27 Byfield
Birtwistle John G draughtsman h 31 Franklin
Black Robert A supt Juniper Hill Cemetery also florist Sherry av nr Bay View av h do
Blackman Ethel bookkeeper (Prov) bds 61 Constitution
Blackman Ida bookkeeper 419 Hope bds 61 Constitution
Blackman Rose clerk bds 61 Constitution
Blackman Samuel fruit peddler h 61 Constitution
Blaisdell Florence D widow Walter L h 68 Constitution
Blaisdell Fred G engineer N I R Co h 68 Constitution
Blaisdell Grace bds 65 Bay View av
Blaisdell Myra A widow Oliver h 65 Bay View av
Blaisdell Myra F textile des bds 65 Bay View av
Blaisdell Ruby M stenographer bds 68 Constitution
Blaisdell Sarah widow Oliver H h 36 Pierce av
Blakeslee Ella E teacher bds 112 Franklin
Blanchard Walter A manager J D Peck h Warren

COLLECTIONS AND CREDIT REPORTS
Our service is as near as your telephone. We will gladly furnish names of clients whom you know, who are satisfied users of our service. Tel. Union 1526

Western Mercantile Corporation,   Providence, R. I.

BRISTOL DIRECTORY, 1917-18.   49

Blease Harold clerk bds 99 Union
Blease John molder h 99 Union
Blease Marion bds 99 Union
Bliven Earl B conductor N Y N H & H h 73 Constitution
Bliven Raymond E (U S N) bds 73 Constitution
Bolster De Witt E rep Bristol Phoenix h 24 Bourn
Booth Sarah Mrs h 135 Wood
Booth Stanley machinist h 135 Wood
Booth Star L florist r 202 High h 202 do
Borg Joseph rubber worker h 104 Bay View av
Bosworth Bradford D conductor N Y N H & H R R h 689 Hope
Bosworth Isabell A E bds 652 Hope
Bosworth Jennie rubber worker bds 112 Franklin
Bosworth Orrin L lawyer (Industrial Trust bldg Prov)) h 652 Hope
Bosworth Sarah D bds 689 Hope
Bottomley Joseph rubber worker h 15 Lincoln av
Bottomley Joseph M printer bds 15 Lincoln av
Bottomley William rubber worker bds 15 Lincoln av
Bourn Alice W bds Hope cor Walley
Bourn Augustus O (Bourn Rub Co Prov) h Hope cor Walley
Bourn Augustus O Jr lawyer (N Y) bds Hope cor Walley
Bourn Elizabeth R bds Hope cor Walley
Bourn Emma E Miss bds 234 Hope
Bourne John E oyster farmer h Little's Narrows
Bovay Ethel E bookkeeper bds 76 Burton
Bovay Mabel M bds 76 Burton
Bovay Walter (Navy) bds 76 Burton
Bovay William H painter h 76 Burton
Bowen Albert summer res Little's Narrows
Bowen Arthur E farmer bds C F Bowler
Bowen Elizabeth A widow George N bds 107 High
Bowen Frank L rubber worker h 22 Burton
Bowen John H fireman h 720 Hope
Bowen John J bds 106 Bradford
Bowen Margaret T at rubber works bds 106 Bradford
Bowen Mary widow Peter h 106 Bradford
Bowen Mary C Mrs (100 years old) at Home for Aged Women 11 Franklin
Bowen Mary E bds 106 Bradford
Bowler Charles fisherman h Kickemuit Shore nr town line
Bowler Charles F h ft of Gooding av
Bowler Charles W fisherman h Kickemuit

R. I. RUG WORKS RUG CLEANING, CARPET CLEANING AND LAYING
678 WESTMINSTER ST., PROVIDENCE. Telephones Union 2203 and 2204

Bowler D Melissa Mrs bds 98 Constitution
Bowler Rebecca S widow of James C h 47 Franklin
Bowler William M h 98 Constitution
Boy Scouts of America club room 679 Hope
Boynton Henry W writer h "Upper Longfield" off Hope opp Gibson road
Bradford Le Baron treas (Prov) h 51 Church
Bradford Mark D'W Mrs bds 51 Church
Bradford Mary Mrs housekeeper bds 725 Hope
Bradford Mary E widow of William J bds 680 Hope
Bradford Sarah Miss h 36 Constitution
Bradford William inspector Bristol and Warren Water works h 680 Hope
Bradic Frederick farmer h 140 Bay View av
Bradic Prescott A driver bds 140 Bay View av
Brady Philip h 275 Wood
Brag Lena rubber wkr h 161 Franklin
Bramhall Nettie J h 468 Thames
Brechin John bds 68 Burton
Brechin John foreman Herreshoff Boat Shop h 68 Burton
Brechin Louise S rubber wkr bds 68 Burton
Brechin Peter steel fitter bds 68 Burton
Breen Annie rubber worker bds 12 Lincoln av
Breen Bernard liquors 5 John h 513 Wood
Breen Bridget mill emp bds 11 Lincoln av
Breen Charles P rubber worker bds 11 Lincoln av
Breen Elizabeth mill emp bds 11 Lincoln av
Breen Elizabeth V rubber worker bds 12 Lincoln av
Breen Hugh J teamster h 11 Lincoln av
Breen Hugh P clerk h 24 Washington
Breen Mary widow of Hugh h 11 Lincoln av
Brelsford Annie Mrs h 15 Milk
Brelsford Pauline forelady bds 15 Milk
Brelsford Samuel machinist h 865 Hope
Brelsford Samuel J (U S A) bds 865 Hope
Brelsford Thomas F oiler bds 15 Milk
Bridd John laborer h 12 Shaw lane
Bridgham Charles B foreman Herreshoff Mfg Co h 42 Union
Briggs Carrie B bds 208 High
Briggs E Herbert sum res (Attleboro) h Little's Narrows
Briggs Ella M h 208 High
Briggs Jennie mill emp h 76 Church
Briggs Lidora Miss h Little's Narrows
Briggs William F saw filing and variety 213 High b 76 Church
Brightman Thomas locomotive engineer h 40 Usher pl
Brightman Thomas P cost mgr 20 Burnside h 40 Usher pl
Brine Joseph T rubber wkr h 118 Bay View av
Bristol Armory off Thames nr Church

WALTER H. JACKSON CO. 435 Industrial Trust Building, PROVIDENCE, R. I.
"DELCO" ELECTRIC LIGHTING & PUMPING PLANTS
WINDMILLS, GASOLINE ENGINES AND TRACTORS

BRISTOL DIRECTORY, 1917-18. 51

Bristol Asylum Asylum lane
Bristol Auto Shop (Joseph Congdon prop) auto repairing and garage 750 Hope
Bristol Casino (Club Rooms) 128 High
Bristol County Court High opp Court
Bristol County Gas & Electric Co 327 Hope wks rear 391 Thames Supt A G Earle
Bristol County Jail 48 Court
Bristol Depot cor Franklin and Thames
Bristol Golf Club Ferry road
BRISTOL HOTEL (James F McLaughlin prop) 24 State —see page 20
BRISTOL PHOENIX Farrally Bros props Joseph F Farrally editor 547 Hope—see page 17
Bristol Police Headquarters Burnside Memorial bldg
Bristol Post Office (Daniel G Coggeshall postmaster) Hope nr State
Bristol Reading Room (William P Gladding steward) 2 Constitution
Bristol R R Station (A D Fraser agt) Thames ft Franklin
Bristol Town Clerk's Office Burnside Memorial bldg
Bristol Town Farm Asylum lane
Bristol Woman's Exchange (Miss Nellie N Read mgr and treas) 331 Hope
Bristol Yacht Club foot of Constitution
Bristol & Warren Water Works (C H Tuttle supt) 553 Hope
Brobosa John rubber wkr h 14 Third School
Brogan Cornelius h 322 Wood
Brogan Josephine student bds 322 Wood
Brogan Margaret teacher bds 322 Wood
Brogan Margaret h 24 First
Brogan Mary rubber wkr bds 322 Wood
Brogan Nora rubber wkr bds 24 First
Brogden James boat builder h rear 875 Hope
Brooks George H gardener h rear 64 High
Brotherton Edith rubber wkr h 432 Thames
Brouillette Augustine mason h 725 Hope
Brown Alice C wid Frank H boarding house 399 Hope h do
Brown Bruce McK at rubber works bds 675 Hope
Brown Edward E clerk 206 Thames h 7 Collins
Brown Emily R rubber worker bds 675 Hope
BROWN GEORGE restaurant 5 Bradford h do—see page 20
Brown George H rubber worker bds 110 Constitution

WHITTEMORE & COLBURN
PRINTERS   15 Pine St., PROV.

JAMES C. GOFF CO. Sole Agents for **ATLAS**
31 to 49 POINT ST.   **Portland Cement**
Providence, R. I.

Brown Henry A shoe stripper h 110 Constitution
Brown Jacob junk dealer State h 28 Central
Brown James B cabinet maker h 92 Burton
Brown James F foreman h 17 Charles
Brown John W rubber worker h 675 Hope
Brown Manuel night watchman h 10 Easterbrooks av
Brown Mary E rubber worker bds 110 Constitution
Brown T Clark (U S A) bds 17 Constitution
Brown Thomas C conductor h Juniper
Brown Veronica stitcher bds 17 Charles
Brownell Catherine summer res h Little Narrows
Brownell Edward I lawyer (Prov) h 120 Hope
Brownell Elnathan P treas The Waldron Brownell Co h 656 Hope
Brownell Frederick B clerk h 113 Constitution
Brune Mary widow h 165 Franklin
Bruneau Hudger W boiler mkr h 256 Hope
Bruno Bros liquor dealers 157 Bradford
Bruno Francesco bartender 157 Bradford
Bruno Giuseppe bartender 157 Bradford
Bruno Paolo retired 157 Bradford
Bruno Sam bartender 157 Bradford
Bryant William E operative h r 110 Thames
Bryden Joseph night watchman h off Metacom av nr town line
Bryden Samuel mill emp h off Metacom nr town line
Budlong Arthur summer resident Hog Island
Buffington Frank H manuf of boxes (Prov) h 693 Hope
Buffington Helen G bds 23 Burton
BUFFINGTON WILLIAM H pharmacist 458 Hope h 23 Burton—see page 20
Buffum John H carpenter h 108 Constitution
Buffum Joseph L contractor and builder h Gooding av
Buffum Samuel farm hand h Metacom av
Bullock Alvin M at rubber works h 116 Mt Hope av
Bullock Arthur (U S A) bds Third School
Bullock Bertram purser h 95 High
Bullock Emiline widow of William H M h 20 Catherine
Bullock Harry H (U S A) bds 95 High
Bullock Henry cutter h 95 High
Bullock James (U S A) bds Third School
Bullock Jasper M rubber wkr h 14 Third School
Bullock Marion G bds 137 Mt Hope av
Bullock Mary maid 35 Union
Bullock Mary E widow Amos K h 23 Oliver
Bullock Robert H laborer h 78 Thames
Bullock Russell D wood dealer h 137 Mt Hope av
Bullock Russell D Jr (U S A) bds 137 Mt Hope av
Bullock Sarah h Third School

RALPH C. WATROUS CO.
Real Estate Auctioneers
437 INDUSTRIAL TRUST BUILDING

Bunn Clara H (M S Bunn & Co) 450 Hope bds 16 Constitution
Bunn Edward E clerk N I R Co bds 89 Constitution
Bunn Gertrude stenographer (Prov) bds 89 Constitution
Bunn Martha S (M S Bunn & Co) 450 Hope h 16 Constitution
Bunn M S & Co (M S Bunn C H Bunn) fancy goods and millinery 450 Hope
Bunn Nathan M carpenter h 89 Constitution
Burg Antoni rubber wkr h 71 Usher av
Burge Manuel rubber wkr bds 215 Franklin
Burgess Almira B at rubber works h 34 Central
Burgess Chester R clerk 678 Hope h 14 Franklin
Burgess Fred S h 47 Constitution
Burgess Georgiana Miss h 34 Central
Burgess Louis teamer h 68 State
Burgess M Marietta school teacher bds 224 Hope
Burgess William N agt Adams Express Co h 680 Hope
Burke James third hand h 307 Thames
Burke John F clerk 563 Hope bds 2 Chestnut
Burke Margaret widow Thomas F bds 126 Thames
Burke Thomas teamster h rear 814 Hope
Burke William fish market 13 State rms 5 Church
Burke William H foreman h 126 Thames
Burlingham ―――― summer res Metacom av nr Griswold
Burnham Herbert B clerk (Prov) h 65 Franklin
Burnham Stella L bds 381 High
Burns Joan C Miss bds 183 High
Burns John J janitor at P O h 183 High
Burns Samuel printer bds 16 Burton
Burrow John E mill emp bds 307 Thames
Burt Mrs Charles D sum res h 1242 Hope
Bush George H painter 142 High h do
Bush George H painter 57 Burton h do
Bush Henry C painter bds 57 Burton
Bush Roy V machinist bds 57 Burton
Buttler Frank rubber wkr h 14 Shaw lane
Byrnes Edward gardener h 10 Bourn
Byrnes Francis L rubber worker bds 77 Bay View av
Byrnes John at rubber works h 77 Bay View av
Byrnes Mary A Miss h 77 Bay View av
Byrnes Thomas H agent Dyer Trans Line h 9 Gooding lane

Cabot Harry H retired h 341 Hope
Cabral Antone rubber wkr h 14 Third School

Blackstone Canal Nat'l Bank | BEST FACILITIES
20 MARKET SQ., PROVIDENCE | **Prompt Attention**

WARREN MONUMENTAL WORKS
Cor. Railroad Avenue and Croade Streets, Warren, R. I.

BRISTOL DIRECTORY, 1917-18.

Cabral Frank rubber wkr bds 165 Franklin
Cabral Mabel A mill emp bds 42 Oliver
Cabral Manuel rubber wkr h 11 Easterbrooks av
Cabrol Antone farmer h 16 Third School
Cabrol Jessie rubber wkr h 161 Franklin
Cady Philo V sheriff (Bristol County) h 69 High
Cahill Albert L Rev asst pastor St Elizabeth R C Church bds 330 Wood
Cahoon Matthew J sail maker h 27 Noyes av
Callan Alice widow Michael h 11 Borden av
Callan Annie M nurse bds 241 High
Callan Bernard M (U S A) bds 241 High
Callan Catherine nurse (U S A) bds 208 Franklin
Callan Charles E (U S N) bds 208 Franklin
Callan John at rubber works h 208 Franklin
Callan John J chauffeur bds 208 Franklin
Callan John J driver bds 241 High
Callan Luke rubber worker bds 30 Byfield
CALLAN L H COL (U S A) general contractor 237 Franklin h do—see page 4
Callan Margaret widow Thomas h 30 Byfield
Callan Margaret M mill emp bds 241 High
Callan Mary widow Michael bds 380 High
Callan Mary A clerk C R Co bds 380 High
Callan Peter B bookkeeper and timekeeper bds 11 Borden av
Callan Rose bookkeeper bds 208 Franklin
Callan Sadie C teacher bds 208 Franklin
Callan Sarah rubber worker bds 380 High
Callan Sarah widow Thomas h 241 High
Callan William J (U S A) bds 11 Borden av
Camara Manuel rubber wkr h 10 Gray
Campanello Giuseppe at rubber works bds 221 Wood
Campanello Joseph (Campanello Bros) bds 221 Wood
Campanello Samuel (Campanello Bros) h 221 Wood
Campbell Andrew teamster h 31 Cole
Campbell John marine engineer bds 16 John
Capocchiano John shoe mkr 572 Wood h 8 Bourne av
Card Elizabeth N widow of John A h 30 Constitution
Card Harry E (Peleg J Card & Son) masons h Barrington
Card Henry F at Benj Church Home 1010 Hope
Card James E boat builder h 10 Washington
Card Martha W bds 10 Washington
Card Mary widow Allen housekeeper bds Hope nr Warren line
CARD PELEG & SON (Peleg and Harry E Card) masons and contractors 10 Washington—see page 21
Card Peleg J (Peleg J Card & Son) masons h 10 Washington
Card Raymond A carpenter h 104 Union
Cardoza Frank C clerk bds 49 Mt Hope av

Carey Belle widow Charles H h 45 Cottage
Carey Harold B (U S A) bds 122 Mt Hope av
Carey John A rubber worker h 74 Constitution
Carey John A Jr at rubber works bds 74 Constitution
Carey see also Cary
Carlos Margaret emp N I R Co bds D'Wolf Inn Thames
Carnes James W blacksmith h 28 Garfield av
Carney Catherine widow John h 91 High
Carney see also Kearney
Carpenter Charles (Prov) summer res h Little's Narrows
Carpenter Edgar summer res Little's Narrows (Attleboro)
Carpenter Henry C summer res h Little's Narrows (Prov)
Carpenter Howard summer res at Edgar Carpenter's cottage (Attleboro)
Carr Anna F bds 84 Walley
Carr Herbert watchman h 7 Burnside
Carr Mabel F bds 84 Walley
Carr Walter M optical wkr h 30 Washington
Carreia Almeida E grocery 281 Thames h do
Carroll Thomas H mill emp bds 48½ Constitution
Carron Anna Mrs h over Buffington's Drug Store
Carter Annie C Mrs dressmaker 736 Hope bds do
Carter Charles N at Benj Church Home 1010 Hope
Carter Evelyn school teacher bds 736 Hope
Carter Madelyn B clerk 444 Hope bds 736 do
Cary Charles H h 104 Constitution
Cary Elizabeth h 104 Constitution
Cary see also Carey
Case Anna bds Daniel R Case
Case Daniel R h Popposquash
Case Helena bds Daniel R Case
Casey Mary E governess bds 132 High
Castriotto John grocer 431 Wood h do
Castriotto L grocer 324 High h 327 do
Cashin James emp woolen mill h 271 Wood
Cavanaugh Annie mill emp bds 83 Burton
Cavanaugh Katherine rubber worker bds 83 Burton
Cavanaugh Mary E h 83 Burton
Cavanaugh Richard rubber worker bds 83 Burton
Cavanaugh see also Kavanaugh
CENTRAL GARAGE James T Haines prop 41 Church— see page 21
Chace Frank I boat rigger h 721 Hope
Chace Harriet L rubber worker bds 721 Hope

Merewether & Dunn
Plumbing and Heating Contractors
31 TURNER AVENUE,   RIVERSIDE, R. I.

Chace Susan F rubber wkr bds 721 Hope
Chace see also Chase
Chadourne Mae A matron D'Wolf Inn Thames
Chadwick Minnie A rubber worker bds 68 Franklin
Chadwick Sarah E widow Ezra h 68 Franklin
Chafee Sarah E h 608 Wood
Champlin Rodman N carpenter h 881 Hope
Chase Clarence E summer res (Prov) h Little's Narrows
Chase Halsey Capt (Prudence Island Transportation Co) h 48 Constitution also Prudence Island
Chase Madeline clerk bds 132 Hope
Chase Rachel school teacher bds 48 Constitution
Chase Rebecca bookkeeper (Prov) bds 48 Constitution
Chase see also Chace
Cheesman Merton A private sec (Prov) h Poppasquash Colt Farm
Cheetham William H chauffeur h 116 Bradford
Chesebrough C L H Mrs widow of E Stanton h 140 Hope
Child Charles salesman (Prov) h Little's Narrows
Children's Home Mrs Theresa B Hay matron 48 Union
Chin Charlie laundryman 577 Hope h do
Christian Harry G electrician h Beach road
Christie Annie rubber worker bds 189 State
Christie Thomas H at rubber works bds 189 State
Church Anna M widow Louis H h 281 Hope
Church Benjamin Home for Aged Men (Charles O Coggeshall keeper) 1010 Hope
Church Charles H farmer h Poppasquash rd
Church Everett LeB insurance agt h 91 Burton
Church Gertrude E school teacher h 46 Constitution
Church Harriet P widow of Hezekiah W bds 46 Franklin
Church Helen W organist bds 281 Hope
Church Howard W dentist 471 Hope h 37 Franklin
Church James C retired h Poppasquash rd
Church John W supt Staples Coal Co of R I local branch h 862 Hope
Church Reba Howe piano teacher 281 Hope bds do
Church Russell S physician 8 Constitution h 12 do office hours until 9 a m 6 to 8 p m Tel
Church Street House (George Smithson prop) 5 Church
Church Thomas C at Benj Church Home 1010 Hope
Cirillo Gaetano shoemaker 261 Wood h 12 Catherine
Clancy Rose A bookkeeper 278 Hope bds 276 do
Clark Eneater teamster h 497 Hope
Clark Frank E mill emp bds 24 Burton
Clark George overseer h 24 State
Clark Gertrude E bds 24 State
Clark Howard L banker (Prov) h "North Farm" Hope nr Warren line

OUR CREDIT REPORTS TELL—Whom to trust;
whom not to trust; who pay promptly; who pay slowly; who never pay their
bills except under pressure.   Telephone Union 1526
Western Mercantile Corporation, Providence, R. I.

Clark Jennie H bds Ella C Munroe Summer
Clark Rose rubber worker bds 697 Hope
Clark Thomas at rubber works h 697 Hope
Clarke & Manchester grocers 96 High
Clarke Charles W clerk 96 High bds 146 High
Clarke James farmer h Metacom av nr Bay View av
Clarkson James U carpenter h 380 High
Clerico Alfred grocer 257 Wood h 133 Constitution
Cleaver Fred G (U S N) bds 19 Bourne av
Cleaver Jennie h 19 Bourne av
Cleaver May E asst forewoman bds 19 Bourne av
Cleaver William H rubber wkr h 10 Munroe av
Clowes Elizabeth W school teacher bds 45 Union
Clowes George carpenter h 45 Union
Clowes Lloyd R (U S A) bds 45 Union
Cobb Charles I summer res (Attleboro) h Little's Narrows
Cobb Emma W rubber worker 96 Franklin B
Cobb Homer summer res (Attleboro) at C I Cobb's cottage
Cobb Mary bds Lidora Briggs
Coggeshall Albert H engineer pumping sta h Poppasquash
Coggeshall Charles fireman bds 42 Dimond av
Coggeshall Charles O keeper Benj Church Home 1010 Hope h do
Coggeshall Charlotte H Miss h 39 Church
Coggeshall Daniel G postmaster h 117 Constitution
Coggeshall Edith W bds 98 Church
Coggeshall Frederick H engineer h 38 Dimond av
Coggeshall George B h 42 Dimond av
Coggeshall George W engineer h 48 Cottage
Coggeshall H Augusta Miss h 39 Church
Coggeshall Helen B clerk 439 Hope bds 30 Constitution
Coggeshall James N station agent Constitution St Station h 817 Hope
Coggeshall J Everett farmer h Little's Narrows
Coggeshall John rubber worker bds 42 Dimond av
Coggeshall John M Town Clerk office Burnside Memorial bldg h 93 Constitution
Coggeshall LeRoy B painter h 733 Hope
Coggeshall Marion E bookkeeper bds 817 Hope
Coggeshall Mary M Mrs h 98 Church
Coggeshall Russell P rubber worker h Chestnut
Coggeshall Walter H painter 30 Constitution h do
Coggeshall William H at rubber works h 733 Hope

R. I. RUG WORKS
Rugs Woven from old and new carpets.   Telephones { 2203 2204
678 WESTMINSTER ST.,   PROVIDENCE

Coggeshall William L farmer bds J E Coggeshall
Cohen Louis F jeweler and watchmaker cor Church and
  Hope h do
Cole Amanda V widow of William h 64 Constitution
Cole Annie M bds 64 Constitution
Cole Bertha R widow of John H bds 103 Bradford
Cole Carrie W h 11 Cole
Cole Elizabeth Mrs dressmaker 108 Union h do
Cole Elizageth A widow of John F h 11 Cole
Cole Elizabeth F chief operator Bristol Exch bds Warren
Cole Freeborn R teamster 64 Constitution bds do
Cole Walter L marine engineer h 142 High
Colfer John H laborer bds 34 Bay View av
Colfer Michael laborer h 34 Bay View av
Collard Etena rubber worker bds 282 Thames
Collard George (U S A) bds 282 Thames
Collard Joseph driver bds 282 Thames
Collard Josephine widow Frederick h 3 Bradford
Collard Lenore rubber worker bds 282 Thames
Collard Peter (U S A) bds 282 Thames
Collins Mary widow Horace h 559 Hope
Collins Olney clerk 30 Bradford bds 721 Hope
Collins Walter (U S A) bds 559 Hope
Cologne Adolph H (U S A) bds 302 Thames
Colt Edith C widow LeBaron C h Smith
Colt LeBaron B Senator h 35 High
Colt Memorial Library Hope cor Bradford
Colt Samuel P pres N I R Co h 500 Hope
Colwell Charles rubber worker h last on Pleasant
Colwell Elizabeth L F bds 104 Constitution
Colwell Wilworth H inspector Public Bldgs Dept Prov h 104
  Constitution
Condon Ellen L nurse 11 Franklin h do
Condon Johannah Miss bds 47 Franklin
Condon John J rubber worker h 98 Church
Congdon Fannie R rubber worker bds 69 Burton
Congdon Giles S florist 69 Court h do
Congdon Joseph B salesman (Prov) also prop Bristol Auto
  Station h 106 Bradford
Congdon Lena H housekeeper h 69 Burton
Congdon May D stenographer bds 69 Burton
Congdon Sadie L rubber worker bds 69 Burton
Conklin Llewellyn boss farmer Metacom av
Conley James E chauffeur h Bay View av nr Metacom av
Conley James H Jr rubber wkr h 248 Hope
Conley John L clerk h 114 Franklin
Conley Margaret M clerk 657 Hope bds 19 Byfield
Conley William C (U S A) bds 19 Byfield

Water Supply Outfits House Pumps	Walter H. Jackson Co. 435 Industrial Trust Building Providence, - R. I.	"Dodd" System Lightning PROTECTION

BRISTOL DIRECTORY, 1917-18. 59

Conley William E insurance agent h 19 Byfield
Conley William E varnishmkr 75 Bay View av nr Sherry av
Conlin Annie E maid 249 Hope
Connell Honora widow James A h 22 Byfield
Connell Joseph E engineer h 34 Byfield
Connery Alicia widow Robert F h 110 Church
Connery Catherine E music teacher bds 110 Church
Connery Charles M pipe fitter bds 121 Constitution
Connery Helen E bds 118 High
Connery Henrietta C bds 118 High
Connery James J insurance agent bds 110 Church
Connery Lillian B stenographer (Prov) bds 110 Church
Connery Mary A bds 110 Church
Connery Mary E at rubber works bds 35 Thames
Connery Moses E carpenter h 121 Constitution
Connery Richard farmer bds Moses Wood Metacom av n Bay View av
Connery Robert J clerk (Prov) bds 110 Church
Connery Thomas J clerk 22 State h 102 State
Connery Thomas P clerk bds 110 Church
Connery William H laborer h Garfield av nr Wood
Connery William L driver h 14 Charles
CONNERY WILLIAM M gents' furnishings clothing and hats 491 Hope h 118 High—see page 18
Connor Emily Mrs summer res h Little's Narrows (Attle)
Connor Fred summer res Mrs E Connor's cottage (Attle)
Connors James T teaming & expressing 380 Thames h 711 Hope
Constitution Street Station James N Coggeshall agent foot of Constitution
Cook James W night watchman h DeWolf av
Cooke Charles rubber wkr h 30 First
Cooke Lydia M Miss h 20 Constitution
Cooke Nellie bds 64 Church
Cooke Nellie widow John J h 8 Prospect
Cooke Robert D plumber 49 Bradford bds 45 Mt Hope av
Cooke Robert J helper h 45 Mt Hope av
Cooke Thomas G machinist h 58 Collins
Corea John W rubber wkr h 116 Bradford
Corey Elias mill wkr bds 57 Bay View av
Cornell Elisha oysterman h 12 Bradford
Cornell George L mechanic h 87 High
Cornell Mary E widow of Alfred L bds 6 Central
Cornell Richard R cutter h 6 Central

WHITTEMORE & COLBURN
PRINTERS 15 Pine St., PROV.

VALENTINE'S Diamond & Star FIRE BRICK

JAMES C. GOFF CO.
31 to 49 POINT ST.
Providence, R. I.

60   BRISTOL DIRECTORY, 1917-18.

Corra Lena widow h 6 Second School
Correiro Estulo teamster h 29 State
Corthell James H h 58 Union
Costa Antone rubber wkr h 118 Bay View av
Costa Jesse rubber wkr bds John Costa
Costa John rubber worker h Metacom av
Costa Manuel rubber wkr h 84 Charles
Cote Arthur operative h 253 Thames
Cote Joseph ins coll h 135 Wood
Cote Leo G mgr Western Union Tel 421 Hope h 98 State
Coughlan Alice rubber worker bds 80 Vay View av
Coughlan John J driver bds 80 Bay View av
Coughlan Michael clerk Post Office h 149 Mt Hope av
Coute J John rubber wkr h 215 Franklin
Coutier Albert carpenter bds 628 Wood
Coyle Bridget widow Daniel h 30 Byfield
Coyle Catherine and Susan Misses h 17 Usher av
Coyle James laborer bds 17 Usher av
Cragin George A genl sales mgr National India Rubber Co h Prov
Crandall Oscar M Capt h 17 Thames
CRANSTON WORSTED MILLS Charles B Rockwell treas Thames near Church—see page 5
Crapo Felix bartender 206 Thames bds 5 Church
Craval Antone rubber wkr bds 213 Franklin
Crispel Daniel carpenter h 64 Charles
Cromer Charles W comp Bristol Phoenix rms 102 State
Cronin William R tel oper Bristol Depot bds 512 Thames
Crowley Alice E stenciler N I R Co bds 189 Wood
Crowley Elenore F widow of James W h 189 Wood
Crowley William J h 597 Wood
Cruz Joseph rubber wkr h 157 Franklin
Culley Annie E housekeeper 169 State
Culley Bride E forelady bds 169 State
Cummings Frank summer res (Attle) h Little's Narrows
Cunniff Margaret mill emp bds Owen Cunniff
Cunniff Mary mill emp bds Owen Cunniff
Cunniff Mary T widow Patrick J maid 105 State
Cunniff Michael J teamer bds Owen Cunniff
Cunniff Owen h Wood nr High
Cunniff Thomas F painter bds Owen Cunniff
Cunue Serefine rubber wkr h 159 Franklin
Curra William rubber wkr bds 7 Easterbrooks av
Curran Elizabeth cook 500 Hope
Curron Ventron rubber wkr h 71 Usher av
Curtis George machinist h 26 Burton
Cute Antone rubber worker h 16 Third School
Cutler Charles W treas Staples Coal Co of R I h Warren

RALPH C. WATROUS CO.
RESIDENTIAL and INVESTMENT PROPERTY
Of All Kinds For Sale
487 Industrial Trust Building

BRISTOL DIRECTORY, 1917-18.   61

DAGENAIS JOSEPH A blacksmith and wheelwright rear 281 Thames h 133 Bradford—see page 21
Dailey James F driver h 512 Thames
Dais Frank rubber worker h 10 Third School
Dais Joseph rubber worker h 10 Third School
Dalrymple Frederick carpenter h 409 Hope
D'Ambrosio Dominic barber F C Pierce h 30 Franklin
Darby Thomas O fisherman h 211 Thames
DARLING HENRY M periodicals 444 Hope h 656 do—see page 20
Darling William A engineer h 103 Constitution
Darling William B fireman bds 103 Constitution
DAVID ABRAHAM tailor dry goods and gents' furnishings 301 Hope h do—see opp page 45
David John tailor for A David bds 301 Hope
Davidson Alexander boat carpenter h 21 Cottage
Davidson James boat builder h 13 Woodlawn av
Davis Charles L chauffeur bds 30 Washington
Davis Clara I Mrs bds 616 Wood
Davis Frank L letter carrier h 40 Church
Davis Lawrence F sub clerk P O h 40 Church
Davis Nellie L maid Hope cor Walley
Davis Wendell R purchaser bds 98 Bradford
Davoren Mary P teacher Miller St School Warren bds 268 High
Days Farnandes rubber worker h 10 Third School
Deconing Edward (U S A) bds 17 Oliver
Deconing Louis (U S N) bds 17 Oliver
Deconing Louis D weaver h 17 Oliver
De Federico Aniello barber 495 Wood
De Federico Francesco grocery Wood
De Felice Bros liquors 164 Bradford
De Felice Gennaro barber 433 Wood
De Laura Alfredo tailor 372 Hope bds 236 State
Del Toro Biagio grocer 23 Catherine
Demarias George truck driver h rear 210 Thames
Demarars Hannah widow Joseph h 326 Thames
Demars Euclid J (U S A) bds 326 Thames
Demars Flora mill emp bds 326 Thames
Dennis John (U S A) h 1 Easterbrooks av
Dennis Manuel rubber worker h 8 Prospect
De Palmer Joseph barber 125 Franklin h 50 Monroe av
de Rocha Verginio J farmer h Metacom av

Blackstone Canal Nat'l Bank | A Progressive Bank
20 Market Sq., Prov. R. I. | Fully Equipped for Service

Warren Monumental Works
Cor. Railroad Avenue and Croade Street, Warren, R. I.

Des Laurier John G treas and sec'y The Franklin Street Garage Co Franklin cor Thames
Deslauriers Annie E Mrs h 129 Hope
Deslauriers Arthur (Franklin Garage) Franklin and Thames bds 35 Central
Desrosier Alex watchman h 39 Oliver
Deveaux Joseph weaver bds 42 Cottage
De Wolf Alice W bds 51 Union
De Wolf Bradford Colt h 35 Union
De Wolf Emma J widow of William R h 31 Catherine
De Wolf Florence E Miss dressmaker bds 31 Catherine
De Wolf Francis Colt student bds 35 Union
De Wolf Francis E h 217 Hope nr Union
De Wolf Harold physician 132 High h do
De Wolf Harriet R Mrs h 82 High
De Wolf John W special agent h 51 Union
De Wolf John W Jr (U S N) bds 51 Union
De Wolf Katherine K H Mrs h 11 Burton
De Wolf Louise H student bds 11 Burton
De Wolf Mary R Miss h 142 Hope
De Wolf Philip broker h 55 Woodlawn av
De Wolf Sophie J widow of James F h 18 Church
Dickerson see Dixon
Dillon Charles H prop Star Theater h Auburn
Dillon William hostler bds 15 John
Diman George W janitor h 29 Burnside av
Dimond Annie C student bds 56 Church
Dimond Charles F grocer High cor Constitution h 56 Church
Dimond Frank M dry goods and clothing 462 and 464 Hope h 60 Church
Dimond F Reginald broker office (Prov) bds 60 Church
Dimond John D Jr carpenter h 145 State
Dimond Martha B widow of John N h 290 Hope
Dimond Roswell B student bds 60 Church
Dimond Samuel C manager 174 High h 123 High
Dio Henry variety and 5-and-10-cent store 439 Hope h do
Dion Albert mason h 227 Thames
Dion George clerk h 38 Congregational
Disilets Ambrouse garage bds 29 State
Dixon Annie R bds 42 High
Dixon Ezra pres Dixon Lubricating Saddle Co 182 High h 42 High
Dixon Ezra Jr salesman h 232 Hope
Dixon Fred Morton bds 42 High
Dixon Mrs Hattie h 85 High
Dixon Lubricating Saddle Co (Ezra Dixon pres) 182 High
Dixon William G salesman 182 High h 129 Hope
Doherty Minnie rubber worker bds 111 Franklin

NATIONAL EXCHANGE BANK, 63 Westminster St., Providence
Stands First on "ROLL of HONOR" Among R. I. Banks. We respectfully ask for Your Account

Donovan Joseph M barber h nr 1290 Hope
Donovan Lillian M stenographer 553 Hope bds 400 High
Doran Dennis J carpenter and builder h 99 Franklin
Doran John J carpenter h 118 Franklin
Doran Joseph E carpenter h 69 Court
Doran William A carpenter h 75 Bay View av
Dorstrom Benjamin painter h 847 Hope
Douglas Elizabeth L at Home for Aged Women 11 Franklin
Douglas George G painter bds 119 High
Douglass Georgianna widow George H h 119 High
Downey Alice Miss h 30 Bourne
Downey Alice F rubber worker bds 88 Franklin
Downey John J laborer bds 30 Bourne
Downey Mary rubber worker bds 97 Franklin
Downey Thomas clerk bds 88 Franklin
Downey Thomas F driver h 88 Franklin
Doyle Louise rubber worker bds 183 High
Doyle Margaret rubber worker bds 165 Wood
Doyle Mary rubber worker bds 289 Wood
Doyle Michael J at rubber works h 183 High
Doyle Thomas rubber worker h 289 Wood
Dracoules Bros (James and Perry) ice cream and confectionery 473 Hope
Dracoules James (Dracoules Bros) 473 Hope bds 15 John
Dracoules Perry (Dracoules Bros) 473 Hope bds 15 John
Draper Le Roy summer res h Little's Narrows
Dreyer Amelia widow Herman bds 18 Church
Drury Gertrude D bds 259 High
Drury John Temple real estate Drury block h 868 Hope
Drury Julia C bds 259 High
Drury Mary R bds 259 High
Duarte R Joseph rubber worker h 10 Read
Dubuc Alfred mill hand h 20 Pierce av
Dubuc Emile stenographer bds Alfred Dubuc
Dubuc Joseph dyer h Hope
Duffy Augustus P undertaker 322 Wood bds do
Duffy Charles C clerk P O bds Providence
Duffy Frank E rubber worker h 320 Wood
Duffy Helena M widow Thomas h 322 Wood
Duffy James F laundryman h 35 Thames
Duffy John H at rubber works h 326 Wood
Duffy Joseph E (U S A) bds 320 Wood
Duffy Joseph L (U S A) bds 322 Wood
Duffy Louise rubber worker bds 320 Wood

Merewether & Dunn
Plumbing and Heating Contractors
31 TURNER AVENUE,   RIVERSIDE, R. I.

Duffy Marguerite M bookkeeper bds 322 Wood
Duffy Thomas rubber worker h 27 Noyes av
Duffy William F physician 79 Constitution h do
Dugas George weaver h 15 John
Dumas Frederick at rubber works h 28 Central
Dunbar Annie E widow George P h 183 Wood
Dunbar Archibald F emp Gas Co h 247 Wood
Dunbar Aribert R at boat shop bds 23 Oliver
Dunbar Arthur P chauffeur h 367 High
Dunbar Charles W clerk bds 23 Oliver
Dunbar Earle K (U S A) bds 23 Oliver
Dunbar Frederick L supt wire dept N I R Co h 208 Hope
Dunbar George N gardener h 13 Summer
Dunbar George N Jr clerk (Prov) bds 13 Summer
Dunbar Howard B cabinet maker 361 Hope h 31 Burnside
Dunbar Iola widow Richard H h 129 Hope
Dunbar Julia B Miss h 48 Oliver
Dunbar Lena R widow Ellery A bds 48 Oliver
Dunbar LeRoy C wire worker bds 59 Burton
Dunbar Mable C bookkeeper 361 Hope bds 183 Wood
Dunbar Robert R laborer h 54 Charles
Dunbar Sarah M widow Robert R bds 23 Oliver
Dupuis Napoleon laborer h 538 Thames
Duquette Charles A engineer h 15 John
Durand Theodore mill emp h 7 John
D'Wolf Inn private boarding house N I R Co (May C Hyde supt) 173 Thames
Dwyer Johanna h 6 Third School
Dwyer John J steel fitter h 3 Howe
Dwyer Margaret shoe maker bds 6 Third School

Dwyer Margaret M rubber worker bds 20 Collins
Dwyer Thomas R chief police h 20 Collins
Dwyer Thomas W jeweler (Prov) bds 20 Collins (U S A)
Dwyer William T plumber 49 Bradford h 7 Howe
DYER TRANSPORTATION LINE T H Byrnes agt ft of State (185 So Water Prov)—see page 11
Dyer William Capt (sum res) (Prov) h Little's Narrows
Dyer William H physician 271 Hope h Prov
Earle Albert O (U S A) bds 239 Franklin
Earle A O Mrs in charge Sperry & Hutchinson Co h 239 Franklin
Earle Alfred G supt Bristol County Gas & Electric Co h 11 Constitution
Earle Henry G bank clerk (Prov) bds 11 Constitution
Easterbrooks Crawford L clerk h 100 High
Easterbrooks Edward G shipping clerk h Sherry av nr Bay View av

LIVE WIRE collectors of **BAD BILLS**
"No Collection—No Charge"
WESTERN MERCANTILE CORPORATION
420-421 Grosvenor Building. Tel. Union 1526 Providence, R. I.

BRISTOL DIRECTORY, 1917-18.   65

Easterbrooks Frank N grocer h 164 Wood
Easterbrooks Frederick A h 232 Hope
Easterbrooks Mary D school teacher bds Edward G Easterbrooks
Easterbrooks William at Benjamin Church Home 1010 Hope
Eastman Ethel M sum res (Attleboro) h Little's Narrows
Eaton Fred L carpenter bds 329 Hope
Eaton Ida Mrs dressmaker bds 329 Hope
Eckersley Joseph ticket collector h 35 Thames
Eckhardt Henry cabinet maker h 12 Prospect
Edgar Edward A prop variety store 1061 Hope h do
Edmonds Albert A (U S A) bds 36 Burton
Edmonds Joseph (U S A) bds 11 Byfield
Edmonds Martin J florist h 40 Burton
Edmonds Thomas J boiler maker h 47 Sherry av
Edson Cyrus H farmer h 195 High
Edson Minnie housekeeper bds 195 High
Edwards John R Admiral h 620 Hope
Eisemberg Augusta rubber worker bds 66 Charles
Eisemberg Julius rubber worker h 66 Charles
Eisenstadt Abraham dry goods 419 Hope h 268 do
Eisenstadt Maurice grocery 1 State h over do
Elhert William E machinist bds 11 Byfield
Elliott Henry W boat builder bds 65 Burton
Emerson Arthur H emp N I R Co h 70 High
Emmons Robert W treas Herreshoff Manuf Co Inc h Boston
Ennis John L (U S A) bds 162 Thames
Ennis John P rubber worker h 162 Thames
Ennis Joseph fireman bds 29 Collins
Enos Frank farm hand bds John Enos
Enos John farmer h Metacom av nr town limits
Entwistle William machinist h 344 Hope
Erno Regina emp N I R Co bds D'Wolf Inn
Estralla Manuel farmer h 1236 Hope
Ethier Almeidos steel worker h 10 State
Ethier George E laborer h 290 Thames
Ethier Joseph rubber worker h 290 Thames
Ethier Sudjsic (U S N) bds 290 Thames

Fair William chef rms Church Street House
Fairchild Daniel summer res Hog Island
Fales Alexander G farmer h Hope cor Fales av
Fales Charles A farm hand bds Alexander G Fales

R. I. RUG WORKS
Furniture Repaired and Repolished, Chairs Reseated
678 Westminster Street, Providence. Telephone Union 2203 and also Union 2204

Fales Nathaniel farmer h Hope cor Fales av
Fales Stephen H farm hand bds A G Fales
Fales Thomas J at Benjamin Church Home 1010 Hope
Farcie John rubber worker h 71 Usher av
Farley Bernard J foreman N I R Co bds 130 Constitution
Farley Mary widow Bernard h 165 Wood
Farley Rose rubber worker bds 165 Wood
Farnandis Adeline widow h 161 Franklin
Farnandis William rubber worker h 161 Franklin
Farr Bentley B (U S N) bds 744 Hope
Farr Herman C (Ryone & Farr) garage h 118 Constitution
Farr Julia A at box shop bds 744 Hope
Farr Lenora E widow Herbert L h 744 Hope
FARRALLY BROS publishers Bristol Phoenix J F Farrally mgr 547 Hope—see page 17
Farrally Doris J bds 83 State
Farrally Joseph F editor Bristol Phoenix 547 Hope h 83 State
Farrally Lavina M Miss h 102 State
Farrally Phyllis R bds 83 State
Farraz Vegan rubber worker h 147 Franklin
Farrin Landoff rubber worker h 211 Franklin
Farrington Lilla R Miss h 103 Bradford
Farrington Philip H correspondent Prov Journal h 27 Usher place
Faulkner Adam laborer h 39 Monroe av
Faulkner James A bds 39 Monroe av
Faux Emily rubber worker bds 675 Hope
Favro Charles laborer h 318 Thames
Fay Annie E Mrs h 597 Wood
Fay James P letter carrier bds 597 Wood
Fay Rose V at rubber works bds 597 Wood
Federico Ambrose rubber worker bds 495 Wood
Federico Aniello barber 493 Wood h 495 do
Federico Frank bds 495 Wood
Fee Joseph W foreman bds 11 Lincoln av
Fee Maria widow of John L h 11 Lincoln av
Felson Joseph fruit and confectionery 376 Hope h Pleasant
Ferraro Vincenzo barber 446 Hope h 73 Franklin
Ferreira Dennis G rubber worker h 34 Cook
Ferries Manuel teamster h 10 Easterbrooks av
Ferro Dominic tailor for A Lollo bds 587 Wood
Ferron Clara emp N I R Co bds D'Wolf Inn
Findlay Lottie emp N I R Co bds D'Wolf Inn
Findlay Margaret emp N I R Co bds D'Wolf Inn
Finley James F carpenter h 57 Church
Finley William night watchman bds 38 Dimond av
Finn John rubber worker bds 213 Franklin
Fish Byron K bds 62 Franklin

WALTER H. JACKSON CO. 435 Industrial Trust Building
PROVIDENCE, R. I.
"DELCO" ELECTRIC LIGHTING & PUMPING PLANTS
WINDMILLS, GASOLINE ENGINES AND TRACTORS

BRISTOL DIRECTORY, 1917-18. 67

Fish George R (U S A) bds 62 Franklin
Fish Ruth A Miss bds 62 Franklin
Fish William A at Benj Church Home 1010 Hope
Fish William J bill poster h 62 Franklin
Fishbein Samuel rubber worker h 20 Lincoln av
Fitch Annie W Miss h 77 Union
Fitch Eliza H Miss h 77 Union
Fitz Howard W sum res h Gibson rd
Fletcher Mary A widow Thomas bds 49 Thames
Flint Albert H Mrs h 875 Hope
Flint Albert H Jr (U S N) bds 875 Hope
Flipe S Francis h 209 Franklin
Flowers Margaret teacher B H S bds 24 Lincoln av
Flowers Roy A night operator Bristol Depot h 65 Burton
Flowers Sanford W rubber worker h 24 Lincoln av
Flynn John W rubber worker h 58 Constitution
Flynn Michael J at rubber works h 60 Charles
Flynn Nellie at rubber works bds 64 Church
Flynn Thomas rubber worker h 3 Howe
Follett Cecil R clerk Bristol Depot h Valley Falls
Forbes Edson W draughtsman also physical director Y M
    C A h 119 High
Forgette Charles emp N I R Co bds 363 Wood
Foster Charles F sum res h Gibson rd B H
Foster Chester E sum res at Charles F Foster's cottage
Foster Ellen Miss sum res at Charles F Foster's cottage
Foster Fred ice cream and confectionery h 40 Cottage
Fountain Levi sum res (Attleboro) h Kickemuit
Fountain Marion L sum res (Attleboro) at Levi Fountain's
    cottage
Francis John rubber worker h 6 Second School
Francis John T farmer h 118 Bay View av
Francis John T Jr farmer bds 118 Bay View av
Francis William rubber worker h 159 Franklin
Franklin Abby A Mrs at Home for Aged Women 11 Franklin
Franklin J Wallace asst supt N I R Co h 47 Cottage
Franklin Louise B nurse bds 47 Cottage
FRANKLIN STREET GARAGE (THE) Thames opp
    Franklin St R R Depot—see page 18
Fraser Alexander D agt Bristol Depot h 49 Woodlawn av
Freeman Edward L at Joseph W Freeman's cottage
Freeman Joseph W sum res h Gibson rd B H
Freitas Joseph J rubber worker h 585 Wood

WHITTEMORE & COLBURN
PRINTERS   15 Pine St., PROV.

King's Fibrous Plaster Board & Hard Plaster
JAMES C. GOFF CO.
21 to 49 Point St., Prov., R. I.

BRISTOL DIRECTORY, 1917-18.

French J Barnard farmer Metacom av
Furtado Antone rubber worker h 30 Second School
Furtado Joseph rubber worker h 283 Thames
Furtado Joseph M grocer 421 Wood h Metacom av
Furtado Joseph R grocer h 229 State
FURTADO L ROSA grocer 229 State h do—see page 19
Gablinske Herman B carpenter h 64 Mt Hope av
Gablinske John S cutter h 96 Union
Gablinske William H (U S A) bds 112 Union
Gallagher James bds 32 Rock
Gallagher John J rubber worker h 49 Catherine
Gallagher Rose emp N I R Co bds D'Wolf Inn
Galligher Thomas emp N I R Co h 391 Wood
Galloway P Robert local mgr The Mayflower Store bds 11 Byfield
Gallup Edward C clerk bds 617 Hope
Gallup Jennie H Miss dentist 617 Hope bds do
Gallup Julius C dentist 617 Hope h do
Galvin Alice M clerk 439 Hope bds 19 Rock
Galvin Annie M rubber worker bds 356 High
Galvin Catherine E rubber worker bds 356 High
Galvin Mary A housekeeper h 356 High
Galvin Nellie L rubber worker bds 356 High
Gamelin Nazaire laborer h 290 Thames
Garcia Frank farmer h Metacom av
Garcia Mary Miss at rubber works h Metacom av
Gardiner William H foreman h 98 State
Gardner Mabel L dressmaker h 145 High
Gardner Paul farm hand bds T J Mahoney
Gasper Peter J boat carpenter h 73 Union
Gayton Annie rubber worker bds 1013 Hope
Gayton Grace Mrs widow of Joseph h 189 High
Gayton James E carpenter h 1013 Hope
Gayton Julia F rubber worker bds 1013 Hope
Gayton Leander M farm hand bds 1023 Hope
Gayton William P (U S A) bds 189 High
Gear Joseph farm hand bds 1200 Hope
Gearns Mary A widow John J boarding house 96 Thames h do
Geho Frank emp N I R Co h 363 Wood
Geisler Alexander E student bds 29 Summer
Geisler Alexander L foreman Herreshoff Mfg Co h 29 Summer
GEISLER FREDERICK A florist 122 Mt Hope av h do— see page 4
Gibson Maria G widow Henry M h Hope cor State
Gifford Frank M driver Adams Express h 675 Hope
Gifford Harold W at rubber works bds 675 Hope

Ralph C. Watrous Co. FARMS and SUBURBAN PROPERTY For Sale
437 INDUSTRIAL TRUST BUILDING

Gifford Joseph W engineer and janitor G A R hall h 55 Mt Hope av
Gifford Josephine L widow of Robert D h 234 Hope
Gifford Marcia L rubber worker bds 675 Hope
Gifford Sophia L widow of William H h 50 Oliver
Gifford William D automobile repairer h Metacom av nr town line
Gilbert Joseph teamster h 554 Thames
Gillan Thomas J Rev pastor St Mary's R C Church h 330 Wood
Gilligan Mary emp N I R Co bds D'Wolf Inn Thames
Gillispie Margaret rubber worker h 141 High
Gillon Carrie B Mrs bds 106 Franklin
Gilroy Charles rubber worker h 111 Franklin
Gilroy John F grocer 75 Franklin h 110 do
Gilroy William milk dealer h Metacom av nr Gooding av
Giunta Joseph barber 475 Hope h 587 Wood
GIUSTIANY PETER grocery and market 247 Thames h 282 do—see page 19
Gladding Elizabeth G widow John A C bds F F Gladding
Gladding Frederick F treas Wardwell Lumber Co Thames h Bay View av near Metacom av
Gladding George T Captain h 22 Noyes av
Gladding Hattie A widow of Nathaniel bds 2 Central
Gladding Mary A Miss h 2 Central
Gladding Nathaniel machinist h Gibson rd
Gladding Samuel W sub letter carrier bds 2 Constitution
Gladding Theodore O oyster dealer and fish market 219 Thames h 83 State
Gladding William P yacht agency 2 Constitution h do
Gladu Arthur weaver h 400 High
Gladu Donat G plumber bds 302 Thames
Gladu George F electrician bds 302 Thames
Gladu Joseph (emp Prov) h 302 Thames
Gladu Leda mill emp bds 302 Thames
Gladu Louis watchman h 16 Bradford
Gladu Louis Mrs widow bds 720 Hope
Gladu Medis driver h 241 Thames
Gladu Peter fisherman h 302 Thames
Goddard Harold boat builder bds 15 Burton
Goddard John H boat builder h 15 Burton
Goddard Madeline stenographer bds 15 Burton
Goettler George wool sorter h 28 Cook
Goettler Gladys M bds 28 Cook

Blackstone Canal Nat'l Bank | Established 1831
20 MARKET SQ. PROVIDENCE | STRONG AND CONSERVATIVE

WARREN MONUMENTAL WORKS
Cor. Railroad Avenue and Croade Streets, Warren, R. I.

Goettler Mildred I stenog 525 Hope bds 28 Cook
Goff Ada M widow Thomas Jr prop Goff's Market 367 High h 8 Lincoln av
Goff Catherine rubber works bds 366 High
Goff Celestina widow Henry bds 728 Hope
Goff Frank painter h 40 Cottage
Goff Henry clerk h 1030 Hope
Goff James W Captain policeman h Bay View av and High
Goff Jeffrey rubber worker bds 366 High
Goff Thomas retired h 366 High
GOFF'S MARKET Mrs A M Goff prop 367 High—see page 20
Goglia Luigi confectionery 374 Wood h do
Golden Frank C rubber worker h 41 Congregational
Goldstein Charles (Goldstein & Schwartz) 581 Hope h 154 Wood
Goldstein Israel dry goods etc 31 State h 428 High
Goldstein & Schwartz (Charles Goldstein David Schwartz) gents' furnishings 581 Hope
Gooding Lillian M widow James M bds 1st on Gooding av
Gooding Marguerite Miss bds Gooding av
Gooding William B driver bds Gooding av
Gorham Amos S clerk 525 Hope h 21 High
Gorham Isaac H foreman N I R Co h 183 Wood
Gorham Julia H teacher Walley School bds 183 Wood
Gorham Mary A bds 67 Constitution
Gorham Washington farmer h 75 Constitution
Gough see Goff
Gould Charles H at boat shop h 685 Hope
Goulet Edward rubber worker h 42 Bradford
Grabert John rubber worker h 148 High
Grabert Rose wire worker bds 404 Wood
Graham Margaret widow Archibald h 68 Bay View av
Graham Martha district nurse 68 Bay View av
Graham Ruth nurse bds 68 Bay View av
Grammont Clarence T Mrs bds 875 Hope
GRAND VIEW HOUSE Chas A Aldrich prop Prudence Island—see page 16
Grant William B h 1290 Hope
Gravelin John B laborer h 740 Hope
Gravelle Augustus A retired 38 Mt Hope av
Gray Beazie E widow Augustus h 141 High
Gray Ella M tel oper 656 Hope bds 28 Dimond av
Gray Harry R driver Adams Express h 1019 Hope
Gray Herbert N rubber worker h 1st on Sunnyside av
Gray John A carpenter h last on Sunnyside av
Gray Percy T farmer h Metacom av nr town line
Gray Robert S carpenter h 28 Dimond av
Gray Vernon A (U S A) bds 984 Hope

National Exchange Bank
63 Westminster St., Prov.

Established 1801
If you think of changing your bank, there is
None better than this

Greago Hope Miss h 10 Bourne
Great A & P Tea Co (The) Thomas Atkinson local mgr 583 Hope
Green Myrtis boxmaker bds 25 High
Greene Alice M widow Patrick bds 84 Franklin
Greene George A h 60 Court
Greene Harold F (U S N) bds 25 Summer
Greene Lillian N W widow Henry A bds 25 Summer
Greene Richard P at rubber works bds 84 Franklin
Gregory Joseph garage bds 494 Thames
Greenwell Fannie G Mrs h 21 Usher pl
Greenwell Laurence S rubber worker bds 21 Usher pl
Grinnell Charles H clerk 573 Hope h 676 Hope
Guerreiro John barber 212 Thames h 985 Hope
Guevremont Aleck truck driver h rear 256 Thames
Guevremont Fred mason h 494 Thames
Guevremont Remie mason h 102 Bay View av
Guevremont Wilfred laborer 118 Church
Guiteras Gertrude E Miss h 291 High
Gyott Arthur summer res h Little's Narrows

Hablin John F laborer h 161 Mt Hope av
Hadfield Edward operative h rear 110 Thames
Hadfield J Edward (U S A) bds 110 Thames
Hagen Bertha clerk bds 58 Constitution
Hagen Fred C sailmaker h 58 Constitution
Haggerty Anna May tel oper bds 129 Hope
Haggerty Frances V rubber worker bds 129 Hope
Haines James J (U S A) bds 41 Church
Haines James T prop Central Garage 41 Church h do
Haines John L machinist bds 41 Church
Hall Benjamin L Capt commander Soldiers' Home h do
Hallowell Emma M bds 57 Church
Hamil David h 494 Thames
Hamil Frederick oyster opener bds 494 Thames
Hamill Cletus wire worker bds 604 Wood
Hamill Dry Goods Store (Miss M G Hamill prop) 499 Hope
Hamill Katherine A Marietta G Misses h 692 Hope
Hamill Margaret G Miss (prop Hamill's Dry Goods Store) h 692 Hope
Hamill Margaret M clerk 499 Hope h 692 do
Hamill Mary Mrs h 604 Wood
Hammill Anna J h 149 State
Hommill Charles L real estate 149 State h do

Merewether & Dunn
Plumbing and Heating Contractors
31 TURNER AVENUE,   RIVERSIDE, R. I.

Hammill Frank H judge 54 State (also Prov) h 41 Woodlawn av
Hammill Joseph lawyer bds 149 State
Hammill William P Dept Sheriff (Prov) h 205 State
Hammon John W sum res (Taunton) h Little's Narrows
Hammond Philip H Mrs h 620 Hope
Hanke Stephanie L rubber worker bds 61 Church
Hanley James J rms Church Street House
Hanson Gustave W rubber worker h 98 Constitution
Harrington May rubber worker bds 371 High
Harrop William rubber worker h 260 Hope
Hart Charles F rubber worker bds 33 Cook
Hart James R engineer bds 25 Lincoln av
Hart John at rubber works h 18 Mt Hope av
Hart Mary A widow Bernard D h 363 Wood
Hart Rebecca E widow William S h 25 Lincoln av
Harvey Joseph boat builder h 881 Hope
Harvey Owen rubber worker h 32 Congregational
Hasbrouck Cornelius J physician and surgeon 115 State h 117 do
Hasbrouck Gertrude M bds 117 State
Hassett Joseph steel worker bds 248 Hope
Hassett Michael gardener h 248 Hope
Hathaway Asa W overseer Herreshoff Mfg Co h 107 High
Hathaway James B adjutant Soldiers' Home h do
Hauke Conrad mill emp h 61 Church
Hauke Victoria widow Conrad bds 61 Church
Hay Theresa B Mrs matron Children's Home 48 Union
Hayes Henry W lawyer (Prov) h 14 Union
Haynes Elizabeth H bds 76 Burton
Hazard John foreman rms Church Street House
Hazen Morris (Liberty Market) 217 High h Fall River
Head Cornelius (U S A) bds 24 First
Head James H bar tender 258 Wood bds 17 Catherine
Head Thomas F carpenter h 64 Church
Head Thomas J bar tender bds 24 First
Head William J teamster bds 24 First
Heilhecker Eugene C at rubber works h 885 Hope
Hempel Chester plumber h 17 Franklin
Henderson James packer h 64 Bay View av
Hern Albert rubber worker bds 720 Hope
Heroux Napoleon carpenter h 51 Oliver
Herreshoff Agnes bds 6 Walley
Herreshoff Alice A h Poppasquash
Herreshoff Clarence DeW draughtsman bds 6 Walley
Herreshoff Eugenia T T widow John B h 64 High
Herreshoff Julia A bds Poppasquash
Herreshoff Lewis h 142 Hope
Herreshoff L Francis (U S N) bds 6 Walley

HERRESHOFF MANUFACTURING CO INC N G
Herreshoff pres R W Emmons 2d treas C W
Young sec'y and ass't treas yacht builders Hope
opp Burnside and 20 Burnside—see page 5
Herreshoff Marine Band (Asa W Hathaway mgr) 25 Burnside
Herreshoff Nathaniel G pres Herreshoff Mfg Co Burnside h 6 Walley cor Hope
Herreshoff Nathaniel G Jr electrician bds 6 Walley cor Hope
Herreshoff Sideny DeW designer bds 6 Walley
Herrmann Christian machinist h 17 Constitution
Herrmann Ida F teacher (N Y) bds 17 Constitution
Herrmann Velma L clerk bds 17 Constitution
Herzig Paul A Capt h 22 Oliver
Hibbert Elisha machinist h 45 Union
Hibbert George cabinet maker h 881 Hope
Hickey Thomas A (U S A) bds 26 Noyes av
Hidden Walter summer res h off Ferry rd
Hill Abbie Mrs h 41 Church
Hill Carlton B clerk N I R Co bds 93 Franklin
Hill Cora M school teacher bds 837 Hope
Hill Eber private secy 182 High h 93 Franklin
Hill Eber Wilcox (U S A) bds 41 Church
Hill Elizabeth widow Joseph H h 33 Borden av
Hill Elwin A letter carrier h 1019 Hope
Hill Frank T (U S A) bds 41 Church
Hill Harold E (U S A) bds 93 Franklin
Hill James E carpenter h 837 Hope
Hill Rachel bookkeeper 573 Hope bds 41 Church
Hilton Jane widow James bds 189 High
Hoar James H retired bds 895 Hope
Hoar Prescott A at rubber works h 48 Oliver
Hoar Sarah C bds 43 Byfield
Hoard Mary E widow James J h 43 Byfield
Hochman William furniture dealer 25 State h 20 Lincoln av
Hodgdon Fred F carpenter h 8 Noyes av
Hodges Edward Walter John summer res (Attleboro) h Little's Narrows
Hodges James summer res (Attleboro) h Little's Narrows
Hodgkinson Richard janitor Industrial Trust Co rms 21 Constitution
Hogan John D trainman h 384 High
Holmes James policeman h 18 Byfield
Holmes Robert C at rubber works h 18 Bourne

Holmes William J machinist h 37 Bourne
Holt Ralph W at rubber works h 956 Hope
Holten John engineer h 885 Hope
Home for Aged Women (Mrs Annie W Tirrell matron) 11 Franklin
Hope Drug Co (B Elmer Mathewson mgr) 297 Hope
Hopkins Stephen W (Talbot & Hopkins) 53 Bradford h 348 High
Horton Amy G widow Edmund h 83 State
Horton William W steward h 34 Burton
Hosmer Ellen P widow Charles bds 341 Hope
HOTEL BELVEDERE (H P Morrissey) Hope opp Post Office—see page 18
Houle Alexander A at rubber works h 4 State
Houlihan Annie J rubber worker bds 701 Hope
Howard Anson B asst minister St Michael's Episcopal Church bds 15 Church
Howe Arthur W h Metacom av opp Woodlawn av
Howe Arthur W Jr bds A W Howe
Howe Frank P summer res h Metacom av nr Griswold av
Howe Wallis E architect (Prov) h 45 Woodlawn av
Huestis J Floyd chauffeur h rear 500 Hope
Huestis Thomas B machinist h Gibson rd
Huftalen Marcus L lobster fisherman h rear Gibson's Hope
Hughes Catherine E rubber worker bds 256 Hope
Hughes Howell R steward (Worcester) h 256 Hope
Hughes Mary bds 118 Franklin
Hughes Sarah C clerk bds 256 Hope
Hughes Theresa Miss milliner 535 Hope h 118 Franklin
Hume Alice emp N I R Co bds D'Wolf Inn Thames
Humphry Edwin bds 156 Mt Hope av
Humphry Harold carpenter h 156 Mt Hope av
Hyde Mary C Miss supt D'Wolf Inn Thames h do
INDUSTRIAL TRUST CO BRISTOL BRANCH C T Sherman mgr 525 Hope—see front cover and insert opp Warren Directory
Ingraham E Daniel farmer h 21 Woodlawn av
Ingraham George E carpenter h 23 Cottage
Ingraham Hezekiah S (U S N) bds 23 Cottage
Ingraham J Ellery bank emp (Prov) bds 1059 Hope
Ingraham John S Jr supt North Burial Ground h 1059 Hope
Ingraham Mary M Mrs dressmaker 1059 Hope h do
Ingraham Sarah Mrs h 980 Hope
Innis see Ennis
Jackson Cyrus A (U S N) h 74 Church
Jackson J Frederick mechanic h 9 Anthony av
James Jennie widow Carroll h 246 Thames
Jamial Albert (Geo Jamial & Sons) dry goods h Warren
Jamial George (Geo Jamial & Sons) dry goods h 45 State

| Water Supply Outfits House Pumps | Walter H. Jackson Co. 435 Industrial Trust Building Providence, - R. I. | "Dodd" System Lightning PROTECTION |

Jamial George & Sons (George and Albert) dry goods and shoes 45 State
Janson George D (U S A) bds 949 Hope
Janson Joseph A grocery and market 22 State h 949 Hope
Jarvin Frederick O overseer h 307 Thames
Jenkins William (Attleboro) h Little's Narrows
Jesse Joseph rubber worker h 10 Silton
Jesse Manuel rubber worker h 10 Gray
Jetty George mason h rear 256 Thames
Johnson Charles A grocer 678 Hope h 631 do
Johnson John machinist h 45 Union
Johnson Thomas E clerk N I R Co h 48 Church
Johnston Algernon L clerk 267 Thames h 108 Church
Johnston Sarah E widow William h 164 Wood
Jones Dr A T summer res h off Ferry rd
Jones John H boiler maker h 116 Wood
Jordan Arthur E marine man h 27 Cole
Joye Annie Miss h 36 Mt Hope av
Kamison Samuel rubber worker h 21 Munroe av
Kavanaugh Edward M (U S A) bds 130 Constitution
Kavanaugh see Cavanaugh
Kearney Elizabeth A bds 45 Bourne
Kearney Charles rubber worker bds 61 Church
Kearney Sarah Mrs widow Maurice h 61 Church
Kearney William H watchman h 44 Monroe av
Kearney see Carney
Kearns Annie emp N I R Co bds D'Wolf Inn Thames
Keating J Frank plumber h 107 Franklin
Keating John W laborer bds 65 Constitution
Keating Lydia widow John h 65 Constitution
Kebrek Minnie B clerk N I R Co bds 11 Prospect
Kebrek Pauline Mrs grocer 255 Wood cor Constitution h 11 Prospect
Keegan Bartley rubber worker h 379 Wood
Keegan John E helper h 37 Congregational
Kelley Hugh F night police h 19 Byfield
Kellogg Clayton A rubber worker bds 29 Lincoln av
Kelton Emma emp N I R Co bds D'Wolf Inn Thames
Kemas Thomas shoe polishing parlor 489 Hope h over do
Kemlik William restaurant 1 Franklin h do
Kempf George W rubber worker bds rear 139 Bay View av
Kempf Herman J care taker h rear 139 Bay View av
Kempf Herman J Jr variety store 681 Hope h 245 High
Kempf Jerome F farmer bds rear 139 Bay View av
Kempf William F machinist bds rear 139 Bay View av

WHITTEMORE & COLBURN
PRINTERS   15 Pine St., PROV.

JAMES C. GOFF CO.
31 to 49 POINT ST.
Providence, R. I.

All kinds of Masons' Materials

Kempt John H mgr Baybery Farm Poppasquash
Kenna George farmer h Metacom av
Kenna John bds George Kenna
Kennedy Alfred clerk bds 62 Oliver
Kennedy Annie bds 62 Burton
Kennedy John J rubber worker bds 62 Burton
Kennedy Margaret h 62 Burton
Kennelly Anna D stitcher bds 189 State
Kennelly James M clerk bds 189 State
Kenney Leon J cashier Bristol County Gas & Electric Co h 262 High
Kenney Margaret G bookkeeper N I R Co bds 25 High
Kenney Pardon T retired h 45 Richmond
Kenney Russell S (U S N) bds 25 High
Kenney Willard S painter h 25 High
Kenney Willard S Jr steel worker bds 25 High
Kenyon Amos D retired bds 17 Thames
Keough Katherine emp N I R Co bds D'Wolf Inn Thames
Kerr Joseph A engineer bds 568 Wood
Kerr Josephine school teacher bds 568 Wood
Kerr Maria widow Michael h 568 Wood
Kerr Walter P foreman Usher av
Kinder Jane widow William H h 54 Garfield av
Kinder Joseph (Samuel Kinder & Bro) florist h 65 Collins
Kinder Ralph h 65 Collins
Kinder Samuel (Samuel Kinder & Bro) florist h 315 Hope
KINDER SAMUEL & BROTHER (Samuel and Joseph) florists 317 Hope—see page 18
King Albert wire worker h 102 Wood
King Annie G clerk 467 Hope bds 593 Wood
King Francis E painter h last on right on Bay View av
King George P motorman h 692 Hope
King Joseph L confectionery and variety 467 Hope h 593 Wood
King Lillian F bds 692 Hope
King Manuel painter h last on right on Bay View av
King Mary at rubber works bds 593 Wood
King (English) see Roy (French)
Kingman Lydia A widow Cassander h 26 Byfield
Kinnicutt Frank T clerk h 963 Hope
Kinnicutt George L bookkeeper bds 963 Hope
Kirby Jeremiah rubber worker h 7 Metacom av
Knight Carlo W summer res Hog Island
Knight Catherine summer res Hog Island
Knight Walter H summer res Hog Island
Knights of Columbus Hall over 485 Hope
KUNZ EDWARD D jeweler and optician 469 Hope h 186 Hope cor Burton—see page 20
Kunze Charles H painter bds 111 High

About Rhode Island

By far the most thickly populated State in the Union—the home of nearly 600,000 prosperous contented people—the busiest hive of human industry in the world ∴ ∴ ∴ ∴

The Providence Journal .. The Evening Bulletin
(BOTH TWO CENT PAPERS)
are the two great newspapers that entirely dominate this wonderful advertising field.

The Providence Journal

"The Rhode Island Bible;" established as a daily in 1829; steadily growing in circulation.

Average Daily Circulation for Year 1917
SWORN NET PAID
28,670

The Evening Bulletin

One of the largest daily newspapers in the United States.

Average Daily Circulation for Year 1917
SWORN NET PAID
52,325

FLAT RATES

Independent alike of political parties or corporate influences

THE W. E. BARRETT CO.

Corner Canal and Waterman Streets

PROVIDENCE, R. I.

1848 — OLDEST SEED STORE IN R. I. — 1918

SEEDS
FOR
Farm, Garden and Lawn

Farm and Garden Tools

EVERYTHING FROM A

"Tractor" to a Hand Weeder

FARM and HOG FENCING, POULTRY WIRE

POULTRY SUPPLIES

SPRAY PUMPS AND INSECTICIDES

Fertilizers -- Best Grades

"Wizard Brand" Sheep Manure

Large Illustrated Catalog Free to All

Get Your Name On Our Mailing List

Ralph C. Watrous Co.
ESTATE MANAGERS. RENT COLLECTION A SPECIALTY
437 INDUSTRIAL TRUST BUILDING

Kunze Emilie L bds 111 High
Kunze Louis W h 111 High
Kunze Oscar O clerk bds 111 High
La Bonte Hortense emp N I R Co bds D'Wolf Inn Thames
La Fleur George E clerk h 9 Constitution
Lafrance Louis H at rubber works h 628 Wood
Lake Elizabeth B nurse bds 85 Union
Lake Mary B Mrs h 85 Union
Lake Mary B bookkeeper (Prov) bds 85 Union
Langello Frank barber 237 State h Richmond
Lannon John M laborer h 21 Pierce av
Lannon Louise rubber worker bds 31 Pierce av
Lannon Peter rubber worker bds 29 State
Lannon Peter J driver h 31 Pierce av
Lanphere Robert E draughtsman h 202 Hope
Lansing Clarence W h 67 Constitution
Lanzieri Giovannina grocery and dry goods Wood h do
Larue Alfred Jr carpenter h 145 State
Lathrop Rev summer res (Prov) h Beach rd
Lavender James F lawyer 54 State h 131 Wood
Lavender John J rubber coat mkr bds cor Wood and Collins
Lavender Louise stenographer bds cor Wood and Collins
Lavender Marie stenographer bds cor Wood and Collins
Lavender Rose widow Michael M h cor Wood and Collins
Lawless Mary G Miss teacher bds 208 High
Lawton Ada F Mrs h 122 Church
Lawton Arthur S jeweler 122 Church h do
Lawton Walter V foreman Herreshoff Mfg Co h 10 Noyes av
Leahy Catherine B rubber worker bds Thomas Leahy
Leahy Edward L lawyer 18 High h do (Prov office 705 Grosvenor bldg)
Leahy James P shipping clerk h 74 Church
Leahy John ice dealer Metacom av nr Chestnut h do
Leahy John E (U S A) bds Thomas Leahy
Leahy John V teamer h Metacom av nr Soldiers' Home
Leahy Margaret A teacher bds John Leahy
Leahy Mary A stenographer bds John Leahy
Leahy Mary M stitcher bds Thomas Leahy
Leahy Nora Miss sec 228 Wood bds John Leahy
Leahy Thomas F engineer h Metacom av
Leahy Thomas S (U S A) bds Thomas F Leahy
Leahy William N, R F D carrier No 1 bds John Leahy
LeClair Eugene mason contractor 19 Thames h do
LeClair Octave painter Constitution nr Wood h 17 Burton

Blackstone Canal Nat'l Bank 20 Market Square PROVIDENCE, R. I.
Capital, $500,000.   Surplus Profits, over $500,000

Warren Monumental Works
Cor. Railroad Avenue and Croade Street, Warren, R. I.

LeClair William J chauffeur h 31 Franklin
Lee James rubber worker h 21 Cook
Lee James Mrs dressmaker 21 Cook h do
Lee Marguerite F stenographer bds 21 Cook
Lee William W Jr principal High School h 342 High
Leighton George E supt Cranston Worsted Mills bds 98 Bradford
LeLois Ambrose B yacht builder h 5 Milk
LeMaire Delima widow George h 29 State
LeMaire Edmund J carpenter h 249 High
LeMaire Laura rubber worker bds 29 State
LeMaire Leon painter h 676 Hope
LeMaire Oliver J (U S A) bds 29 State
LeMaire Wilfred (U S N) bds 29 State
Lemieux George driver h 253 Thames
Lemoine Duriel laborer bds 241 Thames
Lemoine Napoleon watchman h 241 Thames
Lennon see Lannon
Lent Harriet Mrs mill emp Warren bds 195 High
Leroy Emile janitor h 402 High
Leroy Jule weaver bds 402 High
Leroy Serge weaver bds 402 High
Letour Oliver machinist h 42 Bradford
Letts Mrs Florence (N J) summer res h Little's Narrows
Le Valley Andrew fireman h 4 State
Levere Bessie widow John h 363 High
Levere Catherine Miss teacher bds 363 High
Levere John H bds 363 High
Levy Louis boot and shoe repairer 35 State h do
Lewis John V retired h 341 High
Lewis Joseph at rubber works h 12 Collins
Lewis Manuel rubber worker h 14 Third School
Liberty Market (Morris Hazen) 217 High
Lincoln William summer res h Little's Narrows
Lindemuth Benjamin F lawyer 471 Hope also 42 Westminster Prov bds 932 Hope
Lindley Benjamin I confectionery and lunch Thames cor Constitution
Lindsey Edwin F machinist h 122 Church
Liscomb Charles H painter h 88 Burton
Liscomb Elizabeth A bds 232 Hope
Liscomb Hattie F housekeeper 232 Hope
Littlefield Susan S widow Julius h 721 Hope
Livingston Charles farmer h Chestnut nr Metacom av
Locke George L Rev D D rector St Michael's Episcopal Church h 45 Woodlawn av
Logan Mary M Mrs h 999 Hope
Lollo Albert D tailor 483 Hope h 377 High
Lombardi Gaetano grocer 174 Bradford h 501 Wood

NATIONAL EXCHANGE BANK 63 WESTMINSTER ST.
PROVIDENCE
IF YOU ARE LOOKING FOR A STRONG BANK, WHERE A FRIENDLY
Welcome Always Awaits You, Open an Account With Us

BRISTOL DIRECTORY, 1917-18. 79

Lonergan Thomas M bartender 300 Thames h 701 Hope
Lopes Antone farm boss h 1200 Hope
Lorance Joseph rubber worker h 205 Franklin
Lorance Manuel rubber worker h 169 Franklin
Lord Herbert machinist h 97 Union
Lothrop Katherine Mrs bds 96 High
Low William G summer res h off Ferry rd
Low William G Jr summer res h off Ferry rd
Lowney John F foreman N I R Co h 20 Lincoln av
Luddy Elizabeth M housekeeper 41 Union
Lung Dr George A Baybery Farm Poppasquash
Lusk Samuel F supt of construction h 25 Byfield
LUSO-AMERICAN GROCERY AND MEAT MARKET
    157 Bradford—see page 19
Luther Annie L. rubber worker bds 18 Cottage
Luther Charles A farmer h Metacom av town limits
Luther Charles E farmer h Griswold av
Luther Edward summer res h Gibson rd B H
Luther Elizabeth B dressmaker bds 31 Constitution
Luther Frederick W dairy farmer h 1200 Hope
Luther George S plumber h 17 Franklin
Lynch Mary A h 84 High
Lynch William A foreman Narra Rub Co bds 84 High
Macauley Frederick W painter and paper hanger 283 Wood
    h do
MacDonald Charles A boat builder h 84 Franklin
MacDonald Charles H boat builder h 63 Burton
MacDonald Mildred H clerk bds 63 Burton
MacDougall Annie E widow Hugh h 55 Franklin
MacDougall Benjamin M insurance (205 Industrial Trust
    Bldg Prov) h 55 Franklin
Maciel Catherine widow Manuel h 60 Court
Maddox Agnes mill hand bds 106 State
Maddox William plumber h 106 State
Maddox William L rubber worker bds 106 State
Mageau Arthur M janitor D'Wolf Inn bds do
Magee Anna stitcher bds 7 Prospect
Magee E Lillian shoe worker bds 245 High
Magee Elizabeth widow of David h 245 High
Magee Elizabeth L widow of James h 61 Bay View av
Magee Francis A widow of Thomas F h 96 Constitution
Magee George E (U S A) bds 7 Prospect
Magee Helen widow of Thomas h 36 Bourne
Magee Ida M bds 61 Bay View av
Magee James bookkeeper 49 Bradford bds 245 High

Merewether & Dunn
Plumbing and Heating Contractors
31 TURNER AVENUE,   RIVERSIDE, R. I.

Magee Jennie G rubber worker bds 61 Bay View av
Magee John rubber worker bds 36 Bourne
Magee John E electrician h 7 Prospect
Magee John H (U S N) bds 7 Prospect
Magee John J (U S A) bds 61 Bay View av
Magee John R treas (The Waldron Co) 49 Bradford h 89 do
Magee Levi rubber worker bds 36 Bourne
Magee Louis rubber worker bds 36 Bourne
Magee Mary C stitcher bds 7 Prospect
Magee Mary M rubber worker bds 61 Bay View av
Magee Richard H rubber worker bds 61 Bay View av
Magee William at rubber works h 33 Congregational
Maguire Anna emp N I R Co bds D'Wolf Inn Thames
Maguire Elizabeth emp N I R Co bds D'Wolf Inn Thames
Maher Ann L Miss h 25 Congregational
Maher Kate rubber worker h 25 Congregational
Mahnken John H driver bds 234 Hope
Mahnken Lavinia Miss h 234 Hope
Mahoney Anita rubber worker bds 87 High
Mahoney Mary widow Thomas J bds 5 Home
Mahoney Nora rubber worker bds 55 Bay View av
Mahoney Patrick F rubber worker bds 55 Bay View av
Mahoney Thomas J farmer h Metacom av
Maker William B sail maker h 3 Charles
Makowsky Albert clerk 55 State bds 19 Lincoln av
Makowsky Ethel M clerk 55 State bds 19 Lincoln av
Makowsky Max clothing 55 State h 19 Lincoln av
MALAFRONTE DOMINIC grocer 264 Wood h 270 do—see page 19
MALAFRONTE LUIGI liquors 176 Bradford also immigration agt and notary public h 270 Wood—see page 19
Malafronte Tony grocer 239 State h do
Malone John laborer h 82 Thames
Malloney Lillian emp N I R Co bds D'Wolf Inn Thames
Malloney Mary emp N I R Co bds D'Wolf Inn Thames
Manchester Anna B h Hope cor Constitution
Manchester Annie H Mrs clerk bds 61 Constitution
Manchester Arthur H rubber worker h 2 Chestnut
Manchester Charles J h 341 High
Manchester Daniel T rubber worker bds 152 Thames
Manchester Elsie bookkeeper Wardwell Lumber Co bds 33 Central
Manchester Emily F widow J Howard h 115 Bradford
Manchester Eunice G stenographer bds 61 Constitution
Manchester Eva J widow A Frank h 825 Hope
Manchester Harriet A Miss h 34 Thames
Manchester Henry R liquors 206 Thames h 218 Hope
Manchester Herbert W prop 96 High h 146 do

Manchester Jennie L housekeeper bds 61 Constitution
Manchester Mabel school teacher bds 825 Hope
Manchester Martha J rubber worker bds 61 Constitution
Manchester Mary E clerk bds 61 Constitution
Manchester Mary J widow James C h 65 Constitution
Manchester Philip A keeper Almshouse Asylum rd h do
Manchester Sarah B Miss bds Bay View av nr Metacom av
Manchester Susan E widow James T h 895 Hope
Manchester Thomas F rubber worker bds 108 Union
Manchester Thomas S Capt sailmaker h 29 Burton
Manchester William C clerk 176 High bds 61 Constitution
Manchester William H rubber worker h 18 Bourne
Manchester William H R letter carrier bds last on Sunnyside av
Manchester William L sec Wardwell Lumber Co Thames h 33 Central
Manchester William M carpenter h 13 Bourne
Mandell August iron worker bds 31 Catherine
Mandell John L h 31 Catherine
Manley Elmer carpenter h off Broad Common
Manning Helen widow Henry C h 34 Central
Manning Henry C elevatorman h 901 Hope
Mansfield Elizabeth emp N I R Co bds D'Wolf Inn
Mapes Augusta Mrs at Home for Aged Women 11 Franklin
Marall Cristan rubber worker bds 213 Franklin
Markoff Aaron E watch and clock repairer and jewelry 657 Hope h 686 do
Marshall George S carpenter h last on Pleasant
Marshall John rubber worker bds 24 Second School
Marshall Joseph rubber worker h 30 Second School
Marshall Manuel rubber worker h 24 Second School
Marshall Manuel Jr (U S A) bds 24 Second School
Marshall Mary widow h 1 Third School
Martelli Charles rubber worker bds 29 Lincoln av
Martelli Peter carpenter h 404 High
Martin Elmer boat builder h 65 Burton
Martin Frank rubber worker h 222 State
Martin Frederick H farmer h 1231 Hope
Martin James S farmer bds 1231 Hope
Martin Joseph rubber worker h 2 Easterbrooks av
Martin Joseph W pres Staples Coal Co h at Warren
Martin Rock rubber worker h 222 State
Martin Susan Mrs at Home for Aged Women 11 Franklin
Martin William F marine engineer h 1290 Hope
Marz Frederick W at rubber works h 53 Burton

Marz George H piper h 7 Pleasant
Marz Herman clerk 678 Hope h 22 Mt Hope av
Mason A Everett farmer h off Metacom av at town line
Mason Ezra farmer h Metacom av near town line
Mason Ezra W bank clerk (Prov) h off Metacom av near town line
Mason Oliver L bookkeeper Staples Coal Co of R I bds Warren
Matheson John carpenter h 52 Collins
Mathewson B Elmer mgr Hope Drug Co h 48 Constitution
Matta William rubber worker h 10 Third School
Matthewson J rubber worker bds 15 John
Maturi Achille R foreman h 72 Constitution
Maturi Louise M rubber worker bds 72 Constitution
Maxfield William H lather h 113 Union
Maxmean Manuel carpenter h 228 State
Maxmean Mary widow h 19 Congregational
Maxmean William rubber worker bds 19 Congregational
Mayflower Store (The) P R Galloway local mgr 541 Hope
Mayhew Francis P gardener bds 84 Walley
Mayo Annie cook D'Wolf Inn bds do
Mayo Sarah B widow of Charles H V bds 260 Hope
Mayotte Francis driver h 253 Thames
Maytum Charles J shipping clerk h Sherry av nr Cemetery
Maytum Joseph A Capt mariner h 122 Constitution av
McAleese John M shipping clerk h 685 Hope
McCallan Ralph boat builder bds 16 Burton
McCallum James H rubber worker h 636 Wood
McCallum William G rubber worker bds 636 Wood
McCanna Hugh bookkeeper Morris Bros h Warren
McCarron Anne E schoolteacher bds 46 Constitution
McCarthy Dennis J letter carrier h 231 Wood
McCarthy Frank M boilermaker h 46 Collins cor Fox Hill av
McCarthy Margaret E bds 231 Wood
McCarty Frank B rubber worker h 122 Consttitution
McCarty George F rubber worker h 196 State
McCaughey Annie nurse bds 849 Hope
McCaughey Catherine widow William h 859 Hope
McCaughey David A h 384 High
McCaughey Elizabeth J h 849 Hope
McCaughey Irving V bookkeeper Cranston Worsted Mills bds 384 High
McCaughey Margaret nurse bds 849 Hope
McCaughey Margaret E Miss stenographer bds 849 Hope
McCaughey Maria forelady bds 849 Hope
McCaughey Robert A clerk Bristol P O h 864 Hope
McCaughey Sarah Miss h 67 Church
McCaughey Thomas J baggage master Bristol Depot h 4 Washington

WALTER H. JACKSON CO. 485 Industrial Trust Building
PROVIDENCE, R. I.
"DELCO" ELECTRIC LIGHTING & PUMPING PLANTS
WINDMILLS, GASOLINE ENGINES AND TRACTORS

McCaughey William D (U S A) bds 849 Hope
McCaw Annie K widow of William h 8 Bourne
McCaw Arthur reg pharm for W H Buffington h Warren
McCaw Ellen A bds 70 Thames
McCaw Ethel I stenographer bds 123 Constitution
McCaw Jane widow William bds 241 High
McCaw John retired h 70 Thames
McCaw Leon E clerk 176 High bds 169 do
McCaw Mary E bds 70 Thames
McCaw Samuel grocer 176 High h 169 do
McCaw William R machinist h 123 Constitution
McCherry Margaret maid 24 Court
McClure George H wire worker h 31 Bradford
McClure Georgianna rubber worker bds 189 High
McClure Henry caretaker bds 189 High
McClure Oliver rubber worker h 189 High
McClure Peter plumber h 31 Franklin
McCool Sarah cook 79 Constitution
McCormack Jane widow of Thomas h 1051 Hope
McCormack Thomas carpenter bds 1051 Hope
McCormack William H at rubber works bds 1051 Hope
McCormick James teamster h rear 131 Wood
McCormick Richard H farmer bds rear 131 Wood
McCue Bridget waitress 64 High
McDermott Elizabeth V Mrs bds 70 Mt Hope av
McDonough Mary J widow William J h 538 Thames
McElevey Catherine cook 474 Hope
McGann George W plumber 278 Hope h 276 do
McGann May E bds 276 Hope
McGee see Magee
McGeeney Ellen maid 474 Hope
McGilton A Clark Rev pastor State St M E Ch h 129 State
McGinn Charles (U S A) bds 55 Mt Hope av
McGinn Margaret rubber worker h 55 Mt Hope av
McGovern Annie widow of Patrick bds 145 Franklin
McGovern Francis P shipping clerk h 626 Wood
McGovern John J rubber worker h 10 Lincoln av
McGovern Mary E maid 31 Union
McGovern Maud shoe maker bds 67 Burton
McGrath Edward rubber worker h 267 Wood
McGrath Thomas E engineer h 33 Borden av
McGuigan Mathew foreman h 95 Burton
McHale Mary bds 118 Franklin
McHugh Alice B at rubber works bds 106 Bradford
McHugh Charles F clerk bds 106 Bradford

WHITTEMORE & COLBURN
PRINTERS   15 Pine St., PROV.

McIntyre Sarah bds rear 110 Thames
McKale Mary G stitcher bds 41 Franklin
McKale Rose widow of Thomas h 41 Franklin
McKale Teresa stitcher bds 41 Franklin
McKale Thomas H printer (Bristol Phoenix) h 22 Oliver
McKay Elizabeth h 14 Shaw lane
McKay J Henry blacksmith bds 16 John
McKay Mary J housekeeper bds 16 John
McKee William L summer res h Ferry rd
McKelbie Helen maid 509 Hope
McKenna Anna M rubber worker bds 5 Howe
McKenna Frank A at rubber works h 5 Howe
McKenna Margaret J widow of James h 30 Mt Hope av
McKenzie Kenneth oysterman h 3 Franklin
McLaughlin Bessie I bookkeeper bds Bristol Hotel
McLaughlin Elizabeth bds 11 Prospect
McLaughlin James F prop Bristol Hotel h do
McLaughlin Margaret R rubber worker bds 11 Prospect
McLaughlin Robert Jr inspector (Prov) bds 11 Prospect
McLaughlin Sarah R widow Robert h 11 Prospect
McLaughlin William bookkeeper (Prov) bds 11 Prospect
McLaughlin William H bds Bristol Hotel
McLeod Margaret mill emp bds 27 Noyes av
McMahon John boat builder bds 114 Franklin
McMahon Norah widow h 114 Franklin
McManus Ella L clerk N I R Co bds 963 Hope
McNamara Elmer cutter bds 385 High
McNamara John (U S A) bds 385 High
McNamara John night watchman h 385 High
McNeal William rubber worker h 246 Thames
McShane Hugh rubber worker h 241 Wood
McShane Mary J rubber worker bds 241 Wood
McShane William J asst postmaster bds 241 Wood
McVerrish Angus boat builder h 10 Poppasquash rd
McVey Daniel sum res (Taunton) h Little's Narrows
Meagher see Maher
Medaia Antone rubber worker h 243 State
Medearos Frank rubber worker h 104 Bay View av
Medearos John rubber worker h 214 Franklin
Medearos Joseph rubber worker h 214 Franklin
Medeiros Joseph rubber worker h 45 Catherine
Mederaos Antone rubber worker h 10 Silton
Meders Marion rubber worker bds 3 Easterbrooks av
Medras Manuel rubber worker h 49 Prospect
Meiggs Edward H engineer bds rear 139 Bay View av
Meiggs Edward M at rubber works bds 601 Wood
Meiggs Grace M bds rear 139 Bay View av
Meiggs Henry M rubber worker h 16 Pierce av
Meiggs James F machinist helper bds 66 Franklin

RALPH C. WATROUS CO.
Real Estate Auctioneers
437 INDUSTRIAL TRUST BUILDING

Meiggs James W at rubber works h 69 Franklin
Meiggs Lillian at rubber works bds 601 Wood
Meiggs Sarah E widow Andrew B bds 329 Hope
Meiggs Sarah J widow John R bds 6 Washington
Meiggs Thomas J carpenter h 6 Washington
Mello Frank rubber worker h 14 Third School
Mello John rubber worker bds 23 Milk
Mello Manuel rubber worker h 228 State
Mello Phebe h 3 Easterbrooks av
Mello Rego operator h 13 Easterbrooks av
Menard Albert mill hand h 27 Oliver
Merchant see Marchant
Mercier Alfred V truck driver h 307 Thames
Merriman Alfred Mitchell physician 597 Hope h do office hours 2 to 3 and 7 to 8 P M tel
Metcalf John gardener h 132 Hope
Metcalf Mary E bds 132 Hope
Metcalf Ruth A spool tender bds 132 Hope
Metiver Amanda widow Leopold bds 9 Constitution
Metiver Laura rubber worker h 110 State
Metiver Nazare boat builder h 482 Thames
Miano Santa barber 263 Wood h 41 Bradford
Middleton Anna E Alicia H The Misses h Poppasquash rd
Middleton Frances P music teacher (Prov) h Gibson rd B H
Milburn William B carpenter h 18 Byfield
Miles Ella F rubber worker h 404 Wood
Millard George L architect (Prov) bds 50 Franklin
Millard George W stenographer h 50 Franklin
Millard James N carpenter h 984 Hope
Millemaggi Carmel shoe maker 148 Bradford h 435 Wood
Millemaggi Paul C barber 148 Bradford bds 435 Wood
Miller Archibald M groceries and hardware 557 Hope h 825 do
Miller Asahel M agent Poppasquash R R Station h Warren
Miller Horace I at rubber works h 108 State
Miller Julius h 201 High
Millett Mr summer res (Attleboro)) h Little's Narrows
Milligan Joseph A sec'y Y M C A h State
Misto Louis night operator Bristol Depot h Prov
Mitchell William H marine engineer h 721 Hope
Moffitt Hope bds 103 Franklin
Moisan Leontane truck driver h 1013 Hope
Molesky Jacob dry goods 44 State h 46 do
Molasky Louis M grocery 238 Thames h 21 Bradford

Blackstone Canal Nat'l Bank | BEST FACILITIES
20 MARKET SQ., PROVIDENCE | Prompt Attention

WARREN MONUMENTAL WORKS
Cor. Railroad Avenue and Croade Streets, Warren, R. I.

Molasky Samuel foreman h 37 Lincoln av
Monahan Mary Mrs bds 48 Constitution
Montagna Antonio groceries h 594 Wood
Montagna Josephine bds 594 Wood
Montagna Louis rubber worker bds 594 Wood
Montross Ambrose clerk 182 High h 8 Bourne
Moore George F boat builder h 7 Howe
Moore John laborer h 52 Court
Moore Margaret T widow James h 63 Court
Moore Moses engineer h 49 Thames
Moran Joseph blacksmith bds 290 Thames
Moren Felunena widow h 151 Franklin
Morgado Jackmee widow h 213 Franklin
Morgan Alfred L Prof bds 353 Hope
Morgan Milton W Jr emp N I R Co h 133 State
Morgan Ralph M rubber worker bds 608 Wood
Morin Joseph blacksmith rear 281 Thames h 290 do
Moroney Margaret bds 22 Byfield
Morrell Sarah widow John bds 25 Lincoln av
Morris Annie widow h 6 Second School
Morris Bernard V (Morris Bros) bottlers h 41 Union
Morris Bros (Patrick H Bernard V) ice dealers bottlers
    and liquor dealers 300 Thames
Morris Edward L (U S A) 26 Noyes av
Morris Jennie T h 141 State
Morris Lena D Miss housekeeper 41 Constitution
Morris Manuel (U S A) bds 215 Franklin
Morris Margaret J widow Philip h 26 Noyes av
Morris Marguerite G clerk bds 26 Noyes av
Morris Mary E bookkeeper bds 26 Noyes av
Morris Owen h 615 Wood
Morris Patrick H (Morris Bros) bottlers h 923 Hope
Morris Peter R painter h 1063 Hope
Morris Philip rubber worker h 35 Mt Hope av
Morris Philip C foreman bds 923 Hope
Morris Philip J (U S A) bds 923 Hope
Morris Serefine emp Rubber Co bds 11 Easterbrooks av
Morris Terrence P clerk bds 923 Hope
Morrissey Edward C plumber 39 State h 168 High
Morrissey Elizabeth mill hand bds 11 Poppasquash rd
Morrissey Harry P prop Hotel Belvedere h do
Morrissey Johanna M widow Thomas h 11 Poppasquash rd
Morrissey Nellie mill hand h 10 State
Morrissey Thomas F rubber worker h 161 Wood
Morse Emily S teacher bds 210 High
Morse Fannie W h 210 High
Morse Walter A mgr Bristol Auto Station h Prov
Mott Frederick R at rubber works bds 7 Burnside
Mott Helen laundress bds 6 Third School

Mott John H foreman N I R Co h 32 Cook
Mott Samuel A steel worker h 371 High
Mott Samuel R rubber worker h 371 High
Motta John rubber worker h 18 Third School
Motta Joseph rubber worker h 5 Easterbrooks av
Motta Marion rubber worker bds 5 Easterbrooks av
Motta Raniaro weaver h 168 Wood
Mowry Thomas H engineer h 88 Burton
Mudge Margaret widow Henry H h Poppasquash rd
Muller Annie M widow Henry h 97 Constitution
Mulloy Annie M rubber worker bds 111 Bay View av
Munro Albert mariner bds 1039 Hope
Munro Annie Mrs at Home for Aged Women 11 Franklin
Munro Charles F laborer h 88 Bay View av
Munro Cornelius H Mrs (101 years old) at Home for Aged Women 11 Franklin
Munro Ella C h Summer
Munro Ethel M h 321 High
Munro Evelyn bds 275 Hope
Munro George H building mover h 109 Constitution
Munro Harry C machinist h head of Summer
Munro Harry W bookkeeper Cranston Worsted Mills h 8 Church
Munro Helen E rubber works bds 36 Bradford
Munro Helena B bds 275 Hope
Munro Isaac B painter h 9 Garfield
Munro James A rubber worker h 42 Thompson av
Munro Margaret R rubber worker bds 32 Washington
Munro Robert F clerk bds 321 High
Munro Samuel W fireman h 32 Washington
Munro Sarah C Miss h 224 Hope
Munro Sylvester mover h 24 Catherine
Munro Walter H overseer h 712 Hope
Munro William H h 275 Hope
Munro William J at rubber works h 36 Bradford
Munro see Munroe
Munroe Annie M widow Carrington P h 698 Hope
Munroe Carrie H Miss h 23 Summer
Munroe Carrington P gardener bds 698 Hope
Munroe Emma M h 56 Franklin
Munroe Eunice E bds 698 Hope
Munroe Fritz E W crossing tender h 837 Hope
Munroe George C rubber worker h 16 Prospect
Munroe George F (U S A) bds 16 Prospect
Munroe Henry F farmer h 16 Diamond av

Munroe Isabel G clerk 462 Hope bds 106 Franklin
Munroe Lena M rubber works bds 106 Franklin
Munroe Mary E Miss bds 23 Summer
Munroe Mary E rubber works bds 106 Franklin
MUNROE WALTER E dist agt Travelers' Insurance (29 Weybosset rms 46 47 48 Prov) h 23 Summer—see page
Munroe see Munro
Murphy Annie V widow John J h 51 Byfield
Murphy Catherine widow Frank h 70 Franklin
Murphy Catherine widow Jeremiah nurse h 15 Munroe av
Murphy Edward laborer h 50 Oliver
Murphy Hannah B clerk 51 State bds 222 Wood
Murphy Hugh liquors 171 Bradford h 601 Wood
Murphy James F at rubber works bds 42 Congregational
Murphy Johanah widow Daniel h 42 Congregational
Murphy John J (U S A) bds 51 Byfield
Murphy Katherine rubber worker bds 21 Pierce av
Murphy Mary E rubber worker bds 51 Byfield
Murphy Mary J Jennie E Misses h 24 Congregational
Murphy Minnie rubber worker bds 66 Franklin
Murphy Peter h 607 Wood
Murphy Peter Jr at rubber works bds 607 Wood
Myers Chester C rubber worker bds 245 High
Myers George C h 245 High
Nappi Durante barber bds 167 Bradford
Nappi Michelangelo shoemaker 167 Bradford
Naroditzky Samuel boot and shoe dealer and repairer 302 Hope h 38 Byfield
NATIONAL INDIA RUBBER CO rubber goods mfg Wood opp Bradford—see page 6
Negus Anton H machinist helper bds rear 64 High
Nelle Charles F baker 184 Thames h do
Nelle Charles H M rubber worker h 241 High
Nelle Martin T boat builder bds 184 Thames
Nelson Robert M h 647 Hope
Nelson Robert W clerk 525 Hope bds 647 do
Nerone Augustine C clerk (Prov) bds 1 Prospect
Nerone Augustine P boots and shoes 561 Hope h 686 do
Nerone Julia C stenographer bds 686 Hope
Nerone Mary E stenographer bds 686 Hope
Nerone William M clerk 5 John h 1 Prospect
Nettleton Charles Capt mariner h 32 Dimond av
Neumann see Newman
Neveu Albert painter h 538 Thames
Newbold Elizabeth bds 96 Franklin
Newbold Ida rubber worker bds 96 Franklin
Newbold James at rubber works h 96 Franklin
Newbold Joseph at rubber works h 375 Wood

OUR CREDIT REPORTS TELL—Whom to trust; whom not to trust; who pay promptly; who pay slowly; who never pay their bills except under pressure. Telephone Union 1526
Western Mercantile Corporation, Providence, R. I.

Newbold Robert Jr h 121 Franklin
Newbold Robert G clerk 75 Franklin bds 121 do
Newman Abbie A bds 106 High
Newman Arthur T musician bds 22 Cottage
Newman A Russell (Newman Bros) grocers 296 Hope h 110 High
Newman Bros (James A, A Russell) grocers 296 and 300 Hope
Newman Carl A C rubber worker h 40 Catherine
Newman Charles H clerk h 41 Franklin
Newman Edward B painter h 71 Church
Newman George (U S A) bds 71 Church
Newman Howard A rubber worker h 30 Constitution
Newman Howard R clerk 296 Hope h 81 Burton
Newman James A (Newman Bros) grocers h 106 High
Newman John B clerk (Newman Bros) 296 Hope h 59 Burton
Newman Irene M millinery parlor 295 Hope h 41 Franklin
Newman Nelson machinist h 22 Cottage
Newman William J rubber worker bds 71 Church
Newport & Providence Railway Co's Ferry ft of Thames nr Constitution
Newton Julian manufr (Prov) h Hope
Nickleson Lillian emp N I R Co bds D'Wolf Inn Thames
Nicholas Lillian clerk bds 22 Cottage
Nichols Euclid C chauffeur h 725 Hope
Nichols Fred H at box shop (Prov) bds 736 Hope
Nichols Nellie bds 736 Hope
Nichols Stella R bds 38 Cook
Nolan James W bartender 300 Thames bds 5 Church
Norris John F salesman bds 42 Franklin
Norris Lillian R widow John M h 42 Franklin
Norris Maria D Miss h 474 Hope
NORTHUP BROS (George W Charles H) ice cream and confectionery 539 Hope—see page 16
Northup Charles H (Northup Bros) 539 Hope h Anthony R I
Northup George W (Northup Bros) 539 Hope h 80 State
Northup Joseph clerk bds 282 Wood
Northup Philip C clerk bds 80 State
Northup Stephen T rubber worker h 282 Wood
Northup Walter S bds 282 Wood
Norton John P janitor Y M C A rms State
Nunes Joseph rubber worker h 212 State
Nunes Manuel rubber worker h 212 State

R. I. RUG WORKS
Rugs Woven from old and new carpets. Telephones { 2203 / 2204
678 WESTMINSTER ST., PROVIDENCE

Nunes Manuel Jr rubber worker h 49 Prospect
Nussenfeld Samuel prop Washington Market 237 Thames h do
Oberg William carpenter h 342 High
O'Brien Catherine housekeeper 11 Borden av
O'Brien Edmund L mill hand h 48 Constitution
O'Brien James lineman 565 Hope h 10 Prospect
O'Brien Michael J dentist 497 Hope h Warren
O'Brien Ruth mill emp bds 48½ Constitution
O'Connor Elizabeth R rubber worker bds 471 Wood
O'Connor John S H rubber worker h 471 Wood
O'Connor Martin fireman 33 Congregational
O'Connor Mary J housekeeper bds 471 Wood
O'Connor Michael J h 471 Wood
O'Connor William J at rubber works h 106 State
O'Donnell Catherine rubber worker bds 70 Mt Hope av
O'Donnell Jeremiah S painter rms Church St House
O'Donnell Mary A Miss h 70 Mt Hope av
O'Donnell Thomas at rubber works bds 30 Mt Hope av
O'Donnell William T attorney at law 471 Hope h 31 Union
Oliver Anthony P sailor (U S N) bds 41 Bay View av
Oliver Anthony P Mrs h 41 Bay View av
Oliver Frank engineer bds 41 Bay View av
Oliver Isabelle rubber worker bds 41 Bay View av
Oliver Manuel teamster bds 41 Bay View av
Oliver Mary M rubber worker bds 41 Byfield
Olstadt Thomas mariner bds 30 Byfield
Opitz Henry retired h 17 Milk
Opper Manton A carriage painter bds 122 Mt Hope av
Orgelman Charles H foreman h 196 State
O'Reilly Vincent A grocer 52 Mt Hope av h 69 Burton
O'Rourke Arthur P bds 39 Bourne
O'Rourke Herbert L florist Samuel Kinder & Bro bds 39 Bourne
O'Rourke Peter J at rubber works bds 39 Bourne
Orthmann John H retired bds 40 Catherine
O'Shea Daniel farmer h 324 Metacom av nr Bay View av
O'Shea Richard (U S A) bds 324 Metacom av
Ostby Christian master mechanic h 907 Hope
Osterberg Clarence A (U S N) bds 35 Central
Osterberg Esther J at rubber works bds 35 Central
Osterberg Helen J at rubber works bds 35 Central
Osterberg Knut A upholsterer h 35 Central
Ostrander Sylvia DeW widow Cornelius V B (N Y) h 12 Church

Pailthorpe George S clerk bds 11 Cottage
Pailthorpe John C at rubber works bds 11 Cottage
Pailthorpe Sarah widow George h 11 Cottage

Water Supply Outfits | Walter H. Jackson Co. | "Dodd" System
House Pumps | 435 Industrial Trust Building | Lightning
 | Providence, - R. I. | PROTECTION

Paine Stella F and Della E sum res (New Bedford) h Gooding av Little's Narrows
Paine George T laborer h 33 Woodlawn av
Paine William P sail maker bds 33 Woodlawn av
Paley Meyer junk dealer rear 39 Catherine bds 20 Catherine
Palmer Charles A clerk h 11 Byfield
Palmer Julia A widow Frederick bds 11 Byfield
Palumbo Domenico variety store and steamship agent 467 Wood h 6 Bay View av
Palumbo Eva clerk 467 Wood bds 6 Bay View av
PANZARELLA ANGELO C dry goods and shoes 401 Wood h 421 do—see page 19
Panzarella Antonio shoemaker 17 Congregational
Panzarella Salvatore shoemaker 17 Congregational
Paquin Fred rubber worker bds over Buffington's Drug Store
Paquin Joseph oysterman h 221 Thames
Pardey Charles H (U S N) bds 61 Mt Hope av
Pardey Hattie M Mrs h 61 Mt Hope av
Parker William B head nurse Soldiers' Home h do
Partington Joseph at rubber works h 108 State
Pasho John rubber worker h 242 State
Pasho John Jr rubber worker bds 242 State
Pasho Marcan rubber worker h 161 Franklin
Pastime Theater 85 State
Patstone Alfred A glazier h 122 Mt Hope av
Patstone Frederick J (U S A) bds 122 Mt Hope av
Paul John mill emp h 34 Thames
Paul see Paull
Paull Anne M widow Henry E h 22 Oliver
Paull Benjamin produce dealer h 694 Hope
Paull Catherine school teacher bds 889 Hope
Paull Charles farmer h 34 Oliver
Paull Eugenia F widow Seth h 702 Hope
Paull Frank prop (Seth Paull Co) 267 Thames h 649 Hope
Paull Grace C bds 702 Hope
Paull Jeannette Grace Miss bds 900 Hope
Paull J Howard clerk (Prov) bds 649 Hope
Paull Marion H Mrs meat market and grocery 679 Hope h 889 do
Paull Martha B bds 46 Franklin
Paull Prescott B clerk 267 Thames bds 649 Hope
Paull Reba R P bds 900 Hope
Paull Sarah J widow Augustus R h 46 Franklin
Paull Seraphine B Mrs dressmaker h 42 Franklin

WHITTEMORE & COLBURN
PRINTERS   15 Pine St., PROV.

VALENTINE'S Diamond & Star FIRE BRICK | **JAMES C. GOFF CO. 31 to 49 POINT ST. Providence, R. I.**

Paull Seth Co (F Paull prop) coal and lumber 267 Thames
Paull Zebede broker (Prov) h 900 Hope
Payne see Paine
Peabody Frances E widow of Frederick h 93 High
Peabody Ralph shipping clerk h 494 Thames
Pearce Frank C clerk bds 63 Court
Pearce Frank K hairdresser 559 Hope h 63 Court
Pearce see Pearse also Pierce
Pearse Albert S h 154 High
Pearse Edward B h 93 Franklin
Pearse Isabella widow John R h 115 High
Pearse Mabel R dressmaker 115 High h do
Pearse William B bookkeeper Namquit Worsted Co bds 115 High
Pearse see Pearce also Pierce
Peate Grace widow Joseph A bds 46 Byfield
Pebelo Robert emp N I R Co h 32 Rock
Peck Albert P clerk (Prov) bds 35 Burton
Peck Frank farmer bds 34 Oliver
Peck Gertrude F bds 35 Burton
Peck Harriet P widow George H h 35 Burton
Peck John D hay and grain Thames nr Franklin
Peck Louis H F fire insurance (Prov Wash) h 149 High
Peck Lydia J widow of Horace bds 974 Hope
Peck Sarah V G Miss h 932 Hope
Peckham Emily W bds 24 Court
Peckham Harriet L dressmaker bds 702 Hope
Peckham Josiah F h 24 Court
Pedley Harold E wool sorter bds 116 Mt Hope av
Pendleton Charles L emp gas office h 47 Franklin
Pepe Francesco grocer 429 Wood h 39 School
Peper Charles J machinist h 260 Hope
Perkins Lizzie Miss h 148 High
Perry Anna Elizabeth Nellie Misses sum res h Little's Narrows
Perry George E boat carpenter h 341 High
Perry Horatio N h 101 High
Perry Jessie rubber worker bds 157 Franklin
Perry Joseph rubber worker h 5 Easterbrooks av
Perry Joseph rubber worker h 10 Gray
Perry Joseph rubber worker h 175 Franklin
Perry Joseph rubber worker h 9 Silton
Perry Joseph D rubber worker h 41 Bay View av
Perry Manuel bar tender h First School
Perry Manuel rubber worker h 3 Third School
Perry M DeW Miss h 132 High
PERRY STORAGE CO (Wm W Perry) mgr rear Hope cor Perry—see page 21

ESTABLISHED 1873

BROWN'S
FALL RIVER'S LEADING STORE

'IF IT COMES FROM BROWN'S IT'S GOOD'

If you are unable to come to Fall River's Shopping Center, Mail or Phone your orders. Our facilities are unsurpassed for Out-of-Town Service.

WE CARRY THE MOST EXCLUSIVE LINES of WOMEN'S, MISSES and CHILDREN'S MILLINERY, SUITS, COATS, DRESSES, WAISTS, HOSIERY, SHOES, GLOVES, and Dress Accessories in Southeastern Massachusetts. Also Complete Lines of FURNITURE, CARPETS AND FLOOR COVERINGS, KITCHEN UTENSILS, GRAFONOLAS, ETC.

E. S. BROWN COMPANY
168-188 North Main Street, Fall River, Mass.

VALUE OF PHOTOGRAPHY

IT HAS
BEEN
PROVEN
IN
THE PAST

That Photography forms a priceless record of Events and People.

Modern Photography is always appreciated, and our Studio has long Excelled in High-Grade Portraiture

Yᴱ ROSE STUDIO

385 Westminster St.   A. G. Skonberg

RALPH C. WATROUS CO.
RESIDENTIAL and INVESTMENT PROPERTY
Of All Kinds For Sale
437 Industrial Trust Building

Perry William grocery Court also at rubber works h 7 Narragansett av
PERRY WILLIAM W civil engineer also mgr Perry Storage Co h 814 Hope—see page 21
Peters Bridget widow Richard h 76 Bay View av
Peters James sum res (Prov) h Mt Hope Shore end Soldiers' Home rd
Peters Manuel coal worker h 14 Third School
Peters Margaret A bds 76 Bay View av
Peters Philomena D clerk 439 Hope bds 100 Mt Hope av
Peterson Charles boat rigger h 13 Summer
Peterson Henry W master mechanic h 112 Bradford
Peterson Robert H liquors 18 State h 116 Bradford
Petty Ellen F rubber worker bds 78 Thames
Petty Harriet widow John F h 33 Cook
Pevin Frank chauffeur h 14 Washington
Pevin Joseph plumber h 11 Washington
Pevin Philip painter h 152 Thames
Phair John J rubber worker h 14 Bourne
Phenes Isaac tailor 17 State h 49 Catherine
Philleo Winifred B domestic science teacher bds 224 Hope
Pickles Ada J bds 25 Pierce av
Pickles Fred foreman bds 25 Pierce av
Pickles John wire inspector bds 25 Pierce av
Pickett Mae emp N I R Co bds D'Wolf Inn Thames
Pierce Anna Miss teacher bds 53 Burton
Pierce George (U S A) bds 41 Bradford
Pierce James T (U S A) bds 41 Bradford
Pierce Mary A widow of Walker h 53 Burton
Pierce William J rubber worker h 41 Bradford
Pierce William J Jr rubber worker bds 41 Bradford
Pierce see Pearce also Pearse
Pike J P summer res (Attleboro) h Little's Narrows
PIMENTEL & SOUSA props meat market 217 Wood—see page 19
Pischier Louis machinist bds 11 Byfield
Pitman Elizabeth H and Mary A Misses h 38 Franklin
Pitts Gussie stenographer bds 84 High
Place Harold E clerk 485 Hope bds Warren
Place Lenius E variety store 485 Hope h Warren
Poli Alberto teamster cor State and Rock
Polleys Woodbury S stock man at rubber works h 16 Union
Pollock George T foreman h 29 Noyes av
Pollock John B foreman h 92 Constitution
Ponte Joseph rubber worker h 10 Silton

Blackstone Canal Nat'l Bank **20 Market Sq., Prov. R. I.**	A Progressive Bank Fully Equipped for Service

Warren Monumental Works
Cor. Railroad Avenue and Croade Street, Warren, R. I.

Poppasquash R R Station (Asahel M Miller agt) Poppasquash rd nr Hope
Porter George (U S A) bds 9 Prospect
Porter John at rubber works h 9 Prospect
Porter Samuel at rubber works bds 9 Prospect
Post Office Hope near State
Posytan Henry H photographer 56 State h 61 Catherine
Potter Byron T summer res off Ferry rd Ferry Hill
Potter F Helen stenographer bds 825 Hope
Potter Frank W at rubber works h 30 Washington
Potter Fred clerk bds 37 Washington
Potter John H conductor N Y N H & H R R h 825 Hope
Potter John R carpenter h Gooding av
Potter Josiah W engineer h 37 Washington
Potter Marion G stenographer bds 825 Hope
Potter Mary M W widow Walter A h 344 Hope
Potter Minnie A bds 37 Washington
Potts Lyman F fisherman h 14 Bradford
Pozzi Giovanni grocery 139 Bradford h 32 Munroe av
Preble Matthew iron worker bds 19 Collins
Prends C Manuel rubber worker h 147 Franklin
Priest Charles H machinist h 57 Church
Providence Telephone Co Bristol Exchange (S H White mgr) 565 Hope
Provost Joseph mill emp h rear 210 Thames
Prudence Island Transportation Co (Capt Halsey Chase prop) Church St Dock
Prullo P Manuel rubber worker h 9 Silton
Pryor Mary A stitcher bds 341 High
Puggino Alfonso liquor dealer 410 Wood h 163 Bradford
Quinn Daniel at boat shop h 28 Burton
Quinn Edward A liquors 220 Thames h 527 Wood
Quinn Hugh clerk bds 46 Munroe av
Quinn Michael bartender 220 Thames h 46 Munroe av
Quintal Donat weaver h 299 Thames
Quirk Bros (Quirk Edward J) grocers 173 State h 42 Byfield
Quirk Edward J grocer State cor Wood h 40 Byfield
Quirk Mary E bookkeeper Quirk Bros h 46 Byfield
Rafferty Marion emp N I R Co bds D'Wolf Inn Thames
Rainville Alfred laborer bds 9 Constitution
Rainville Annie mill emp bds 9 Constitution
Rainville Charles carpenter h 21 Milk
Rainville Simeon mill emp h 9 Constitution
Rapano Edward Mrs h 36 Bourne
Rawson Elizabeth housekeeper bds 202 High
Rawson Frank S rubber worker h 44 Oliver
Rawson Jasper R salesman Wardwell Lumber Co h Prov
Rawson John F (U S N) h 41 Cottage

Rawson Susan D Mrs milliner h 41 Franklin
Rawson William A painter h 96 High
Read Alma stenogragher bds 84 High
Read Helen N mgr and treas Bristol Women's Exchange
    h 31 Constitution
Read see Reed also Reid
Rebello Antonio P Rev pastor St Elizabeth's R C Church
    h 577 Wood
Reed A F boat builder bds 65 Burton
Reed Charles E teamster h 8 Second
Reed Charles F wire drawer h 245 Thames
Reed House Furnishing Co (Daniel J Sullivan local mgr)
    30 Bradford
Reed John F engineer h 9 Anthony av
Reed Stella bds 9 Anthony av
Reed see Read also Reid
Rego Antonio mill emp bds 55 Court
Reid Mary G maid 249 Hope
Reid see Read also Reed
Reilly Bernard D laborer h 387 High
Relle Edward E at rubber works h 42 Oliver
Relle Edward H rubber worker bds 42 Oliver
Remieres Frank T hardware etc 573 Hope h 94 Church
Remieres Walter T Mrs prop Revere House h do
Remieres Walter T clerk h 9 Church
Remieres William H bookkeeper 573 Hope h 12 Pierce av
Remington Henry W h 105 State
Renaud Alfred weaver h 62 Oliver
Reposa John rubber worker h 10 Gray
Reposa Manuel rubber worker h 169 Franklin
Revere House (Mrs Walter T Remieres prop) board and
    room 9 Church
Reynolds Alonzo rubber worker bds Jeremiah Kirby
Reynolds Charles B watchman bds Moses Whiting
Reynolds Charles B Jr clerk bds 48 Oliver
Reynolds Elliott P farm hand bds M Warren Whitney
Reynolds Madeline private secy bds 999 Hope
R I Boy Scouts Bristol Troup No 1 681 Hope George R Fisk
    scout master
Riccardi Carlo barber 359 Wood h 32 Pierce av
Rice Vern L pattern maker h 943 Hope
Richardson George carpenter h 56 Union
Richmond Virginia T Miss h 145 High
Rickson Edward bds 17 Union
Rickson James R boat builder h 17 Union

Merewether & Dunn
Plumbing and Heating Contractors
31 TURNER AVENUE,   RIVERSIDE, R. I.

Riley Caroline widow Richard bds 40 Cottage
Rilley Cornelius h 37 Bourne
Rinaldi Saverio bartender 176 Bradford h 32 Constitution
Rinaldi Severio rubber worker h 32 Congregational
Rishe Daniel A rubber cutter h 408 Wood
Rishe Elmer rubber worker bds 283 Wood
Rishe Mary E rubber worker bds 408 Wood
Robertson David rubber worker h 114 Constitution
Robertson James T marine engineer h 40 Constitution
Rockwell Charles B pres and treas Cranston Worsted Mills h 610 Hope
Rockwell Charles B Jr asst treas Cranston Worsted Mills h 180 Hope
Rockwell Martha B S Convalescent Home Mrs Bessie G Wilbur matron 41 Usher pl
Roderick Antoine furniture mover 20 State h do
Rodrick Burt rubber worker h 104 Bay View av
Rodrick Joseph rubber worker h 94 Bay View av
Rogers Free Library (George U Arnold librarian) 525 Hope
Rogers Joseph rubber worker h 6 Easterbrooks av
Rohrman Henry retired h 149 Mt Hope av
Rohrman John at rubber works h 13 Prospect
Rolf Henry N truck driver h 554 Thames
Romano Domenico restaurant 175 Bradford h do
Romano John (U S N) bds 175 Bradford
Romano Pasquale grocer 220 State h do
Romi Nunrio meat dealer 162½ Bradford bds 26 Charles la
Rosa Manuel rubber worker h 18 Rock
Rose Antone coal worker bds 6 Easterbrooks av
Rounds Archie H carpenter h 114 Union
Rounds Charles V general repairer r 17 Pierce av h 165 High
Rounds Eugene A carpenter h 40 Church
Rounds Frank A sailmaker h 17 Charles
Rounds Maria bds Lidora Briggs
ROUNDS SPENCER carpenter and builder also building mover 60 Constitution h 17 Pierce av—see page 21
Rourke see O'Rourke
Rushneck John clerk bds 271 Wood
Russell Rachel May clerk Bristol Depot h Prov
Ryan Frank D laborer bds 16 Shaw's lane
Ryan John J laborer h 16 Shaw's lane
Ryone Eugene S (Ryone & Farr) garage h Gibson rd
Ryone Francis E cutter h 43 Church
Ryone & Farr (E S Ryone H C Farr) garage Constitution nr Hope
St Angelo Angelo foreman h 235 Wood
St Germain Jeremiah mill hand h 19 Lincoln av
St Germain Walter H shipping clerk h 126 Thames

St Lawrence Henry machinist bds 11 Byfield
Saints Emanuel stone worker h 1 Easterbrooks av
Saints Marian rubber worker h 18 Third School
Saldaniour Neta cook 64 High
Salisbury George shipping clerk bds 96 Burton
Salisbury Gertrude D widow James C h 96 Burton
Salisbury Mabel B Miss music teacher 96 Burton h do
Sanders see Saunders
Sanford Charles F h 1222 Hope
Sanford Helen T at rubber works bds 183 High
Sanford Leonard P boat builder h 25 Burton
Sansone Joseph meat market 121 Bradford bds 123 do
Sansone Pasquale grocer 117 Bradford h do
Sansone Peter garage High bds 123 Bradford
Sants Manuel rubber worker h 147 Franklin
Santulli Joseph barber for Nicholas Santulli bds 328 High
Santulli Lawrence rubber worker h 249 High
Santulli Nicholas barber 57 State h 328 High
Sarra Michael grocer 213 State h do
Saucier Edward chauffeur h 248 Thames
Saucier John laborer h 248 Thames
Saunders Charles A day watchman h 180 High
Saunders Ethel J teacher bds 180 High
Savory Ruth emp N I R Co bds D'Wolf Inn Thames
Sawyer Gertrude E school teacher bds 46 Constitution
Sawyer Lillian F Mrs h 18 Cottage
Sawyer Renne A bds 18 Cottage
Scanlon Annie principal Walley School bds 42 Union
Scanlon Julia widow Dennis F rubber worker h 593 Wood
Scanlon Katherine E teacher Walley School bds 42 Union
Scanlon Rose A bds 42 Union
Scanlon Thomas P clerk (Prov) h 42 Union
Schafft Fredricka N widow Andrew h 512 Thames
Schwartz David (Goldstein & Schwartz) 581 Hope h 5 Williams
Schlosser George vice-pres National India Rubber Co h Woonsocket
Schoorel Cornelius W K gardener 500 Hope h rear do
Scott Charles H rubber worker h 24 Lincoln av
Scott George summer res h Little's Narrows
Scott Mary F rubber worker bds Bay View av
Scott Winifred B housekeeper h Bay View av
Sellers William machinist helper bds 55 High
Serbst Frederick J Jr rubber worker bds Revere House
Serbst Henry F keeper Bristol County Jail 48 Court h do

Serbst James J laborer bds Revere House
Servant Joseph carpenter h 326 Thames
Sharkey Neil B steel worker h 19 Collins
Sharp Harriet E Miss bds Chas E Thomas B H
Shaw Clarence H wire inspector h 132 Hope
Shaw George E chief clerk h 165 Wood
Sheldon Newell B pur agt Herreshoff Mfg Co h 59 High
Shepard Emma J clerk bds 205 Thames
Shepard John C F fisherman also mgr fish market 205 Thames bds do
Shepard Marie T clerk 205 Thames bds do
Shepard Sophie J stenographer bds 205 Thames
Shepard Wilhelmina widow John fish market and oyster dealer 205 Thames h do
Shepard William J fisherman bds 205 Thames
Sherman Benjamin F h 381 High
Sherman Clinton T mgr Industrial Trust Co h 44 Church
Sherman Estelle emp N I R Co bds D'Wolf Inn Thames
SHERMAN HAROLD G druggist 399 Wood h at Prov
—see page 19
Sherman Marion student bds 44 Church
Sherman Mary emp N I R Co bds D'Wolf Inn Thames
Sherman Samuel E teamster h 90 Union
Sherman Sarah E widow Andrew J h 142 High
Shield Grace school teacher bds 58 Constitution
Shippee David laborer h 30 Oliver
Shippee George H freight clerk Bristol depot h 715 Hope
Shippee Harold D clerk bds 715 Hope
Siegal Oswald R physician 159 High h do office hours until 9:30 a m 2 to 3 and 7 to 8 p m telephone
Silva Anthony rubber worker bds 29 State
Silva Anthony rubber worker h 49 Catherine
Silva Joseph carpenter h 14 Easterbrooks av
Silva Joseph R liquor dealer 162 Bradford h 11 Easterbrooks av
Silva Manuel rubber worker h 93 Bay View av
Silvia Frank J clerk bds 29 State
Silvia Gabriel farmer h 22 Third School
Silvia John rubber worker h 116 Bay View av
Silvia John Jr teamster bds 116 Bay View av
Silvia Leo (U S A) bds 11 Easterbrooks av
Silvia Manuel rubber worker h 212 State
Silvia Manuel J rubber worker h 161 Franklin
Silvia Mary widow h 11 Easterbrooks av
Silvia Vegan rubber worker h 153 Franklin
Simioli Carlo bartender h 24 Mt Hope
Simmell William R yacht captain h 17 Woodlawn av
Simmons Emily widow h 215 Franklin

Simmons George W Estate of undertakers and emblamers (E L F Colwell prop) rear 104 Constitution
Simmons Hattie L dressmaker 27 Cook h do
Simmons Henry A farmer h 1302 Hope
Simmons Joseph (U S A) bds 215 Franklin
Simmons Joseph E farmer h Ferry rd
Simmons Margaret widow Jason h 67 Church
Simmons Richmond J machinist bds Alfred Dubuc Hope
Simmons Rodney D oysterman bds 67 Church
Simmons Walter E stock clerk h 27 Cook
Simmons William T (U S A) bds 67 Church
Simon Hilma A tel opr h 43 Church
Sinkerson William emp N R Works h 249 High
Sisson Annie D student bds 158 Wood
Sisson George T clerk 174 High h 158 Wood
Sisson George T Jr (U S N) bds 158 Wood
Sisson James (U S N) bds 158 Wood
Sisson William H clerk h 8 Cole
Sisters of Mercy 350 Wood
Skinner Harriett D bds 259 Hope
Skinner Miriam W bds 259 Hope
SKINNER P JR fire insurance and investment securities 259 Hope h do—see page 28
Slade Bertha E housekeeper bds 254 Hope
Slade Carrington P gardener h 250 Franklin
Slade Cecelia G Miss dressmaker 103 Bay View av bds do
Slade Dora M inspector N I R Co bds 254 Hope
Slade Fannie M mill emp h 254 Hope
Slade Florence L Miss milliner bds 103 Bay View av
Slade Francis A chauffeur bds Smith
Slade Lillian M asst matron Children's Home 48 Union
Slocum Charles A fisherman h Kickemuit (Warren)
Smith Bridget widow Robert bds 96 Thames
Smith Charles H foreman h 941 Hope
Smith Daniel machinist h 122 Constitution
Smith Joseph rubber worker h 184 Thames
Smith Maurice C treas & secy National India Rubber Co h Prov
Smith Raymond P painter and paper hanger 31 High h do
Smith Richard sum res (Warren) h Kickemuit
Smith Samuel J (U S N) bds 14 Bradford
Smith William salesman (Prov) h Little's Narrows
Smith William A driver h 78 Thames
Smith William F milk dealer Kickemuit av h do
Smith William T farm hand h 24 Washington

King's Fibrous Plaster Board & Hard Plaster
JAMES C. GOFF CO.
81 to 49 Point St., Prov., R. I.

Smithson George prop Church Street House 5 Church h do
Sodini & Guesti (Joseph Sodini Louis Guesti) bakers 51 State
Soper Edward marine engineer h 29 Garfield av
SOUSA ANTHONY J prop Luso-American 157 Bradford h do—see page 19
Sousa August grocer h 240 Franklin
Sousa Emily widow h 3 Easterbrooks av
Sousa Emlia widow Joseph h 23 Milk
Sousa Joseph grocer h 240 Franklin
Sousa John (U S A) bds 23 Milk
Sousa Manuel rubber worker h 161 Franklin
Sousa Mary h 161 Franklin
Sousa Mary mill emp bds 23 Milk
Sousa Minnie groceries h 240 Franklin
Sparks Albert E rubber worker h 55 Constitution
Sparks Albert E Jr (U S N) bds 55 Constitution
Sparks Albert M h 72 State
Sparks Charles H (U S A) bds 320 High
Sparks Charles W card writer h 320 High
Sparks Gerald B carpenter bds 72 State
Sparks Isabel M widow Joseph B h 111 Franklin
Sparks Marion G stenographer N I R Co bds 320 High
Sparks Nathaniel W rubber worker h 889 Hope
Sparks Samuel O watchman bds 111 Franklin
Spencer Frank F. steel worker bds 11 Byfield
Spencer George L naval architect h 69 Burton
Sperry & Hutchison Co The (Mrs A O Earle in charge) 495 Hope
Splain Rachel A mill emp bds 19 Hope
Splain Sarah A widow John P h 19 Hope
Spooner Frank E at rubber works h 1045 Hope
Spooner Lydia M widow Edward M h 41 Cottage
Spooner Mary E Miss teacher Oliver School h 41 Cottage
Spooner Sarah E widow William H h 693 Hope
Spooner William B rubber worker bds 693 Hope
Springer Franklin (U S A) bds 84 Burton
Springer Herbert L purser h 70 Thames
Springer John C h 84 Burton
Stanley Grace A Mrs milliner 70 State h at E Prov
Stanton Abbie and Harriet L Misses h 706 Hope
Stanton Emma B Miss registrar Brown University Providence bds 706 Hope
Stanton Fred machinist h 75 Burton
Stanton Margaret D B widow George F h 706 Hope
STAPLES COAL CO OF RHODE ISLAND Joseph W Martin pres 239 Thames—see page 5
Star Theatre (C H Dillon prop) 537 Hope
Starkey Henry steel worker h 87 Burton

State Armory Thames foot Church
Stearns John rubber worker rms Church Street House
Steen Rebecca bds Samuel J Steen
Steen Samuel J farmer h Metacom av near Woodlawn
Stewart John G rubber works bds 63 Burton
Stewart see Stuart
Stillwell Elsie actress bds 325 High
Stillwell Leonora Mrs h 325 High
Stoddard Paul carpenter h 11 Pleasant
Stokes Alfred retired h 39 Franklin
Stoughton Ada L housekeeper bds 96 High
Stoughton James F h Ferry rd
Straight Clark H real estate and auctioneer 329 Hope h do
Straight Fred M musician h 697 Hope
Straight Freda M tel operator N I R Co bds 329 Hope
Stuart Charles H bds 97 Constitution
Stuart John A blacksmith h 88 Church
STUART RICHARD S blacksmith steamboat wharf h 97 Constitution—see page 21
Stuart see Stewart
Sullivan Anna E school teacher bds 833 Hope
Sullivan Daniel J local mgr Reed House Furnishing Co h 60 Richmond
Sullivan Dennis B conductor bds James Tobin
Sullivan Florence F mgr N R Co h 2 Mt Hope av
Sullivan James E electrician h 833 Hope
Sullivan Michael rubber worker rms Church Street House
Supple Mary A h 189 State
Suso Joseph rubber worker h 13 Easterbrooks av
Sutcliffe Albert roller coverer h 710 Hope
Sutcliffe J William (U S A) bds 710 Hope
Sutcliffe Thomas E mill hand bds 710 Hope
Suzman Fred E clothing 533 Hope h 551 do
Swain James general mgr Herreshoff Manuf Co Inc h 68 Union
Swanson Elnora C school teacher bds 14 Franklin
Sweeney Thomas F yard foreman Wardwell Lumber Co h Fall River
Sylvester Annie M Miss bds 13 Rock
Sylvester Charles rubber worker bds 13 Rock
Sylvester Charles A (U S A) bds 62 Burton
Sylvester Frank rubber worker h 13 Rock
Sylvester Frank W bds 262 Wood
Sylvester Hannah E rubber worker bds 62 Burton
Sylvester James repairer bds 262 Wood

WARREN MONUMENTAL WORKS
Cor. Railroad Avenue and Croade Streets, Warren, R. I.

Sylvester Madeline I housekeeper bds 13 Rock
Sylvester Martha A widow Roscoe h 62 Burton
Sylvester Myrtle F bds 62 Burton
Sylvester Nellie M mill emp bds 62 Burton
Sylvester Pauline rubber worker bds 62 Burton
Sylvia Henry J rubber worker h 168 Mt Hope av
Sylvia Manuel F bds 168 Mt Hope av
Syortrito G fish dealer 170 Bradford
Syperiano Virginia rubber worker bds 116 Bay View av
Taft Herbert A chief electrician h 13 Summer
Talbee Edward janitor Colt Memorial School bds cor 60 Church
Talbot Walter O (Talbot & Hopkins electricians) h 44 Constitution
TALBOT & HOPKINS (Walter O Talbot Stephen W Hopkins) electrical contractors 53 Bradford—see page 4
Tammaro Carlo shoe maker 419 Wood h 136 Mt Auburn av
Tani Alfred meat market 12 State h 218 Thames
Tanner Samuel B farm hand bds 1200 Hope
Tarvis Manuel M farm hand h Metacom av nr Gooding av
Tattrie Allen U blacksmith R C Stuart h 135 Mt Hope av
Tattrie Arthur C carpenter h 18 Mt Hope av
Taylor Mildred Miss stenographer bds 240 Hope
Taylor Nancy R widow Samuel A h 2 Howe
Taylor Nellie A rubber works bds 2 Howe
Taylor Raymond F carpenter h 240 Hope
Taylor Rosina Mrs bds 2 Howe
Taylor William H clerk h Metacom av nr Warren line
Teller Henry L Jr physician 118 Bradford h do
Teria John rubber worker h 92 Bay View av
Terra Frank farm hand h cor Hope and Church B H
Thayer William H farmer h off Metacm av nr Kickmuit av
Thiele Herman G furniture 211 State h do
Thierbach Elsa F maid 64 High
Thomas Charles E cotton mfg h Gibson rd B H
Thomas Charles R bds Chas E Thomas B H
Thompson Abby A widow Charles H bds 129 Hope
Thompson Anna R Miss h 730 Hope
Thompson Charles O F bookkeeper (Prov) h 11 Munroe av
Thompson George L oyster opener bds Fred Thompson
Thompson Fred watchman oyster beds h ft of Asylum rd
Thompson Henry M h 198 High
Thompson M Ella Miss bds 98 High
Thurston Winthrop G town treasurer h 49 Woodlawn av cor Dunbar
Tilley Abbie A widow George h 927 Hope
Tilley Annie H widow William J h 16 Burton

Tilley Elizabeth M emp N I R Co bds 927 Hope
Tingley Edward H marble (at Prov) h 23 Union
Tingley Harleigh V S student bds 23 Union
Tingley Helen student bds 23 Union
Tirrell Annie W widow Charles matron Home for Aged Women 11 Franklin h do
Tirrell Charles E clerk bds 963 Hope
Tobin Annie M teacher bds James Tobin
Tobin Bessie B clerk bds 66 Franklin
Tobin Charles R trav salesman bds James Tobin
Tobin Ellen rubber works bds 66 Franklin
Tobin Emily F teacher bds James Tobin
Tobin Grace at rubber works bds 513 Wood
Tobin James h Hope near Warren line
Tobin Johannah bds 66 Franklin
Tobin John A painter h 363 High
Tobin Josephine school teacher bds 66 Franklin
Tobin Margaret rubber works bds 66 Franklin
Tobin Margery M clerk bds 66 Franklin
Tobin Michael J undertaker 66 Franklin h do
Tobin Sarah E widow Thomas h 513 Wood
Tobin Thomas Jr clerk bds 513 Wood
Tobin William J dentist 101 Bradford bds James Tobin
Toole John iron worker bds 19 Collins
Tooloonjian Burson rubber worker bds 152 Thames
TORREY ERNEST F painter bds 1039 Hope—see page 21
Torrey William E master mariner h 1039 Hope
Town Edgar third hand bds 72 Constitution
Town Herbert wool sorter h 72 Constitution
Trainor Edward cutter h 211 State
Trainor Owen cutter h 10 Munroe av
Travos Elvene rubber worker bds 3 Easterbrooks av
Traynor Anabel stenographer bds 47 First
Traynor Annie h 47 First
Traynor Edward laborer bds 47 First
Traynor Edward L plumber bds 27 Collins
Traynor Jennie L nurse bds 27 Collins
Traynor John summer res Little's Narrows
Traynor Patrick H rubber worker h 27 Collins
Trinity Church Parish House cor Bradford and Hope
Troiano Matteio grocer 570 Wood h 7 Usher av
Trotter A Ramsay (U S A) bds 814 Hope
Trotter Edith W bds 814 Hope
Trotter Helen H school teacher bds 814 Hope
Trotter William R rector Trinity Church h 16 Burton

Merewether & Dunn
Plumbing and Heating Contractors
31 TURNER AVENUE,   RIVERSIDE, R. I.

Trudeau Amos rubber worker bds 83 Franklin
Trudeau Amos Jr machinist h 83 Franklin
Trudeau Arthur boat builder h 494 Thames
Trudell Henry P (U S A) bds 156 Mt Hope av
Trudell Henry P teamster h 9 Second
Trudell John C teamster bds 14 Second
Trudell Nelson at rubber works h 156 Mt Hope av
Trudell Nelson J Jr supt L H Callan Construction Works h 17 Borden av
Trudell Peter F clerk bds 156 Mt Hope av
Tucker Frank Ramsey adv writer bds 30 Union
Tucker John H h 30 Union
Tucker John Hyrne Jr mgr Allen & Reed Corp (Prov) h 128 High
Turrillo Michael shoe dealer h 346 Wood h Bourne
Tuttle Charles H supt Bristol & Warren Water Works 553 Hope h 7 Smith
U S RUBBER CO rubber goods mfg Wood opp Bradford —see page 6
Usher Irene F Miss summer res h 417 Hope
Usher John h 1230 Hope beyond Gooding av
Usher John H farmer bds 1230 Hope
Usher John Jr farmer 1230 Hope 6th beyond Gooding av
Usher R Harold deck hand bds 1230 Hope
Usher Willard F farmer bds 1230 Hope
Vachon Napoleon mill emp h rear 210 Thames
Vallee Louis J at rubber works h 57 Constitution
Vallely Thomas A bartender 18 State bds opp do
Van Voast Denice mill emp bds 36 Congregational
Van Voast Louise S rubber worker bds 36 Congregational
Van Voast Robert H at rubber works bds 36 Congregational
Van Voast William H at rubber works h 36 Congregational
Van Voast William H Jr cutter h 11 Munroe av
Vargas Antonio grocer 198 Thames h do
Vargas J Frank rubber worker h 242 State
Varolo Peter shoe repairer 43 Bradford h 149 do
Vavares Manuel S rubber worker h 41 Bay View av
Vera Abel rubber worker h 3 Easterbrooks av
Vera John salesman h 320 Wood
Vera Manuel emp Rubber Co h 7 Easterbrooks av
Vera Manuel rubber worker bds 147 Franklin
Vera Manuel rubber worker h 205 Franklin
Vera Manuel rubber worker h 165 Franklin
Vera Manuel Jr rubber worker h 165 Franklin
Vera Mary widow h 3 Third School
Verboncoeur C Edward at rubber works h 27 Oliver
Vermette Alphonse iceman 410 Thames h do
Vermette Charles carpenter h 410 Thames
Vermette Ulric A foreman h 48½ Constitution

A Scientific Collection Service Based On The Principle of
HONESTY.
Western Mercantile Corporation, 420-421 Grosvenor Building Prov. R. I.   Tel. Union 1526

Vermette Wilfred carpenter h 402 High
Vickery Molly G tel operator Western Union Tel & Cable Co 421 Hope h Prov
Voccia Gennaro shoemaker N I R Co Bay View av
Voccia Giuseppe grocer 217 State
Wah Sam laundry 577 Hope h do
Waitt Ernest B box maker bds 16 Burton
WALDRON-BROWNELL CO (THE) (L B Waldron pres E P Brownell treas) 49 Bradford—see page 2
Waldron Caroline widow Charles A h 100 High
Waldron Company (The) (L B Waldron pres John R Magee treas) plumbing steam and gas fitting kitchen furnishings etc 49 Bradford
Waldron Ella H Mrs h 55 High
Waldron Ella M Miss teacher Oliver St School h 55 High
Waldron Harriet D Miss h 108 Union
Waldron Lewis B pres The Waldron-Brownell Co and pres The Waldron Co 49 Bradford h 44 Constitution
Walker David blacksmith h 6 Prospect
Wall Charles W carpenter and contractor 278 Hope h 28 Pierce av
Wall John H h 290 Hope
Walsh Catherine F rubber worker bds 43 Congregational
Walsh James J asst supt Prudential Life Insurance Co Bristol branch h 34 Bourne
Walsh Mary rubber worker bds 205 State
Walsh Mary A mill hand bds 43 Congregational
Walsh Patrick H second hand bds 43 Congregational
Walsh Patrick P at rubber works h 43 Congregational
Walsh Roger rubber works h 49 Bourne
Walsh Timothy E (U S N) bds 348 Wood
Wardwell Annie E widow Samuel D h 843 Hope
Wardwell Belle M Miss h 509 Hope
Wardwell Elizabeth S Miss h 328 Hope
Wardwell Frank M foreman h 974 Hope
Wardwell Harriet P Miss h 509 Hope
Wardwell Hezekiah C pres Wardwell Lumber Co h Metacom av near Bay View av
Wardwell James D h 10 Constitution
WARDWELL LUMBER CO lumber hardware etc Thames ft of Bradford—see head lines
Wardwell Samuel C boat builder bds 843 Hope
Warner Arthur W deck hand bds 1225 Hope
Warner Frederick L farmer h 1225 Hope

R. I. RUG WORKS Oriental Rugs Cleaned and Repaired.
Tels. Union 2203 and 2204
678 WESTMINSTER STREET, PROVIDENCE, R. I.

Warner Herbert A farmer h 37 Burton
Warner Thomas H painter h 270 High
Warren George B h 93 Bradford
Warren George W messenger Adams Exp Co h 93 Bradford
Warren Harriet N housekeeper 15 Church
Warren Helen B vocalist bds 93 Bradford
Warren Ina P Miss teacher Reynolds School bds 15 Church
Washington Market S Nussenfield prop 237 Thames
Watson Mary A widow John G bds 105 State
Weaver Charles E machinist h 39 Oliver
Weaver Ernest W contractor h 34 Pierce av
Webb Walter H pattern maker h Ferry rd nr Hope
Weeden Isabella F Miss bds 94 Church
Welch see Walsh
Wells Amanda shoe maker bds 78 High
Wells Edward gardener h 78 High
Wells Lida shoe maker bds 78 High
Wells Nelson Jr h 38 Bourne
Wells Sarah rubber worker bds 628 Wood
Wennerstrand Ivy mill emp bds 83 Burton
Wennerstrand Violet housekeeper 328 Hope bds do
Wennerstrand William rubber worker h 83 Burton
West Charles H at rubber works h 63 Charles
West Eva M clerk bds 25 Summer
West Everett carpenter h 168 Wood
West Gardiner chauffeur h Broad Common
West Harriet W bds Ferry rd
West James rubber worker h 15 Prospect
West James N farmer h 996 Hope
West J Nelson retired h 25 Summer
West John A rubber worker h 996 Hope
West Julia M h Ferry rd
West Mary E student bds 67 Burton
West Minnie bds Ferry rd
Western Union Telegraph & Cable Co (Leo G Cote agt) office 421 Hope
Weston Frank G nurseryman h 1191 Hope
Wheeler Henry butler 500 Hope
Whipple Charles clerk (Prov) bds 43 Byfield
White Annie widow of Luke h 57 Bay View av
White Annie E packing clerk N I R Co bds 348 Wood
White Ernest sum res (Attleboro) h Little's Narrows
White Isabelle Mrs sum res (Attle) h Little's Narrows
White James J second hand bds 348 Wood
White John R rubber worker h 97 Union
White Mary rubber worker bds 57 Bay View av
White Matthew rubber worker h 348 Wood
White Seth L at Benj Church Home 1010 Hope

Water Supply Outfits House Pumps	Walter H. Jackson Co. 435 Industrial Trust Building Providence, - R. I.	"Dodd" System Lightning PROTECTION

Whitley John E Rev pastor 1st Congregational Church h 35 Church
Whitney Elizabeth Miss sum res (Taunton) at John W Hammond's cottage
Whitney Frederick M sum res (Attle) h Little's Narrows
Whitney M Warren farmer h Metacom av nr town limits
Whittemore Alfratta M Miss dressmaker 201 High bds do
Whittemore Jane G widow of Samuel E h 201 High
Whittington Ann widow Edward h 37 Congregational
Wilbur Bessie G Mrs matron Martha B S Rockwell Convalescent Home 41 Usher pl h do
Wilbur Fred undertaker h 38 Union
WILBUR GEORGE M undertaker 38 Union also 209 So Main Warren h do—see page 22
Wilcox George G farm hand h Kickemuit av
Wilcox George S farmer h Gooding av opp Broad Common lane
Wilcox Henry Clay packer bds James H Wilcox
Wilcox Howard sum res h "The Plaza" B H
Wilcox James H farmer h nr foot Kickemuit av
Wilcox Mabel F boxmaker bds James H Wilcox
Wilcox Mary L widow Solomon bds George S Wilcox
Wilkinson Edward E foreman N I R Co h 39 Byfield
Wilkinson Edward J clerk h 38 Byfield
Wilkinson John J tailor 481 Hope h 875 do
Williams A Louisa wid Fielding L h 366 Hope cor Church
Williams Frederick W physician 249 Hope h do office hours 8 to 9 a m 2 to 3 and 7 to 8 p m tel
Williams Joseph rubber worker h 16 Thompson av
Williams Lillian emp N I R Co bds D'Wolf Inn Thames
Williams Mae emp N I R Co bds D'Wolf Inn Thames
Williams Mary E bookkeeper bds 564 Wood
Williams William F Jr (U S A) bds 249 Hope
Williston Amasa C clerk 361 Hope h 18 Church
Williston Elizabeth A stenographer (Prov) bds 18 Church
Wilson Ann E Mrs at Home for Aged Women 11 Franklin
Wilson Benjamin K rubber worker h 171 Wood
Wilson Charles C machinist h 239 Franklin
Wilson Elizabeth rubber worker bds 239 Franklin
Wilson Elizabeth H widow of Orrin h 30 Lincoln av
Wilson Frederick F clerk bds 239 Franklin
Wilson Lillian T milliner 450 Hope bds 36 Bradford
Wing Moy laundry 33 State h do
Witherell Carl C watchman h 11 Noyes av
Witherell Edward E carpenter h 73 Constitution

WHITTEMORE & COLBURN
PRINTERS 15 Pine St., PROV.

Witherell M E summer res (Prov) h Little's Narrows
Wood Ellen bds 59 Collins
Wood Frank E at rubber works h 1055 Hope
Wood James R plumber bds 59 Collins
Wood John h 59 Collins
Wood Joseph bank clerk h 114 Bradford
Wood Joseph S clerk 176 High h 15 Cottage
Wood J William clerk 525 Hope bds 59 Collins
Wood Lillian emp N I R Co bds D'Wolf Inn Thames
Wood Mary J rubber worker bds 59 Collins
Wood Moses farmer h Metacom av nr Bay View av
WOOD OTIS L livery stable 23 Court h 4 Bay View av cor High—see page 21
Wood Sarah F Miss h 332 High
Woodward Eugene F sum res (Attleboro) h Kickemuit
Wright Amos farmer h Metacom av nr Gooding av
Wright Frederick A at Benj Church Home 1010 Hope
Wright John W Jr clerk h 26 Burton
Wright Sarah R widow Allan G h 41 Constitution
Wyatt A Bertha and Madeleine W Misses h 89 State
Wylie Elizabeth G stitcher bds 11 Cottage
Wylie James F clerk h 11 Cottage
Xavier Julius F groceries Franklin cor Wood h 135 do
Xavier Mariano rubber worker h 133 Franklin
Yarlasabetsky Hyman storekeeper h 167 Franklin
Yergeau Omer blacksmith h 253 Thames
Young Bessie Mrs h 52 Court
Young Charles W sec and asst treas Herreshoff Mfg Co h 212 Hope
Young Charles W Jr stenographer and bookkeeper Herreshoff Mfg Co Inc h 31 Burton
Young Charlotte A school teacher bds 244 Hope
Young Harry I machinist h 21 Constitution
Young James h 31 Cottage
YOUNG J H & CO registered pharmacists 479 Hope h 244 do—see page 20
Young Leah B asst town clerk bds 69 Franklin
Young Men's Christian Association Y M C A building 448 Hope Joseph Milligan secretary
Young Sophia R bds 82 State
Young Vincent C (U S N) bds 212 Hope
Young William E shipping clerk bds 69 Franklin
Young William H retired h 69 Franklin

Industrial Trust Co.

49 WESTMINSTER STREET
PROVIDENCE, R. I.

TRANSACTS A GENERAL BANKING AND TRUST BUSINESS

Is authorized to act as Trustee, Executor, Administrator, etc.
Interest paid on Deposits, subject to check at sight.
Issues **Certificates of Deposits** for sums of money not subject to check, and allows a special rate of interest thereon.
Issues **its own Drafts and Travelers' Circular Letters of Credit** available in all parts of the world.
Offers to **Executors, Administrators, Guardians and Trustees, and Women** unaccustomed to the details of business, as well as **Religious and Benevolent Institutions**, special banking facilities.
Trustees, Executors, Administrators, Guardians and Assignees depositing their funds or property with this Company are **exempt by law** from all personal liability.
Acts as **Registrar and Transfer Agent** for Corporations.
Participation Account Quarters close the 15th days of February, May, August and November.
This account offers to depositors the advantages of **Savings Banks** with the additional security of the **Capital and Surplus** of the Company.

BRISTOL BRANCH,
525 Hope Street, Bristol, R. I.

EZRA DIXON, Chairman of Board
　　　　　　　　　　CLINTON T. SHERMAN, Manager

BOARD OF MANAGERS

Ezra Dixon	Nathaniel G. Herreshoff	Samuel P. Colt
P. Skinner, Jr.	W. F. Williams	H. Martin Brown
Eber Hill	Charles H. Church	Charles B. Rockwell
	Clinton T. Sherman	Russell S. Church

Accounts of Individuals, Firms, Corporations and Trustees respectfully solicited

Industrial Trust Co.

49 WESTMINSTER STREET
PROVIDENCE, R. I.

TRANSACTS A GENERAL BANKING AND TRUST BUSINESS

Is authorized to act as Trustee, Executor, Administrator, etc.
Interest paid on Deposits, subject to check at sight.
Issues **Certificates of Deposits** for sums of money not subject to check, and allows a special rate of interest thereon.
Issues **its own Drafts and Travelers' Circular Letters of Credit** available in all parts of the world.
Offers to **Executors, Administrators, Guardians and Trustees, and Women** unaccustomed to the details of business, as well as **Religious and Benevolent Institutions**, special banking facilities.
Trustees, Executors, Administrators, Guardians and Assignees depositing their funds or property with this Company are **exempt by law** from all personal liability.
Acts as **Registrar and Transfer Agent** for Corporations.
Participation Account Quarters close the 15th days of February, May, August and November.
This account offers to depositors the advantages of **Savings Banks** with the additional security of the **Capital and Surplus** of the Company.

WARREN BRANCH
Main and Market Streets, Warren, R. I.

JOSEPH W. MARTIN, Chairman of Board
EDWIN A. CADY, Manager

BOARD OF MANAGERS

Luther Cole	Francis E. Dana	Edwin A. Cady
Joseph G. Luther	Frank Hail Brown	Clarence H. Seymour
Joseph W. Martin	John H. Brown	Jeremiah Goff
Samuel L. Peck	James B. Drown	Samuel P. Colt
	H. Martin Brown	

SAFES in our Fire and Burglar Proof Vault to Rent at from $5 to $25 per year.

Ralph C. Watrous Co.
ESTATE MANAGERS.   RENT COLLECTION A SPECIALTY
437 INDUSTRIAL TRUST BUILDING

WARREN
GENERAL DIRECTORY

COPYRIGHT 1918, BY UNION PUBLISHING CO.

ABBREVIATIONS.—Ab., above; agt., agent; av., avenue; bds., boards; bet., between; B. H., Bristol Highlands; bldg., building; blk., block; bey., beyond; cor., corner; ct., court; do., ditto; E., East; exp., express; fr., from; ft., foot; f. n., factory number; h., house; ins., insurance; manuf., manufacturer; mfg., manufacturing; N., North; N. I. R. Co., National India Rubber Company; nr., near; opp., opposite; pl., place; P. O., Post Office; pres., president; prop., proprietor; Prov., Providence; N. Y., N. H. & H. R. R, New York, New Haven & Hartford Railroad; r., rear; rd., road; rms., rooms; R. R., Railroad; S., South; sec., secretary; sq., square; st., street; supt., superintendent; treas., treasurer; U. S. A., United States Army; U. S. N., United States Navy; W., West. After the name of the street, the word "street" is omitted.

Abbot Charles W Major (retired U S A) h 15 Miller
Abbot Marion bds 11 Miller
Abbot Sarah C widow of Capt Trevett Abbot U S N h 11 Miller
Abrahams George mule spinner h Market
Abrahams Martha weaver bds Market
Abrahms Herbert mill emp h Market
Abrahms John T mill emp h Market
Ackerman Abraham second hand dealer Water h cor State and Water
Ackerman Samuel bds cor State and Water
Adam John oyster opener bds 7 Union
Adams Annie bds 168 S Water
Adams Emma h 168 S Water
Adams Express Co Frank J Conley agt office S Main cor Joyce
Adams George W clerk 191 S Main h off Metacom av
Adams John H retired bds 88 Child
Ainsworth Ernest second hand h 6 Federal
Ainsworth Ethel L bds 38 Child

Blackstone Canal Nat'l Bank 20 Market Square PROVIDENCE, R. I.
Capital, $500,000.   Surplus Profits, over $500,000

Warren Monumental Works
Cor. Railroad Avenue and Croade Street,   Warren, R. I.

Ainsworth Harold tinsmith bds 30 Wood
Ainsworth James E emp Electric Light Co h 30 Wood
Ainsworth Mary E mill emp bds 30 Wood
Ainsworth Robert overseer Warren Mfg Co h Child cor
    Adams
Aldrich Ada F Mrs clerk 462 Hope h 73 Constitution
Aldrich Charles A farmer h 73 Constitution
Alger Beatrice rubber worker bds 19 Cole
Alger Joseph C rubber worker h 19 Cole
Allard Charles h 31 Pierce av
Allen Annie S Rev pastor Pentecostal Church h 154 Wood
Allen Eunice M bds 154 Wood
Allen Florence S teacher Joyce St School h 55 N Water
Allen Fred summer res h Touisset Neck
Allen Grace R Mrs stenographer Narragansett Worsted Co
    h 12 Baker
Allen M Mrs housekeeper Colt Farm Poppasquash
Alletag Josephine rubber worker bds 30 Child
Alletag Otto J grocer's clerk 28 Child h 30 do
Alletag Rudolf (U S A) bds 30 Child
Almeda John rubber worker bds Market
Amedee Napoleon track walker h 10 Asselin
Amedee Wilfred laborer h 8 Asselin
Andrew Alice widow Samuel bds 9 Baker
Andrews Corella P housekeeper bds 21 State
Andrews Edwin L bds E J Young Metacom av
Andrews Jack farmer h Poppasquash rd
Andruszewski Dymitr speed tender h Company block
Andruszewski Michael bds 65 Bowen
Angell W H Hardware Co (W H Angell prop) South Main
Angell William H prop W H Angell Hardware Co h Touisset
Anjers Jean Baptiste laborer h 78 Child
Anthony Maude P Mrs stenographer Industrial Trust Co
    h 20 Washington
Ardecka Charles spinner bds Main
Ardecka Josephine weaver h Main cor Water
Armstrong M Louise h 64 North Water
Armstrong Simon driver h 64 North Water
Armstrong Simon Jr driver bds 64 North Water
Armstrong William laborer bds 64 North Water
Arnold Edwin B engineer bds 341 South Main
Arnold George B tag manuf 341 So Main h do
Arnold J Albert salesman h 22 Market
Ashton Rachael rubber worker bds 252 Wood
Ashton William W caretaker h Poppasquash rd
Asp Anna bds 59 Market
Asp August rubber worker h 59 Market
Asselin Amanda bds 59 Market
Asselin Diana teacher (piano) bds Napoleon Asselin

Asselin Donat clerk bds Napoleon Asselin
Asselin Ernest loomfixer bds 3 Asselin's plat
Asselin Ernest loomfixer h 59 Market
Asselin Hector prop Premier Bakery 89 Market bds 3 Asselin's plat
Asselin Joseph J loomfixer h 3 Asselin's plat
Asselin Napoleon liquor dealer 29 Market h opp do
Atkinson Edwin T (U S N) bds R P Atkinson
Atkinson Robert P Capt oyster boat h Green's Landing S W
Atwood H & R J (W Goodspeed mgr) wholesale oyster dealers foot of Washington
Atwood Sarah A widow Charles bds 6 Barney
Aubin Albert weaver bds 26 Metacom av
Aubin Aldridge machinist bds 26 Metacom av
Aubin Clephas widow of John h 64 Kickemuit av cor Metacom av
Aubin Dora weaver bds 26 Metacom av
Aubin Elizabeth mill emp bds 26 Metacom av
Aubin Joseph carpenter bds 26 Metacom av
Aubin Mary mill emp h 26 Metacom av
Aubin Wilfred carpenter h 3 Metacom av
August Dennis teamer h Miller
August Emma V bookkeeper Reed House Fur Co h Bristol
August Enos laborer h 59 Company
Auld John at Gas Works h 201 South Main
Autieri Moroy rubber worker h 168 Wood
Backus John W spinner h 167 Brown
Bacon Agnes Mrs h 15 Church
Bacon Alfred printer The Warren and Barrington Gazette bds 15 Church
Bacon Maria bds 15 Church
Bacon Oliver boot and shoe repairer 100 S Water h do
Bain Anna widow bds 21 Manning
Baker Catherine A shoe worker h 45 Bowen
Baker Virginia Miss principal Miller Street School h 6 School
Baldiga Joseph h Cutler
Baldiga Marcel laborer bds 11 Metacom av
Baldwin Arthur lighthouse keeper Bristol Ferry Light h do
Baldwin John weaver h 40 Bowen
Ballou Charles h Woodlawn av
Bander Joseph M clothing and shoe dealer 135 S Main h 302 do
Bandurck Julian slubber tender bds Company blk Union
Bardsley Henry fireman h 184 South Water

Barker Ellen bds 19 Vernon
Barker Francis P florist Middle off Child h do
Barker George florist Metacom av cor Parker av
BARKER LOUIS F florist Barker h do—see page 25
Barnaby Frank D farmer bds Touisset rd head of Child
Barney Ann E widow John W h Manning and Washington
Barney Bros florists Metacom av and Parker av
Barney Charles E oysterman bds Asylum rd cor Child
Barney Francis R farmer h Asylum rd near Child
Barney Herbert T oysterman bds Asylum rd cor Child
Barney Milton E physician Manning cor Washington h do
Barnstead Robert brass fitter bds 96 Constitution
Baron Belle rubber worker bds 16 Catherine
Baron Max rubber worker h 16 Catherine
Barre (French) see Barry (English)
Barrington William H clerk bds Hope
Barrows Edward sum res Woodlawn av
Barrus Jerome L crossing tender h 14 Croade
Barrus Jerome L Mrs bookkeeper h Croade
Barry Helen stenographer bds 40 King
Barry James F janitor h 40 King
Barry James F Jr clerk bds 40 King
Barry James P watchman h 10 Luther
Barry John A surveyor h Handy's lane near Market
Barry Susie widow Edward L bds 40 King
Bartlett Edward E supt Parker Mill No 2 100 Metacom av h 142 Child
Bartlett Frank teamer h Cole
Bartlett Jean Mrs h 142 Child
Bartlett Joseph mill operative h Cole
Bartlett Louis D asst supt (Prov) bds 4 Washington
Barton Alfred C clerk Warren Mfg Co h 17 Washington
Barton Edwin S clerk 124 S Main h 21 Manning
Barton Mary Mrs mill emp h Market
Bartusicwicz Adam laborer h 98 Johnson
Batchelor John B grocery and market S Main cor Child h 9 Miller
Batchelor Mary J widow James h 9 Miller
Bateman Samuel emp Warren Mfg Co bds Market
Battey David C h foot of Maple
Beals Charles R (U S A) h 1183 Hope
Beauchaine Arthur driver h 77 North Main
Beauchaine Fred (U S A) bds 15 Liberty
Beauchaine George mill emp h 15 Liberty
Beauchaine George Jr clerk bds 15 Liberty
Beauchaine Henry H mill emp bds 7 Liberty
Beauchaine Noe bartender h 18 Hope
Beauchamps Joseph loomfixer h f n 137 North Main
Beaudrice Beaulerice spinner bds 11 Hope

Beaupre Alfeda bds Mulberry
Beaupre Ernest mill emp bds Mulberry
Beaupre Irving laborer bds Mulberry
Beaupre Joseph spinner bds Mulberry
Beaupre Samuel laborer bds Mulberry
Beaupre Wilfred weaver h Mulberry
Beauparlant James spinner h 24 Wood
Beauparlant Joseph mill emp h 2 Nobert
Beauparlant Joseph A spinner h South Water cor Church
Beauparlant Ludgar mill emp bds 11 Warren av
Beauregard Radric carpenter h Market
Beauregard Walter emp Nar Elec Co h 136 Child
Bedard Delphice L cigars tobacco and confectionery 96½ N Main h r 91 N Main
Bedard Louis oysterman bds rear 91 North Main
Beetle Frank W Capt oyster boat h 49 King
Belanger Avide station agent h 26 Child
Belanger Frank laborer h Buffalo av
Bell Harry painter bds 262 High
Bellaire Arthur boat builder bds 8 Vernon
Bellaire Henry (U S A) bds 8 Vernon
Bellaire Napoleon boat builder h 8 Vernon
Benjamin Lewis grocer 254 Wood h 73 Burton
Bennett Eva G teacher (Arlington R I) bds 11 Federal
Bennett Florence S supervisor of drawing Warren Schools bds 11 Federal
Bennett Sidney J h 204 South Main
Bennett William S (W S Bennett & Co) Main cor Joyce h 11 Federal
BENNETT W S & CO (W S Bennett H K DeWolf) registered pharmacist Main cor Joyce—see page 27
Benoit Thomas D loomfixer h 20 North Main
Bento Joseph farm hand h 20 Wheaton
Berard Emile retired h 16 Luther
Berard Ernest H clerk 154 S Main nr Child bds 7 Handy
Bergeron G Gernon physician 230 South Main h do
Bergeron Hortense teacher bds 230 South Main
Bergeron Louise bookkeeper bds 230 South Main
Bergeron Rosetta teacher bds 230 South Main
Bergeron Yvonne teacher bds 230 South Main
Bernard Louis mill emp h 3 Nobert
Bernard Louis mill emp bds 3 Nobert
Bernatchey Charles h 15 Market
Bernatchey Delaire mill emp bds 15 Market
Bernatchey Gerard painter bds 15 Market

WARDWELL LUMBER CO.
BRISTOL, R. I.
All Kinds of
BUILDING MATERIAL
at
LOWEST PRICES

Bernatchey Joseph bds 15 Market
Bernier Joseph F crossing tender h 49 Market
Bernier Regina clerk 165 S Main bds 49 Market
Bernier Wilfred bds 12 Union
Besaw Charles J gent's furnishings and dry goods Saugy bldg h 8 Vernon
Besaw George E mason h 8 Barney
Besaw Margaret operative bds G E Besaw
Bettencourt Manuel S farmer h Kinnicutt av
Bezak Peter mill emp h Company blk Bowen
Bicl John farmer h Swamp rd
Bidon Amanda widow Maxim h 22 Market
Bidon Lumina school teacher bds 22 Market
Biel John farmer h Birch Swamp road
Biernacki Andrew h 86 Company
Biernacki Joseph weaver bds 100 Company
Biernacki Michael carder bds 91 Johnson
Bird John P plumber h South Main cor Vernon
Bizier Napoleon carpenter bds 10 Asselin
Black David C h 256 South Main
BLACKMAR CHARLES R JR electrical contractor also agt Westinghouse Lamp 2 Church h River road Barrington—see page 22
Blaine James G Jr sum res Ferry Hill
Blais Alexena mill emp bds 1 Union
Blais Emile laborer bds 75 North Water
Blais Eugene B mill emp bds 1 Union
Blais Harameede oysterman bds 75 North Water
Blais James rubber worker h 123 South Water
Blais Joseph mill emp h 162 Park
Blais Lydia mill emp bds 1 Union
Blais Mary widow Nazaire h 75 North Water
Blais Mary bds f n 134 North Main
Blais Philomene widow Samuel h 162 Park
Blanchard Delia h 402 High
Blanchard Maud A bookkeeper bds 9 Green
Blanchard Wallace A mgr Peck's Grain Store Bristol h 9 Greene
Blanchard Wilfred rubber worker bds 402 High
Bleming A Carrie maid D H Child South Main
Bliss Benjamin A h 24 Washington
BLISS CHARLES C newsdealer stationery etc Goff's Hotel bldg bds 24 Lyndon—see page 25
Bliss Charles H 24 Lyndon
Bliss Frank W liquor dealer bds 24 Lyndon
Bliss George E com traveler bds 24 Lyndon
Bliss & Co wholesale liquors 105 Child
Block Joseph B electrician h 2 North Main
Blouin Albert electrician bds 14 Wood

WALTER H. JACKSON CO. 435 Industrial Trust Building
PROVIDENCE, R. I.
"DELCO" ELECTRIC LIGHTING & PUMPING PLANTS
WINDMILLS, GASOLINE ENGINES AND TRACTORS

Blouin Elzear carpenter h 14 Wood
Blouin Ida mill emp bds 14 Wood
Blouin Leonidas carpenter h 10½ Hope
Blount Byron B (U S N) bds 7 Wheaton
Blount Eddie B oyster dealer S Water bey Wheaton h 7 Wheaton
Blount Florence L musician bds 7 Wheaton
Blount Will E capt of oyster boat bds 7 Wheaton
Boardman Hollis B traveling salesman bds 78 State
Bochcuski Walter fruit peddler h Market
Bodzian Michael carder h Metacom av
Boisvert Wilfred loomfixer h 54 Child
Booth Florence inspector Parker Mill bds 157 Child
Booth William E iron moulder h 11 Church
Boothman George P acting agt Narra Worsted Co h Haile
Borkin Bridget maid 192 South Main
Borkowski Ksavery carder h Market
Bosworth Charles E (E B Bosworth & Son) machinist Manning h 18 Baker
Bosworth E B & Son (Charles E Bosworth mgr) machinists' and jewelers' tools Manning
Bosworth Grace B widow Martin L h 92 State
Bosworth James A florist h 204 Wood
Bouchard Charles second hand h 8 Metacom av
Bouchard Lucien third hand bds 8 Metacom av
Bouchard Zoe Mrs h off Parker av
Boucher Alfred laborer h 4 Company
Boucher Drendonne h 41 Metacom av
Boucher Joseph teamster h 17 Metacom av
Boucher Ovid mill emp bds 12 Metacom av
Boucher William teamer bds 41 Metacom av
Boudreau Arthur oyster opener h Market
Boudreau Etienne rubber worker bds 9 Martin
Boudreau Ettinenne rubber worker h 15 Hope
Boudreau Joseph rubber worker bds 15 Hope
Boudreau Joseph rubber worker h 9 Martin
Bouffard Albert carpenter bds 39 Arlington av
Bouffard Isaac chauffeur bds 30 Franklin
Bouffard Leo mill emp bds 7 Union
Bouffard Simon embossing bds 39 Arlington av
Bouffard Wilbroad mule spinner h 39 Arlington av
Boulard Albert laborer h 5 Company
Bourassa Franc h 128 Child
Bourassa Leo emp Parker Mill bds 128 Child
Bourassa Louis electrician h 3 West

WHITTEMORE & COLBURN
PRINTERS   15 Pine St., PROV.

Bourque (French) see Burke (English)
Boutin Anna mill emp bds 21 Market
Boutin Cyrille mechanic h 52 Child
Boutin Edmond mill emp bds 21 Market
Boutin Emma mill emp bds 82 North Main
Boutin Eva mill emp bds 52 Child
Boutin Gideon mill emp h 3 Handy
Boutin Julie Mrs widow h 82 North Main
Boutin Myvel housekeeper 5 Mason
Boutin Onesime h Martin
Boutin Solomon bds C Boutin
Boutin Ulric farm hand h 21 Market
Boutin Wilfred bds C Boutin
Bovard Robert steel worker bds 114 Constitution
Bowden Bertha stitcher bds 14 Broad
Bowden Jesse L dep com shell fish h 14 Broad
Bowden Mrs h South Water cor Miller
Bowen Bessie H bds 189 South Main
Bowen Elizabeth S widow Daniel K h 19 Child
Bowen James h 139 South Water
Bowen Lucy A Miss bds 341 South Main
Bowen Mary S dressmaker 189 South Main h do
Bowen Olive E bds 6 Federal
Bowen Rebecca C Miss h 11 Washington
Boyce Clara C teacher Child bds 32 North Water
Boyer Mitchell mill emp h ft of Baker
Boylan Ann widow Felix h 51 Child
Boylan Ellen rubber worker bds 51 Child
Boylan James mechanic bds 139 Child
Boylan John S retired h 139 Child
Boylan John S Jr h 139 Child
Boylan Mary E clerk 4 Market bds 51 Child
Boylan Rose supervisor bds 51 Child
Boylan William M salesman h 139 Child
Boyle William piper h 23 Joyce
Boynton Benjamin L clerk h 8 Federal
Brady Charles P rubber worker h 265 South Main
Brasley Marjorie bds 4 North Main
Bray John M supt Duitt Mfg Co bds 9 Baker
Brayton Stephen F carpenter h 19 Manning
Breault David G mill emp h 7 Liberty
Brechin Jessie bds 173 South Main
Brelsford Elizabeth widow George bds f n 152 Warren av
Brelsford Frederick W (U S A) bds 161 Park
Brelsford George L spinner h 161 Park
Breniegar Samuel loomfixer 93 Kickemuit rd
Brennen Catherine B mill emp bds f n 194 Warren av
Brennen Daniel J bricklayer bds f n 194 Warren av
Brennen Helen V mill emp bds f n 194 Warren av

RALPH C. WATROUS CO.
Real Estate Auctioneers
437 INDUSTRIAL TRUST BUILDING

WARREN DIRECTORY, 1917-18. 117

Briand Angus bds Thomas A Briand
Briand Thomas A painter h cor Wood and Martin
Bristol County Gas & Electric Co (C H Sparks agt) 124 South Main
Bristol & Warren Water Works State nr South Main
Bristow Dennis F carpenter h Child
Bristow Mabel M bds Child
Brito Joseph mill emp h South Water cor Baker
Brochu Calista rubber worker bds 6 Hope
Brochu Cyrille carpenter h 6 Hope
Brochu Felix plumber 4 Martin h do
Brochu F Xavier retired h 1 Martin
Brochu Frank X Jr laborer bds 1 Martin
Brochu Napoleon spinner bds 1 Martin
Brochu Oliver spinner bds 1 Martin
Brochu William J rubber worker bds 1 Martin
Brochu Xavier retired h 1 Martin
Brouillette Theodore mule spinner h 130 Brown
Brouillette Theodore Jr moving picture operator h 82 N Water
Brown Anita G widow Frederick H h 14 Federal
Brown Annie weaver bds 7 North Water
Brown Desire weaver h 7 North Water
Brown Edward V fish market r 183 S Water h 183 do
Brown Emma bds 7 North Water
Brown Emma L Miss h Church cor S Water
Brown Frederick H Jr clerk 14 Child h rear 14 Federal
Brown Gertrude O bds 36 North Water
Brown John H real estate and auctioneer 34 N Water h 36 do
Brown Joseph loomfixer h 8 Barney
Brown Lavinia C bds 36 North Water
Brown Martin R (U S A) bds 14 Federal
Brown Mary widow John grocery 211 South Main h do
Brown Mary E Mrs h 15 Baker
Brown Montrose h Manning cor Wheaton
Brown Nancy N housekeeper bds 14 Federal
Brown Oscar mechanic bds 7 North Water
Brown Sarah B Miss clerk P O h Church cor S Water
Brown Stanley H operator bds 30 Child
Brown Thomas foreman h Congregational
Browne Katherine housekeeper 114 North Main
Brownell Gerald rubber worker h 252 Wood
Brownell John P (Potter Collamore & Co) also plumber South Water cor Wheaton bds 24 Washington

Blackstone Canal Nat'l Bank | BEST FACILITIES
20 MARKET SQ., PROVIDENCE | Prompt Attention

WARREN MONUMENTAL WORKS
Cor. Railroad Avenue and Croade Streets, Warren, R. I.

Brule David loomfixer h Child
Bruley Julie Miss mill emp h 145 South Water
Bruno Bros props Hotel Ferncroft 157 Bradford
Bryden John electrician for C R Blackmar Jr bds Hampden Meadows
Bryden Ruth E stenographer bds John Bryden
Bryden Samuel stripper h Metacom av
Buckingham Buell N produce dealer (Prov) h 3 Cherry
Buckingham B Son (E M Buckingham prop) oyster growers foot of Miller
Buckingham Erastus M prop (B Buckingham's Son) oyster grower also produce dealer (Prov) h 15 Washington
Buckley Johanna bds 36 Mt Hope av
Bucler   mill emp h 37 North Water
Buczck Ludwik weaver h 98 Company
Budasz Albert card fixer h Metacom av
Buff Luigi liquor dealer 42 N Main h N Water
Buffington David P (U S A) bds 100 N Main
Buffington George machinist h 21 State
Buffington J Alvin B bookkeeper (Prov) bds 100 N Main
Buffington James bookkeeper (Prov) bds 100 North Main
Bulley George F chauffeur h 7 Metacom av
Bullock Andrew J farmer h 67 High
Bullock Elizabeth S bds 142 South Main
Bullock Edward J C wire insulator (Prov) bds 142 S Main
Bullock George S civil engineer h 142 South Main
Bullock Irene R bookkeeper bds 243 South Main
Bullock Mary C widow of Dr Otis h 12 Baker
Bullock Mary W Mrs widow Dr George S h 142 S Main
Burdge William J steel worker h 27 Cottage
Buregard Serrett bds 4 Market
Burgeson Gustave engineer h 28 King
Burgess Harriet F bookkeeper h 12 Baker
Burgess William A bicycle dealer 20 Miller h cor Water and Washington
Burke Arthur E boat builder bds 37 Market
Burke Elizabeth widow James h 53 North Main
Burke James W blacksmith foot of Church h near do
Burke Lucy rubber worker h 2 Chestnut
Burke Martin grocer 45 Market h 41 do
Burke Mary J bds 41 Market
Burke Michael R bartender 35 Market h 37 do
Burleigh Louis E foreman Narra Elec L Sta h 175 S Water
Burnes John J moulder h S Water nr Baker
Burns Anna widow Edward bds 29 Lyndon
Burns Bernard house man h Poppasquash rd
Burns Clara A bds 15 Child
Burns Katherine rubber worker bds 27 Lyndon

NATIONAL EXCHANGE BANK One of the Oldest and Strongest Banks
63 Westminster St., Providence In Rhode Island

Burns Mary h 27 Lyndon
Burns Mary Miss clerk h 197 South Main
Burns Thomas bartender h 117 Child
Burns Thomas R mill emp bds 27 Lyndon
Burns Thomas R Jr mill emp h 21 Sowamsett av
Burt Ida D h 14 Bowen
Burtch Sarah widow Henry S h 29 Lyndon cor Wheaton
Burtis Hiram O painter 250 South Main h do
Bushee (English) see Boucher (French)
Bushnell Fred summer res Touisset Point
Butler Antone laborer h Market
Butler Bridget M widow Patrick H h 72 N Water
Butler Emma E bds Market
Butler Joseph laborer bds 72 N Water
Butler Joseph A instructor Warren High School h 248 S Main
Butler William P prop Butler's Shoe Store 452 Hope h Pawt
Butterfield Clara M bds 25 Market
Butters Carl W (U S A) bds 13 Woodlawn av
Butterworth Benjamin farmer h Child cor Touisset rd
Butterworth Joseph farmer h Child cor Touisset rd
Byfield School High cor Church
Byrne Thomas bartender Martin W O'Neil 117 Child
Cabral Adline bds Market
Cabral Henry farmer h Market
Cadera John T rubber worker h Juniper lane
Cady Charles J tool maker h 325 South Main
Cady Edwin A mgr Warren Branch Industrial Trust Co South Main near Bristol line
Cady H Dewees teacher Brown University h 259 S Main
Cady Henry N artist (oil marine) h Union cor Liberty
Caffot Emile spinner h 75 North Water
Caffot Joseph spinner h r 47 North Water
Cain Edward factory man bds 30 Market
Calagno Joseph barber 8 Market h 10 Luther
Calcagno Rose bds Ellis av
Campbell Barney rms 265 South Main
Campbell Ella M teacher of drawing 119 Child h do
Campbell Florence M teacher (Pawt) bds 119 Child
Campbell John student bds 119 Child
Campbell Mary E widow Thomas A h 119 Child
Campbell Mary E bds 119 Child
Cape Ann Fish Co (C Norgaad mgr) Green's Landing
Capuccilli Michele barber cor N Main and N Water h nr do
Card Charles F painter h 112 Union
Cardozo Agusto farm hand C H Seymour h rear do

Merewether & Dunn
Plumbing and Heating Contractors
31 TURNER AVENUE,   RIVERSIDE, R. I.

Carnes Benjamin J (U S N) bds 28 Garfield av
Caron Elphege Rev pastor St John the Baptist R C Church h cor N Main and Hope
Caron Eugene oysterman h rear 91 North Main
Caron Eugene laborer h 26 Baker
Carpenter Alvin mason h 132 Child
Carr Caleb A jeweler h just off 155 South Water
Carr George A bookkeeper h 321 South Main
Carr William J second hand h 163 Park
Carter Edwin H loomfixer h Parker av
Cary see also Carey
Case Frank E fisherman h Metacom av cor Parker av
Case Leon spinner h 94 Kickemuit rd
Case Mary L bds 94 Kickemuit rd
Cashin William T printer bds 271 Wood
Caulomb Napoleon h rear 15 Hope
Chace Charles farmer h 19 King
Chace Elsbeth A teacher bds William P Chace
Chace Hattie B bds 19 King
Chace Myra F bds 19 King
Chace William P farmer h Bushee rd
Chace see also Chase
Chadwick Isabella cloth inspector bds Market
Chamberlain Horace C h 7 Barney
Champagne Arzely bds 43 Arlington av
Champagne Octave operative h 43 Arlington av
Champeau Mary housekeeper Liberty cor Union
Champlin H Frank head clerk Warren Mfg Co h 10 Miller
Champlin Jennie H bds 10 Miller
Chapman Joy mill emp h 7 Federal
Chappell Stafford W retired h 8 Federal
Chaput Arthur oyster opener bds 123 S Water
Chaput Phoebe widow Elzeard h 123 South Water
Charron J George loomfixer h 16 Brown
Chase Joseph A farmer bds 45 Arlington av
Chase William R h 45 Arlington av
Chase see Chace
Chermeer John junk dealer h 56 Market
Chermeer Tressia bds 56 Market
Cheshire William wool sorter h 61 Charles
Chevalier Octave mill emp h 16 Church
Chevalri Joseph mill emp h 43 North Water
Child Charles E electrician h 18 Bridge
Child Daniel H trav salesman h S Main at R R crossing
Child Frank C painter and paper hanger h 200 Wood
Child Frank C Jr chauffeur bds 200 Wood
Child Lillian A Miss h 8 Vernon
Child St Nursery (Geo E Sherman prop) 93 Child

OUR CREDIT REPORTS TELL—Whom to trust; whom not to trust; who pay promptly; who pay slowly; who never pay their bills except under pressure. Telephone Union 1526
Western Mercantile Corporation, Providence, R. I.

Childs William B mgr R S Reed Fur Co 14 Child h 11 Bridge
Cholette Joseph teamster h 7 Asselin's plat
Christy Frank B laborer bds Mrs M J Christy
Christy George B mill emp bds Mrs M J Christy
Christy Harrison S mill emp bds Mrs M J Christy
Christy Martha J widow James h ft of Miller
Christy Morton E clammer bds Mrs M J Chrisy
Church Annie L school teacher (Prov) bds 87 N Water
Church Benjamin A farmer h 275 S Main nr Maple
Church Edward P bds A H Coggeshall
Church Emily L bds B A Church
Church Gilbert L physician 87 N Water cor Miller h do
Church Gordon B photographer and picture framing 145 S Main h do
Cichon Ignatus rubber worker bds 5 Johnson
Cichon Joseph weaver bds 58 Company
Cicpicla And laborer bds Child
Ciniglio Luigi restaurant 47 North Water bds North Main
Clairmont Anne Mrs bds 37 North Water
Clancy Thomas M h 11 Wood
Clark Alice M stenographer Main cor Miller bds Charles E Clark
Clark Annie H bds S K Clark
Clark Charles E teamster h Metacom av
Clark Charles S marine engineer h 615 Wood
Clark Chester W bookkeeper bds C Clark
Clark Raymond C (U S A) bds John E Johnson
Clark Solomon K engineer h Bradford
Clarke Amanda F widow John h 349 South Main
Clayton John coremaker h 132 Child
Clayton Julie E widow Henry G h S Water cor Church
Clayton William coremaker h 38 Baker
Cloutier Anthony bds 8 North Main
Cloutier Dora E stenographer bds 10 Hope
Cloutier Edwardian mill emp bds 18 Hope
Cloutier Emile mill emp h 168 Brown
Cloutier Ernest (U S A) bds 10 Hope
Cloutier Joseph towerman (Prov) h 17 Brown
Cloutier Joseph M M mill emp h 123 Child
Cloutier Rosana handkerchief shop bds 18 Hope
Cloutier Rose stenographer (Prov) bds 10 Hope
Cloutier Treffle J conductor N Y N H & H R R h 10 Hope
Cocks Herbert janitor h 182 South Water
Coen Sylvester salesman h Sowamsett av cor King

R. I. RUG WORKS
Rugs Woven from old and new carpets. Telephones { 2203 / 2204
878 WESTMINSTER ST., PROVIDENCE

Coggeshall Chandler H h Colt Farm Poppasquash
Coggeshall Daniel W (U S A) bds 117 Constitution
Coggeshall Frederick W (U S A) bds 38 Dimond av
Coggeshall Josiah farmer h Touisset Neck
Coggeshall Mary E widow William W h Touisset Neck
Coggeshall William D farmer h Touisset Neck
Cole Charles E laborer h 18 Bridge
Cole Ellen F Miss h 229 South Main
Cole Elmer E milk dealer h off Touisset rd 4th beyond R R
Cole Everett F clerk 27 Baker h 47 King
Cole Frank B Mrs nurse bds 7 Miller
Cole Frank H trav salesman h 156 South Water
Cole Frederick B chemist h 13 Vernon av
Cole George G janitor Industrial Trust Co h 252 S Main
COLE GEORGE R grocery and market also garage 27 Baker h 12 Broad—see page 23
Cole Gilbert R retired h 3 Federal
Cole Harry L clerk 27 Baker bds 14 Lyndon
Cole James A janitor Town Hall h 258 South Main
Cole Katherine bds 7 Federal
Cole Kenneth C overseer bds 13 Vernon
Cole Luther h 158 South Water
Cole Martha W Miss h 200 South Main
Cole Mary E widow Samuel bds 13 Vernon
Cole Mildred clerk bds 13 Vernon
Cole Patience Miss h School next Episcopal Church Chapel
Cole William L h 195 South Main
Cole William R blacksmith and horseshoer Market at R R crossing h 3 Federal
Coleman Sarah J bds 229 South Main
Colgan Edward J pastor St Mary's R C Church h 215 S Main
Collamore Elsie P telephone operator bds 24 North Water
Collamore Cinther widow Luther h Birch Swamp rd
Collamore James S (Potter Collamore & Co) h 24 N Water cor Bowen
Collamore John H musician bds 24 North Water
Collins Anne C teacher h Taylor cor King
Collins Emelyn F teacher h Taylor cor King
Collins Horace rubber worker h 41 Congregational
Collins Marion mill emp bds Felix Hebert
Collins Mary L bds Henry F Hull
Collins Michael molder h 57 Child
Cologne Delima Mrs h 5 Nobert
Cologne Eva mill emp bds 5 Nobert
Cologne Napoleon mill emp bds 5 Nobert
Commercial Club The 137B South Water
Condon Elizabeth bds 98 Church
Condon Helen A school teacher bds 98 Church

Condon John J Jr (U S A) bds 98 Church
Conklin Grace L bds V H Conklin
Conklin Henry R Dr veterinary surgeon Maple n S Main
Conklin Reba Mrs bds 23 Vernon
Conklin Vincent H carpenter h Maple
Conley Catherine widow Patrick bds Thomas Kilroy
Conley Elizabeth bds 5 State
Conley Esther J widow John E h 111½ North Main
Conley Esther W school teacher bds 111½ North Main
Conley Frank J Adams Exp agent bds 5 State
Conley Gertrude school teacher bds 111½ North Main
Conley James H rotary operator N Y N H & H R R h 5 State
Conley Lena T bookkeeper (Prov) bds 5 State
Conley William M electrician bds 5 State
Connery Margaret bds 121 Constitution
Connolly James h Market 2d beyond Kickemuit rd
Connolly James E laborer b Market 2 bey Kickemuit rd
Connolly Mary E bds James Connolly
Connolly Thomas H prop Warren Oyster Co h Barrington
Connolly Thomas S prop Warren Oyster Co
Conrick Edmond J clerk Market cor Main bds 18 Child
Conrick Edward J (U S N) bds 18 Child
Conrick Ellen J bds 18 Child
Conrick Fanny bds 18 Child
Conrick Thomas variety store also painter cor Market and Main h 18 Child
Conroy Frank E bds Mrs M P Conroy
Conroy Mary P widow Michael B h 3d on Green
Constand Joseph lather h 20 Arlington av
Contois Albert loomfixer Parker Mill h Child
Contois Alice Mrs bds Child
Contois Clifford weaver bds f n 143 North Main
Contois Malvina widow Rudolph h 3 Nobert
Contois Matilda weaver bds f n 143 North Main
Contois Noe loomfixer h Middle
Contois Samuel laborer h Arlington av
Contois Trefle h f n 143 North Main
Contois Viateus weaver bds f n 143 North Main
Conturre Exina bds Market
Conturre Wilfred engineer h Market
Conway John J physician 93 N Main h do
Cooke Ella F widow William H h 165 High
Cooke George L lawyer 145 South Main and 15 Westminster (Prov) h Providence

**VALENTINE'S
Diamond & Star
FIRE BRICK**

**JAMES C. GOFF CO.
31 to 49 POINT ST.
Providence, R. I.**

Cooper Christopher D boat builder h 10 Vernon
Corcoran Marie V stenographer bds 30 Wood
Corcoran Rose M stenographer bds 30 Wood
Corea Frank emp N I R Co h 1 Usher
Corey Winifred farmer h Birch Swamp rd
Coristine Charles second hand h 87 Kickemuit rd
Coristine Thomas F night asst engineer Warren Pumping Station h Barker av
Corvia Samuel mule spinner h 31 Metacom av
Cory Joseph carpenter h 206 Warren av
Cory see Corey
Costa Joseph rubber worker bds 23 Metacom av
Costa Mary housekeeper 23 Metacom av
Costa Tony rubber worker bds Market
Cote Jasezphine bds Market
Cote William A reg phar Standard Pharmacy h Campbell
Cottell Harry piano dealer h rear 12th off Metacom av
Coughlan Alice E widow Michael P h 80 Bay View av
Coulruier Joseph at dye house h 70 Union
Coupe Henry plumber bds J J Coupe
Coupe John J carpenter h Maple
Covo George H boat builder rear 121 S Water h 121 do
Coyle Matilda music teacher 6 Broad h do
Crabb Frank A farm supt h Poppasquash rd
Craig James overseer Parker Mill h 64 Arlington
Cranston Frank L waste inspector h 17 State
Crapo Florence L bds P E Crapo
Crapo Phineas E farmer h South Main at Bristol line
Crawley Emma L widow William H h 23 Lyndon
Crawley Mary Etta bds 23 Lyndon
Cree Helen Mrs bds 8 Baker
Creech Edward fitter h 68 Metacom av
Creedon Elizabeth H emp 168 South Water h do
Cripps George M pool South Main h 211 do
Critchley Alice mill emp bds 79 Arlington av
Critchley Katherine mill emp bds 79 Arlington av
Critchley Daniel T h 79 Arlington av
Croke Mary widow Jeremiah h North Main cor Church
Cronin Ellen widow James h 18 Lyndon
Cronin James J policeman h 10 Crode
Cronin Nora mill emp bds 18 Lyndon
Crossley George L master mechanic Mt Hope Co h cor Child and Metacom av
Crowell Georgiana C widow William B h 7 Miller
Crowell Mary C tutor bds 7 Miller
Cseylis Joseph weaver bds Summer
Cummings Charles C local mgr The Liberty Stores Co h Swansea

RALPH C. WATROUS CO.
RESIDENTIAL and **INVESTMENT PROPERTY**
Of All Kinds For Sale
487 Industrial Trust Building

Cummings Charles I decorator (Prov) h 228 S Main
Cummings Ethel A bookkeeper bds 228 South Main
Curran George D emp N Y N H & H R R h 18 Child
Curtis Alice C mill emp bds 5 Barney
Curtis John H crossing tender h 5 Barney
Curtis William E salesman (Prov) h ft of Bridge S W
Cushing Charles laborer h Parker av
Cushing Thomas weaver bds Parker av
Custance Mary A Rev pastor Pentecostal Church h 154 Wood
Cutler Charles W cashier Staples Coal Co of R I h 18 State
Cutler Edward R ass't mgr Industrial Trust Co h 18 State
Cutler Lydia L widow Charles R h 18 State
Cutter John J printer h 21 Washington
Cutter Mary E treas Warren Printing & Publishing Co h 21 Washington
Cygan Walenty emp M l Nelle h Bowen
Cyrulik Martin fireman h Kickemuit rd
Cyzanowski Paul speed tender h Company blk Company
Czekajowski Mieczislav shoe repairer for John Natel h 72 North Water
Daigneault Michele rubber worker h 54 North Water
Dailey Rodericka E rubber worker bds 7 Lyndon
Dalenta Joseph carder h 20 Cutler
Dallaire Edward (Gauthier & Dallaire Co) 78 N Water h Child
Dalpe Albert twister h 90 Market
Dalpe Amanda bds 90 Market
Daniel Angelo shoemaker 29 N Water h 22 Warren av
Daniels Jane bds 229 South Main
Daniels Sarah widow James h 229 South Main
Darling Joseph E clerk (Prov) h 28 Locust
Darowski Adam picker boss h 22 Arlington av
Davenport Herbert D (Lightfoot Davenport & Co) 151 Bradford h Fall River
Davis Belbadora bds Child first bey Asylum rd
Davis Charles I boat builder h 5 Sowamsett av
Davis Charles M mason h Child 1st beyond Asylum road
Davis Frank M mason bds Child 1st beyond Asylum road
Davis Fred B farmer Poppasquash rd
Davis George B bricklayer h 15 Bridge
Davis Harriet L rubber worker bds 5 Sowamsett av
Davol Charles S bookkeeper Staples Coal Co of R I h 3 Washington
Davoren Margaret J widow Thomas F h 262 High

Blackstone Canal Nat'l Bank | A Progressive Bank
20 Market Sq., Prov. R. I. | Fully Equipped for Service

Warren Monumental Works
Cor. Railroad Avenue and Croade Street, Warren, R. I.

Day Elizabeth A bds 41 Woodlawn av
de Alcazar Mary bookkeeper (Prov) bds 14 Lyndon
de Alcazar Sarah widow Joaquin h 14 Lyndon
De Bease Vincenzo grocery and market 25 North Main h Barrington
Deblois Eli carpenter h 12 Union
Deblois Henry machinist h ft of Summer
Deblois John bds 20 Union
Deblois John B blacksmith h 20 Union
Deblos David carpenter h 16 Wood
De Coudres Thomas H supt of schools h 281 High
Delaney George mill emp h 12 Barney
Delano Lloyd S designer h f n. 135 North Main
Delckta Michal weaver and clerk h 98 Johnson
De Lengis Louise comb winder h 98 Market
Dellaire Amelia mill emp bds Franklin
Dellaire Celia widow Frederick h 11 Hope
Dellaire Edward carpenter h Franklin
Dellaire Edward plumber h 17 Child
Dellaire Romeo plumber bds 11 Hope
Dembkowski Joseph fireman h Kickemuit rd
Denby Garfield dentist (Prov) h 9 Bridge
Denby John dentist 172 S Main h 155 S Water
Dennis Edmund rubber worker h cor Child and Metacom av
De Puis William rubber worker h 351 Wood
Derosier Rosanna Mrs bds 54 North Water
Deschamps Lena mill emp bds 133 Child
Deschamps Oliva bds 133 Child
Deschamps Oliver h 133 Child
Desilets Dianna Y mill emp bds 24 Franklin
Desilets Edmond weaver h 24 Franklin
Desilets Henry S loomfixer bds 24 Franklin
Desilets Ledger (U S A) h 5 Wood
Desilets Mary J mill emp bds 24 Franklin
Desmarais Abraham foreman B & W Water Wks h 94 Market
Desmarais Albert chauffeur bds 94 Market
Desmarais Delima bds 94 Market
Desmarais Joseph N baker 89 Market bds 95 Market
Dessonier Alfred farmer h 7 Liberty
Deszcz Michal weaver h Company blk Warren
Devlin Joseph J station agt Nayatt h 104 North Main
Devol Margaret H rubber worker bds 11 Lyndon
Devol William L chauffeur h Union nr Liberty
Devol see Davol
Devolin Frank poultry dept Colt's farm bds Allen
Dewire see Dwyer
De Wolf Howard K (W S Bennett & Co) Main cor Joyce h 125 Main

Dickerson Earl R oyster opener h 30 Market
Dickerson William H oyster opener h Green's Landing S W
Dickinson Harry timekeeper bds B M Hall
Dill Samuel N clerk (Prov) h 203 South Main
Dillaire Louis carpenter Franklin
Dillon William F mill emp h 170 South Main
Dimick A W treas Warren Mfg Co h Providence
Diniz Jacintho F sewing machine agency (Singer) 141 South Main bds 150 Market
Dion Joseph mill emp h 89 Market
Dion Treffley weaver h f n 134 North Main
DIONNE CHARLES grocer 140 Child h do—see page 25
Dionne Gilbert J dresser tender h 93 Cutler
Direct Importing Co local agt Henry B Stevens 139 South Main cor Church
District Court Room 5th District at Town Hall
Doherty Charles peddler bds Mary Doherty
Doherty Edward teamster bds Mary Doherty
Doherty Mary widow Timothy h Vernon nr Park
Doherty Sarah mill emp bds Mary Doherty
Doherty Timothy farmer bds Mary Doherty
Doherty William farmer bds Mary Doherty
Domayalu Mary rubber worker bds Cole
Domayalu Simon speed tender h Cole
Donohue John W marine engineer h 27 Broad
Donohue Mary dressmaker bds 27 Broad
Donohue Michael fisherman bds 27 Broad
Donovan Bridget widow David h 31 Joyce
Donovan James E laborer h Bradford nr S Main S W
Donovan Jerome mason h 400 High
Doran Charles J (U S A) bds 145 South Water
Doran Charles W rubber worker h 145 South Water
Doran Genevieve bds 99 Franklin
Doran Helen B V stenographer bds 145 South Water
Doran Mary rubber worker bds 607 Wood
Doran Nellie rubber worker h 167 State
Dougette Joseph rubber worker h 8 Parker
Dougherty see Doherty
Dow George V trav salesman h S Water cor Bridge S W
Dow Joseph S shoemaker Kickemuit rd h do
Dowd Mary F h Franklin nr mill
Drainville Amos O loomfixer h 16 Wood
Drainville George N loomfixer h 16 Wood
Dreadnaught Hook Ladder and Hose Co High cor Church

Drickienicz Ignacy laborer h 100 Water
Driscol Annie Miss h 169 So Water
Drown Annie G widow Wm B h 26 Union
Drown Charles teamster h 17 Federal
Drown Charles W teamster bds 26 Union
Drown Dorcas needle work bds 10 Vernon
Drown George L town sergeant h 10 Vernon
Drown George L Jr emp N I R Co h 45 Richmond
Drown Hannah forelady bds 10 Vernon
Drown James B h 3 Washington
Drown John clerk h 62 King
Drown Josephine bds 10 Vernon
Drown Louise F h 2 Lyndon
Drown Ruth E Miss h 2 Lyndon
Drysdale Edward (U S A) bds 39 Market
Drysdale Richard printer h 98 Constitution
Drysdale William rubber worker h 39 Market
Drysdale William Jr molder bds 39 Market
Dube Edward R mason h 136 Child
Dube Ernest J general contractor 30 Franklin h do
Dubois Arthur driver Adams Express bds 23 Joyce
Dubois Charles W painter bds 23 Joyce
Dubois Henry painter bds 23 Joyce
Dubois Ivan painter h 12 Union
Dubois Ivan B painter bds 23 Joyce
Dubois Louis painter bds 23 Joyce
Dubois William B painter h 23 Joyce
Dubuque Eliza Mrs h 169 Brown
Duchaine Joseph mill emp bds 30 Market
Duchaine Victor blacksmith h 69 No Water
Dudek John laborer bds 50 Union
Dudek Sebastyan carder bds 50 Union
Dudkicrcz Joseph fireman h Baker
Dudzik Albert laborer h 50 Union
Duffy Gregory F rubber worker h 126 Constitution
Dugan James bartender h 16 Luther
Dugan Margaret mill emp bds 16 Luther
Duitt Mfg Co (H B Howland mgr John M Bray supt) hand-
  kerchief mfg 197 South Main
Dunaj Walter weaver h Company blk Brown cor Main
Dunbar Archibald F Jr clerk N I R Co bds 247 Wood
Dunbar Chester H foreman h 49 E
Dunbar George N reg phar bds 24 King
Dunn Harvey boat builder h Green's Landing S W
Dupues Emma widow Archie h 36 Harris av
Dupues Nora mill emp bds 36 Harris av
Dupues Romeo mill emp h f n 37 Harris av
Dwyer Nora E stenog bds 20 Collins

Dyman Thomas carder h 90 Company
Dzialo Wawrzyniec carder bds 164 Park
Dzicdzic Joseph speed tender h Meadow rd
Earle Ida F bds 189 South Main
East Warren School Child opp West st
Easterbrooks Clara B Miss bookkpr (Prov) bds Liberty cor Union
Easterbrooks Nora C widow E Otis h Union cor Liberty
Eaton Augusta R rubber worker bds 10 School
Eaton Edward B rubber worker h 10 School
Eaton Howard H (U S N) bds 10 School
Eaton Maude at handkerchief shop bds 10 School
Eckersley Hannah widow William bds 30 Child
Eddy Helen F bds 1 Lyndon
Eddy Mary S Miss h 200 So Main
Eddy Mary T Miss h 1 Lyndon
Edge James gardener h Ferry rd
Edge Samuel gardener h Ferry rd
Emerson Robert S pres Narragansett Rubber Co office 402 Industrial Trust bldg Prov h Pawt
Emery Ambrose carpenter h 52 Arlington av
Emery Harold plumber h 18 Church
Emery John B mill emp h 4 West
Emery Mary F widow John A h 156 So Water
Emery Philip driver h 19 Church
Emmery William h Touisset Point
Emmett Robert (U S A) bds 37 North Water
Emmett Samuel weaver h 37 No Water
Ennis Edward T farmer h Child 1st bey Kickemuit river
Ennis Rebecca bds 36 Pierce av
ESTES CHARLES land surveyor and civil engineer Touisset rd h do—see page 24
Evers Herbert rubber worker h 126 Child
Evers Jacob teamster bds 126 Child
Excelsior Grocery and Market (B W Viall) mgr 191 and 193 So Main
Fafara Frank h 63 Sisson
Fafara Ignatius (Polish interpreter) painter h cor N Main and Brown
Fafara Jan h 106 Company
Fafara Leo Polish interpretor bds 63 Sisson
Fafara Mary rubber worker bds 63 Sisson
Fahey Edward J tea coffee and spices S Main nr Maple h do
Family Drug Store The Dr C E Scott 27 Child

Farris Karen laborer h 88 North Water
Fartardo Roselina A maid bds 104 Constitution
Faryniasz Karolina weaver bds 132 Main
Faulkner William tailor 147 South Main h 68 Metacom av
Feeney Ambrose station and freight agt Warren h Prov
Feereira Tridorio C farmer h Touisset rd
Ferreira Adolph barber 155 Bradford h 360 Wood
Ferzan Elias A oriental goods (Prov) also Arabic newspaper correspondent (N Y) h f n 70 Sisson
Field Warren F sailor h 23 Metacom av
Fielding John ins agent h f n 151 Warren av
Figueiredo Antonio farm hand h Kickemuit rd
Finberg Joseph mfg jeweler sum res Touisset rd
Finley L Arthur supt (Pawt) h ft of Locust
First Baptist Church High
Fitten John spinner h 4 North Main
Fitzmaurice David laborer h rear 16 No Main
Flet Samuel second hand h Washington cor Eddy
Flet Samuel H rubber worker bds Samuel Flet
Fletcher Paul W Lieut (U S N) bds 15 Miller
Flynn Annie C stitcher bds 124 Wood
Flynn James M boiler maker bds 60 Charles
Flynn John A (U S A) bds 60 Charles
Flynn Mary A shoemaker bds 124 Wood
Flynn William J gardener h 124 Wood
Fogg Emile spinner h 2 Nobert
Foley M Loretta mill emp bds John Hacklin
Fontain Celaise housekeeper 4 Mason
Fontain Omer mason helper bds 4 Mason
Fontaine Ernest G clerk h Market
Foreman Florence G bookkpr Prov bds 19 King
Forest Mary A widow Mederic h 1 Nobert
Forest William E clerk 135 S Main h 1 Nobert
Fortier Albert weaver bds 22 Union
Fortier Alfred weaver h 10 Warren av
Fortier Arthur weaver h Middle
Fortier George loomfixer h 22 Union
Fortier Napoleon laborer h Middle
Fortin Albina spinner bds f n 133 North Main
Fortin Arthur mill emp bds f n 133 North Main
Fortier Donat P loomfixer bds 22 Union
Fortin Frank mill emp bds f n 133 No Main
Fortin J George A mill emp bds f n 133 North Main
Fortin John spinner bds f n 133 No Main
Fortin Joseph weaver h f n 133 No Main
Fortin Napoleon laborer h 17 Hope
Fournier Adelard machinist h f n 144 North Water
Fournier Adelard Jr weaver bds f n 144 North Main

WALTER H. JACKSON CO. 485 Industrial Trust Building
PROVIDENCE, R. I.
"DELCO" ELECTRIC LIGHTING & PUMPING PLANTS
WINDMILLS, GASOLINE ENGINES AND TRACTORS

WARREN DIRECTORY, 1917-18.   131

Fournier Alexandrena mill emp bds f n 136 North Main
Fournier Arthur deckhand h 86 North Main
Fournier Fabian wood chopper h 321 Sisson
Fournier Gule retired bds f n 136 North Main
Fournier John mill emp bds f n 144 No Main
Fournier Joseph mill emp h f n 136 No Main
Fournier Julia housekeeper bds 57 Market
Fournier Marion mill emp bds f n 136 North Main
Fournier Mediric carpenter h 57 Market
Fournier William machinist bds f n 144 North Main
Fox Margaret J housekeeper h 65 Market
Fox Michael h 65 Market
Fox Michael F machinist bds 65 Market
Francis William P rubber worker h 29 Collins
Francour Alphonse chauffeur h 46 Market
Francour Eva bds 46 Market
Franklin Harry brakeman N Y N H & H R R h 95 Cutler
Fratus Delphine washwoman h 23 Metacom av
Frechette Albert mill emp h Parker
Frederico Frank grocer 215 Wood h do
Freeborn Elizabeth J Miss h 2 Lyndon
Freeman Frank retired h off Metacom av
French Byron A foreman Warren Monumental Works h 23 Washington
French Mfg Co (George F Waters mgr) Cutler
Frey Carl A loomfixer h 18 Church
Fritz John bartender h 10 Liberty
Frodyma Joseph laborer h 91 Johnson
Frye John bartender h Liberty
Fuller Seraphine widow Cornelius bds 72 King
Fyans Fraser & Blackway second hand textile machinery Croade cor Cole office 56 Main Fall River Mass
Fyans Thomas F (Fyans Fraser & Blackwell) second hand textile machinery dealer h at Fall River Mass
Gagné Arcardus retired bds 18 Metacom av
Gagnon Henry C garage and auto agency Market at R R tracks h cor State and Water
Gagnon Joseph engineer bds 121 South Water
Gagnon Malvina clerk 165 S Main bds State cor Water
Gagnon Peter engineer h State cor So Water
Galazka Bronislaw farmer h Child
Gale Albert carpenter h 30 Garfield av
Gallagher John M policeman h 97 Franklin
Gallo Louis H rubber worker bds 97 Constitution

WHITTEMORE & COLBURN
PRINTERS   15 Pine St., PROV.

King's Fibrous Plaster Board & Hard Plaster
JAMES C. GOFF CO.
31 to 49 Point St., Prov., R. I.

Galuszka Blazj emp mill h Market
Galuszka Henry rubber worker bds Market
Galuszka Walter rubber worker bds Market
Galvin Thomas poultry dept Colts Farm h Poppasquash
Gambardella Luigi grocer 26 Mt Hope av h 28 Mt Hope
Gancusz Joseph carder bds 50 Union
Gancz Elizabeth M mill emp bds 18 Union
Gancz John M machinist (Newport) bds 20 Union
Gancz Mary widow Stephen bds 18 Union
Gancz Stephen machinist Newport h 18 Union
Ganey Ella at laundry bds 3 Joyce
Gannon Bridget M housekeeper 215 South Main
Garceau Amede (U S A) bds Isaac Garceau
Garceau Delia Mrs h f n 171 Bowen
Garceau Henry (U S A) bds Isaac Garceau
Garceau Isaac master mechanic Parker Mill No 2 h North Main cor Liberty
Garceau Joseph carpenter bds A Plante
Garczyca Sygnacy organist h 100 North Main
Gardiner Elizabeth W teacher High School h 2 Lyndon
Gardiner Harriet bds 2 Lyndon
Gardner David V cigar mfg 8 Croade h do
Gardner Elizabeth S h 192 South Main
Gardner George B farmer h 94 Child
Gardner Georgianna Miss h 9 Washington
Gardner Georgianna E bds 9 Washington
Gardner Henrietta J Mrs h 114 North Main
Gardner Horace R bds 9 Washington
Gardner Israel sum res h 6th on Touisset rd
Gardner S Elizabeth teacher Touisset Neck School bds A C Gardner
Gardner William G cigar maker 8 Croade h Fall River
Gareis Augusta bds Market
Gareis Johann farmer h Market
Garis Barbara widow Nicholas bds Adolf Kaiser
Garrem George mill emp h Miller cor North Water
Garvin Charles W retired bds Jesse Oliver
Garvin Frederick E clerk bds 12 Cook
Garvin George E overseer h R R av near depot
Garvin George J emp I R Co bds R R av near depot
Garvin Wallace W overseer h 12 Cook
Gauthier Ernest driver 114 North Main
Gauthier Eva M bookkeeper 78 N Water bds 76 do
Gauthier Gideon J (Gauthier & Dallaire Co) 78 N Water h 76 do
Gauthier & Dallaire Co (Gideon J Gauthier Edward Dallaire) plumber 78 North Water
Gayton George W cutter bds 189 High

Ralph C. Watrous Co. FARMS and SUBURBAN PROPERTY For Sale
437 INDUSTRIAL TRUST BUILDING

Gebski Frank weaver bds Child
Gee Chin laundry 6 Baker h do
Gempp George G loomfixer h 9 Liberty
Gempp Herman loomfixer bds 9 Liberty
Gempp William loomfixer bds 9 Liberty
Gempp W Louise stitcher bds 9 Liberty
Geoffrey Emanuel mill emp h 22 Union
Geoffrey Osias weaver bds 22 Union
Geoffroy Joseph liquor 71 N Water bds 22 Union
Gerard Joseph weaver h cor Metacom av and Parker av
Gerlak Mary widow Antoni h Bowen
Gerula Dymitr machinist h 14 Union
Gerula Michal carder bds Bowen
Gibbons Catherine mill emp bds 104 North Main
Giblinske Oscar F rubber worker h 112 Union
Gibson Charles DeWolf Mrs h Longfield
Gibson Josephine Miss h Longfield
Gifford Charles E milk dealer S Main at Bristol line h do
Gifford Nellie D Miss bds 14 Broad
Gildert Nellie T carder bds 67 Child
Gildert Peter dry goods and groceries 140 Child h 136 do
Gildert Thomas E laborer h 67 Child
Giles Angeline B housekeeper 72 State
Gillon Edmund V (U S A) bds Vernon
Gillon James (U S N) h Vernon
Gillon William (U S A) bds Vernon
Gilleran Lawrence F dentist Saugy bldg h Campbell
Gilleran Theresa M at rubber works bds L F Gilleran
Gilmore James farmer h Touisset rd 1st bey the R R
Gilmore Josephine widow James bds James Gilmore
Ginalski John laborer bds Company
Ginalski Paul weaver h 95 Johnson
Gingras Joseph A blacksmith bds 82 North Main
Girard Joseph weaver h Metacom av cor Parker av
Gireoux Donat barber h 18 Metacom av
Gladue Joseph C rubber worker bds 11 Hope
Gladue Metille widow Cyriac h 249 High
Glancy Frederick bicycle dealer 70 N Water h 61 Union
Glancy Sarah bds 61 Union
Glancy Walter laborer bds 61 Union
Gliotton Charles (mgr Butler's shoe store) bds 11 Cole
Gluszak Mary speed tender bds 146 Warren av
Gnot Joseph laborer h Kickemuit rd
Gober Russell lineman bds 10 Luther

| **Blackstone Canal Nat'l Bank** | Established 1831 |
| 20 MARKET SQ. PROVIDENCE | STRONG AND CONSERVATIVE |

WARREN MONUMENTAL WORKS
Cor. Railroad Avenue and Croade Streets, Warren, R. I.

Godck Stanley weaver h 60 Metacom av
Godek Walter carder h Arlington av
Goettler Harvard W (U S A) bds 28 Cook
Goettler Mildred I stenographer bds 28 Cook
Goff Henry C jeweler h 11 Broad cor Manning
Goff Lillie M widow Walter I h 235 South Main
Goff Mabel D stenog Industrial Trust Co h 237 S Main
Goff Nathan D bds 235 South Main
Goff Rufus H (U S A) bds 11 Broad
Goff Sally S cashier bds 235 South Main
Goff's Hotel (formerly Coles Hotel) John F McDonough prop South Main cor Joyce
Goggin Samuel A signalman N Y N H & H R R h 250 South Main
Golen Michael weaver h Company
Goldstein Charles merchant 154 Wood
Goloski Blazy slubber tender h Market
Goloski Carolina bds Market
Goloski Elizabeth widow Joseph h Metacom av 9th south Vernon
Goloski Elsie mill emp bds E Goloski
Goloski Henry speeder tender bds Market
Goloski John (U S A) bds E Goloski
Goloski Lawrence mill emp h Child nr Touisset av
Goloski Lawrence farmer also owner h Child
Goloski Peter laborer h Meadow
Goloski Walter speeder tender bds Market
Golowski Elizabeth widow Joseph groceries h Metacom av
Golowski Lawrence weaver h Child
Golowski Peter laborer h Ward
Gonzenbach Charles A (mgr Swiss Textile Co absorbent cotton and sanitary napkin mfrs) Joyce h 9 State
Gonzenbach Paul treas Swiss Textile Co bds 9 State
Gooding Sarah widow James M bds 356 South Main
Goodreau George J mason h 2 Nobert
Goodspeed Joseph W mgr H & R Atwood oyster dealers h 141 South Water
Gorczyea Ignatus organist h 100 North Main
Gorham Isaac W (U S A) bds 183 Wood
Gorman Katherine stenographer bds Thomas Gorman
Gorman Louis carpenter h Locust
Gorman Thomas overseer h Avenue A
Gorman Thomas Jr druggist clerk bds Thomas Gorman
Gough see Goff
Goulet John fireman h Franklin bey the mill
Goulet Lucien at handkerchief shop bds John Goulet
Gourley Hugh student bds 41 North Water
Gourley Hugh J supt Warren Mfg Co h 41 North Water
Gourley Thomas H mill operative h 38 Child

National Exchange Bank Established 1801. If you think of changing your bank, there is
63 Westminster St., Prov.   None better than this

WARREN DIRECTORY, 1917-18.   135

Gracyalny Cora rubber worker bds 161 South Water
Gracyalny Frank mill emp h 161 South Water
Grady Margaret J weaver bds cor No Main and Brown
Grady Mary E h cor North Main and Brown
Graham Bridget E widow Michael h Child 1st bey Kickemuit river
Graham Mary A widow Charles h Child 1st bey Kickemuit river
Graham Mary F bds Child
Grangere Arture plumber bds 43 North Water
Grangere Euclid (U S A) bds 43 North Water
Grangere Joseph wood chopper bds 43 North Water
Grangere Moses wood dealer Johnson h 43 North Water
Grant Edward T mill emp 27 Lyndon
Gravelle Frank J farmer h 37 Cottage
Gray Howard B clerk (Prov) bds 28 Dimond av
Great A & P Tea Co (Edmund H Horton local mgr) 135 Main
Greaves Alfred twister bds 118 Child
Grebin John third hand h ft of Baker
Green Mary E bds 36 Child
Green Maude M music teacher bds 36 Child
Greene Alice W student bds 305 South Main
Greene Charles W town treas also insurance agent h 305 South Main
Greene Charlotte M stenographer Town Hall bds 305 S Main
Greene Frederick C mgr Warren Shoe Co h Haile
Greene George T oyster dealer Greene's Landing h do
Greene Oscar T R compositor (Prov) h 36 Child
Greene Robert H oysterman h 21 Beach av South Warren
Greene Ruth housekeeper 8 Croade
Greenhalgh Daniel rubber worker h 157 Child
Greenhalgh Harry mill emp bds 157 Child
Greenwood Benjamin weaver h 138 Child
Greenwood Ernest weaver h 75 Arlington av
Greenwood James weaver bds 64 Arlington av
Greenwood J Fredrick tel operative Warren depot h Franklin 2d beyond mill
Greenwood William loomfixer h 64 Arlington av
Gregory George clerk 84 North Main bds 24 Union
Gregory Virginia widow John D h 24 Union
Grenier Elyear rubber worker h 8 Broad
Griffin Michael P teller Industrial Trust Co h 300 S Main
Gryszko Heromin weaver h Water

Merewether & Dunn
Plumbing and Heating Contractors
31 TURNER AVENUE,   **RIVERSIDE, R. I.**

Grzbian Edward owner also weaver h 35 Arlington av
Grzbian Stanley owner also carder widower h 20 Cutler
Grzbian Zygmund grocery and market 69 N Main h 84 Child
Grzcbien Edward rubber worker h 39 Arlington av
Grzcbien Stanislaw carder h 20 Cutler
Grczbien Zygmont grocer h Child
Grzechocki Frank weaver h 90 Company
Guillemette Maxime loomfixer h 43 North Water
Guillemette Savere apprentice machinist bds 43 N Water
Guisti Luigi baker h 11 Pleasant
Guli Stanley barber 65 North Water h over do
Guralczyk Baltazy laborer h Sisson
Guralczyk Julian emp mill h 51 Union
Gurka Anna widow Gustave speed tender bds 1 Brown
Hacklin John ins agt h Franklin 2d beyond mill
Hackney Clara widow of Walter S sum res Ferry rd
Hafliger Charles (U S N) bds f n 172 Bowen
Hafliger Emma mill emp bds f n 172 Bowen
Hafliger Fritz (U S A) bds f n 172 Bowen
Hafliger Hedwig bds f n 172 Bowen
Hafliger Samuel weaver h f n 172 Bowen
Hail George Free Library Miss Emilie A Ide librarian 184 South Main cor Croade
Hall Alice W bds 9 Wood
Hall Benjamin M supt h Cherry
Hall Clara T Miss h 62 North Water cor Liberty
Hall John R W Lieut (U S A) bds 9 Wood
Hall Preston I carpenter h South Main cor Cherry
Hall Preston I Jr (U S N) bds Preston I Hall
Hall Nelson Read physician 9 Wood h do
Hall William h South Main cor Cherry
Hall William B driver bds Preston I Hall
Hallock Mary A widow Charles R h 16 Church
Hambly Gladys stenographer bds 1039 Hope
Hamel Bruno B asst engineer h 204 South Main
Hamel Henry deckhand h 86 North Main
Handy George E farmer h 133 Metacom av
Handy Walter L machinist h 1st on Greene
Hanley Aylward J clerk Adams Express Co bds 26 N Water
Hanley John W fruit dealer h 26 North Water
Hanley Nell M Miss h 26 North Water
Hanover Bertha h 41 Market
Hanover Charles T overseer h 41 Market
Hanson Ruth tel operator bds 98 Constitution
Hargraves John fireman h 25 Washington
Harrington Edward J oysterman bds 16 Wheaton
Harrington Evelyn M widow Cornelius h 20 Washington

Harrington John J comber boss h 113 South Water
Harrington Sarah C widow Edward S h 16 Wheaton
Harris Ella L J Miss h 22 Washington
Harris Joseph h off Metacom av nr Bristol town line
Hart George W Capt h Bradford
Hathaway Lena stenographer bds 2 Haile
Hawser Raymond P brick maker h 3 Federal
HAWTHORNE HUGH grocer 174 S Main h 9 Baker—see page 25
Hayes Edward M bookkeeper Warren Oyster Co h Cranston
Hayes George P engineer h S Main nr Bristol town line
Head Margaret M rubber worker bds 39 Richmond
Head Nellie C h 39 Richmond
Healey Alice clerk N I R Co bds 38 Market
Healey Alice E mill emp bds 30 Child
Healey Annie J drawingin hand bds 38 Market
Healey Charles H hairdresser 141 S Main h 1 Church
Healey Earl J operator h 30 Child
Healey Ellery B carpenter h Locust
Healey George H teamster bds E B Healey
Mealey Howard M asst engineer h 37 Market
Healey John C hair dresser h 20 Child
Healey John E weaver h 6 Wood
Healey John H h 30 Child
Healey John S spinner h Parker
Healey Joseph E hair dresser 5 Child h 38 Market
Healey Joseph H clerk R I Freight Co bds 38 Market
Healey Loretta teacher bds 38 Market
Healey Mary cloth inspector bds 38 Market
Healey Matilda G teacher bds 38 Market
Healey Solomon mule spinner h Parker av
Hebert Felix carpenter h Metacom av
Heck Adelaide P bds A Martin
Hedge John F wire chief Warren Exchange h 10 Haile
Henderson George W machinist h 11 Lyndon
Henderson William night crossing tender h Warren av
Hennesey Joseph molder bds 96 Constitution
Henniberry John T bartender Hotel Warren bds do
Henry Thomas shoemaker bds 41 Congregational
Heon Alexander J prop Main St Garage 107 N Main h 105 do
Heon Edward F dry goods 63 North Water h over do
Herbert Felix carpenter h 8th south Vernon-Metacom av
Hevery Joseph mill emp h 26 Wood

Higgins Annie stenographer bds 18 King
Higgins Catherine widow John h 18 King
Higgins Charles E clerk French Mfg Co bds 18 King
Higgins Edward (U S N) bds 13 Liberty
Higgins Francis J express agt bds 18 King
Higgins Maurice J baker h 13 Liberty
Hill Eber mgr h 93 Franklin
Hill Harold E (U S A) bds 93 Franklin
Hilliard Nellie emp Warren Mfg Co bds 46 Market
Hillman William carpenter bds 30 Child
Hinckley William carpenter h 139 South Water
Hnatow Dymitr weaver h Company
Hnatow Eliasz weaver h Company
Hoar Arthur L oyster opener h 45 North Main
Hoar Clara Mrs bds 29 Child
Hoar Emilie M and Nellie C Misses h 58 N Water
Hoar Joseph B retired h 29 Child
Hoar Sadie Mrs bds 29 Child
Hoar Williard B clerk Warren Mfg Co bds 29 Child
Hoch Frances Mrs bds R D A Rogers
Hochman Louis second hand store N Water h 10 Union
Hodgkinson Adam rubber worker bds 24 Cook
Hogue Frank brakeman h 33 Child
Hojnochi Alexander weaver h 45 Water
Holbrook Forrest C (U S N) h 168 High
Holland James E spinner h 75 Arlington av
Holton Amelia laundress h 48 Garfield av
Holton Maud laundress bds 48 Garfield av
Hop Katarzyna weaver bds 93 Johnson
Hop Michael laborer h 70 Water
Hope Pharmacy (B W Quick prop) 127 S Main cor Baker
Hopkins Henry W physician and surgeon cor Miller and Union h do
Horton Edmund H local mgr The Great A & P Co h 7 Sowamsett av
Horton E Francis engineer h 220 South Main
Horton George B engineer h 220 South Main
Horton Gertrude M rubber worker bds 220 South Main
Horton Jennie D Miss shoemaker bds 83 State
Hotel Ferncroft (Bruno Bros props) 157 Bradford
Hotel Warren (James H Lonergan prop) S Main cor Joyce
Houle Alphonsine Mrs bds Market
Houle Maxime h Market
Hounessey Salum yarn tender h Arlington av
Howard George clerk bds William Howard
Howard Minnie at rubber works bds William Howard
Howard William at rubber works h Massasoit cor Cherry
Howarth George carpenter h 104 North Main
Howe Mary widow Herbert M sum res h Ferry rd nr Ferry

| Water Supply Outfits House Pumps | Walter H. Jackson Co. 435 Industrial Trust Building Providence, - R. I. | "Dodd" System Lightning PROTECTION |

Howland Henry P mgr DeWitt Mfg Co h 298 S Main
Howland Laura W bds 298 South Main
Hoxie John emp State roads h 19 Metacom av
Hoxie William emp State roads bds 19 Metacom av
Hoye Francis sec'y Warren Dye Co h Providence
Hoyle Harry overseer Narragansett Worsted Co h 1 Sowamsett av
Hoznar Anna weaver bds Main
Hudson John janitor h Market next to R R crossing
Hudzik Adolf weaver bds Water
Huftalen Floyd laborer h ft of Greene
Hull Annie B Mrs (John) bds James Skuce r 60 Market
Hull Charles watchman h Metacom av
Hull George E watchman bds C Hull
Hull Henry F police officer bds Metacom av 12th south from Vernon
Hunt Charles L night watchman bds 16 Wheaton
Hunt Harry clam digger bds 88 Child
Hunt Robert marine engineer h 28 Wheaton
Hutcheson Joseph pres Warren Mfg Co h 168 S Water
Hutcheson Sarah F h 168 South Water

Ide Emilie A librarian George Hail Free Library h E Prov
Ideal 5 & 10c Store (William A Cote prop) Saugy bldg
Iervolino Michele barber 54 N Water h 4 Company
Ikacz Michal weaver bds 146 Warren av
INDUSTRIAL TRUST CO Warren Branch Edwin A Cady mgr Main cor Market—see front cover and opp Warren Directory
Isimsana Joseph barber 43 Prospect

Jackson J Fred wire worker h 9 Anthony av
Jacobson Ellen Mrs bds 28 Market
Jamiel Albert (George Jamiel & Son) h Miller cor S Water
Jamiel George (George Jamiel & Son) Miller cor Water h Bristol
Jamiel George & Son (George and Albert Jamiel) dry goods Miller cor Water
Jamrock Joseph mule spinner bds 64 Sisson
Jamrog John carder h 64 Sisson
Jamrog Walter mill emp h f n 150 Warren av
Jamrog Walter mule spinner h 155 Warren av
Jamuszkiewicz Karol mill emp h 132 Main
Jannetti Angelo fruit and grocery 41 N Water h N Water
Janorek Andro weaver h 7 Arlington av
Janorek Karol carder bds 24 Arlington av

WHITTEMORE & COLBURN
PRINTERS   15 Pine St., PROV.

JAMES C. GOFF CO.
31 to 49 POINT ST.
Providence, R. I.

All kinds of Masons' Materials

Janson Alphonse grocery and market 79-81 N Water h Bristol
Januszkicurcz Klemens comb tender h 38 Bowen
Jarvais Ben machine apprentice h 113 Market
Jarvais Carrie housekeeper 113 Market
Jarvais Cecilia spinner h 103 Market
Jarvais Delia spinner bds 113 Market
Jarvais Henry doffer bds 103 Market
Jarvais Wilfred spinner bds 113 Market
Jastrzembska Teresa weaver bds 155 Park
Jaworck Andrew weaver h 7 Arlington av
Jaworck Karol carder h 7 Arlington av
Jayne Josephine Miss h Church cor South Water
Jayne Seraphine Miss h Church cor South Water
Jefferson Harry H clerk h 74 North Water
Jefferson Myrtle second hand h rear 4 North Main
Jeffery Joseph rubber worker h 43 North Water
Johnson Betsy weaver bds 184 South Water
Johnson Charles fireman h 16 Brown
JOHNSON FREDERICK I electrical contractor 7 Lyndon h do—see page 24
Johnson John E agt Standard Oil Co h Cherry
Johnson Manne S (U S A) bds 16 Brown
Johnson William summer res h Metacom av
Joly Alice weaver bds 18 Asselin Plat
Joly Desire loomfixer h 18 Asselin Plat
Joly Doria spinner bds 18 Asselin Plat
Joly Wilfred weaver bds 18 Asselin Plat
Jones Annie M bds A H Coggeshall
Jones Clifford R printer h Bradford
Jones Emma widow William H h 18 Vernon
Jones Grace cloth inspector bds Market
Jones Harold R clerk h 18 Vernon
Jones Howard electrician h Coomer av
Jones Mary widow Robert h Market
Jones Nellie M district nurse 11 Lyndon h do
Jones Norman H driver bds 18 Vernon
Jones Roland T packer bds 18 Vernon
Jones Sarah K school teacher h Bridge
Jordan Harry B brakeman h 43 Market
Jordan Mary bds 43 Market
Joseph Mary bds 112 Market
Jovin Charles rubber worker h 49 North Water
Jurczyk Valentine mill emp h 50 Child
Kaiser Adolf weaver h Market
Kaiser Barbara bds Market
Kaliff Abbie weaver bds 50 North Water
Kalitnik Zophia weaver bds Water
Karders Frank speed tender h Sisson

Ralph C. Watrous Co.
ESTATE MANAGERS.   RENT COLLECTION A SPECIALTY
437 INDUSTRIAL TRUST BUILDING

Karpienski Vicenty mill emp h Metacom av opp mill
Kasprzck Jack bartender bds Company
Katt William tailor 31 North Water h Providence
Kaus William loomfixer h Summer and North Water
Kavanaugh Michael janitor Byfield school h 130 Constitution
Kay Charles clerk 6 Market bds 7 Union
Kearney William H (U S N) bds 61 Church
Keating J Frank Jr student bds 107 Franklin
Keating Mildred H clerk bds 107 Franklin
Kebrek Esther rubber worker bds 11 Prospect
Kee Howard W farmer h off Touisset rd 2d from R R crossing
Keefe see O'Keefe
Keegan M Amanda Mrs h 100 North Main
Keeler Ase sewing machine repairs bds 67 Child
Keeler James agent Singer Sewing Mach h 67 Child
Keeler Mary bds 67 Child
Keil Dora cloth inspector h Laurel lane
Kelley Howard J (U S A) bds 32 North Water
Kelley John J paymaster (Bristol) h 8 Bridge
Kelley William W bookkeeper E M Martin Lumber Co h 32 North Water
Kellogg Florence school teacher Walley School bds 262 High
Kelly Thomas L Rev retired h 109 North Main
Kemlik William restaurant 141 Bradford bds 1 Franklin
Kemp Adele teacher Joyce St Sch bds S Main cor Cherry
Kemp Paulina teacher Miller St Sch bds S Main cor Cherry
Kemp Thomas F fireman h S Main cor Cherry
Keroic Charles carpenter h 10½ Hope
Kickemuit Grange Child 3d bey Kickemuit river
Kierklewski George F mill emp h 15 Child
Kilroy Annie bds Thomas Kilroy
Kilroy Arthur L farmer h S Main beyond Maple
Kilroy Margaret bds Thomas J Kilroy
Kilroy Thomas J farmer South Main beyond Maple
Kinder Jane h 54 Carfield av
King James F bds George P Stone
King Mary bds 593 Wood
Kingsley Frank H farmer h 356 South Main
Kirby Morris J at rubber works (Prov) h 71 Market
Kirke Pauline E widow Frank F bds 24 King
Kirouac Anselime bds Mitchell Boyer
Kirouac Emile mill emp h 3 Nobert

Blackstone Canal Nat'l Bank 20 Market Square PROVIDENCE, R. I.
Capital, $500,000.   Surplus Profits, over $500,000

Warren Monumental Works
Cor. Railroad Avenue and Croade Street, Warren, R. I.

Knowlton Lavinia bds 34 Pierce av
Knox Agnes rubber worker bds 351 Wood
Knox Max h 351 Wood
Kochanck John laborer h 7 Arlington av
Koechling A G violin teacher Saugy bldg h Pawtucket
Kolusa Andrew weaver h 80 Company
Korinsky Julian fireman h 31 Metacom av
Kosior Anthony weaver h Company
Kotowski Antoni carder h 94 Company
Kozik Sabastian shoemaker h 12 West
Krawczyk John grocery and market 66 N Water bds 68 do
Krawszyk Mary wid Gregory grocery 66 N Water h 68 do
Krevolin Jacob P watchmaker and jeweler 139 S Main h 10 Croade
Krzywoblocki Arthur h 14 Union
Krzywoblocki Henry weaver h 147 Warren av
Kubicki Casimir laborer h 1 Arlington av
Kulponicz Antoni carder h 59 Water
Kumiega Joseph laborer h 101 Company
Kunicki Julian fireman h 11 Metacom av
Kuros Ludwig clerk 86 N Water h 23 Arlington av
Kurowzki Alexander weaver h 159 Park
Kurzawa Clara widow Joseph dressmaker h 72 N Water
Kuszcj Anthony emp mill h Warren av
Labelle Wilfred weaver h f n 192 Park
La Brie Mitchell J chauffeur h 102 Wood
Labrun Oliver mill emp h 82 North Water
Lach Gabryel laborer h 44 Kelly
Lach John speed tender bds 48 Union
Lach Michael machinist bds 162 Park
Lachance Stanislas J spinner h Arlington av
Lachapelle Moses loomfixer h 13 Church
Laduc Anna Mrs bds ft of Summer
Laferriere Anna housekeeper h off Cole
Laferriere Francis J deck hand bds off Cole
Laferriere Fred E mill hand bds off Cole
Lafferriere Donat (U S A) bds 91 North Main
Lafferriere Gedeon J h 91 North Main
Laflamme Clara bds 54 Child
Laflamme Fred mill emp h 54 Child
Lafleur Adolph J chief engineer Bristol & Warren Pumping station Child nr Barker av h opp do
Laforge Albert clerk 1 North Water h 16 Wood
Laforge Armedos weaver h 18 Wood
Laforge Augustine laborer h 14½ Wood
Laforge Joseph Mrs h 86 North Main
Laforge Mederic weaver h 14 Wood
Lafrance Wilhelmina Mrs boarding house ft of Summer
Lajeunesse Jeffrey chauffeur h 20 Warren av

Lajeunesse Mary Mrs clerk Warren Shoe Co h 20 Warren av
Lajoie Donat painter h 2 Wood
Lally Mary widow James bds 11 Liberty
Lamarch Mederic loomfixer h 53 Summer
Lambert Hermine Miss bds 27 Child
Lambert Joseph bds 26 Baker
Lambert Otto mule spinner h Baltimore av
Lamora Celi mill emp bds rear 10 North Main
Lamora Charles mill emp h rear 10 North Main
Lamora Jennie bds rear 10 North Main
Landry Ida widow Frederick bds rear 91 North Main
Laneau Amos driver h Liberty cor Union
Langelier John barber h 1 Nobert
Langlois Evariste mill emp h 10 Warren av
Lanue Amos driver h 13 Liberty
Lanue Avila (U S N) bds 13 Liberty
La Page Louis laborer h 23 Market
Lapane Adelard J carpenter h Cornell av
Lapane Medause mill emp Arlington av
Lapane Peter farmer h 40 Metacom av
Lapare Edward weaver h 19 Metacom av
La Point Thomas bartender 29 Market h Parker av
Larivee Adelard electrician h 61 Child
Larivee Albina bds 95 Market
Larivee Charles bartender 29 Market h 95 do
Larivee William machinist bds 5 Wood
Lariviere Hermine millinery 159 South Main h 5 State
Larned Emma Mrs widow Edward C h Poppasquash rd
Laroche Joseph carpenter h Buffalo av
Latourneau Emile weaver h 12 Barney
Lavender Fred E engineer h nr Wood
Lavergna Albert at rubber works bds 26 Market
Lavergna Matilda mill emp bds 26 Market
Lavergne Joseph Mrs h 26 Market
Lavigueur Herbert stationery Main h Market
Lawrence Joseph laborer h 51 Market
Lawson William contractor h 118 Child
Leach Albert E district mgr Phoenix Mutual Life Insurance Co 1205 Union Trust bldg Prov h 12 Miller
Leach Fred A cutter bds 118 Child
Leahy Maurice rubber worker bds 93 North Water
Leahy Nora Miss sec'y and treas Narragansett Rubber Co h Metacom av
Leahy Thomas S (U S A) bds Metacom av

33 Canal St. CHARLES J. JAGER CO. Providence
ELECTRIC AND GASOLINE PUMPS AND PRESSURE SYSTEMS
We carry the largest stock of this kind in New England

144   WARREN DIRECTORY, 1917-18.

LeBart Harriett Miss bds 237 South Main
Lebicda John carder h 97 Johnson
Lee Ernest J painter h 22 Warren av
Lee George mill emp bds 26 Warren av
Lee Joseph mill emp h 26 Warren av
Lee Louis mill emp h 22 Union
Lee Mary E bds Market
Lee William mill emp h Market
Leeson James H local mgr the Mayflower Store h 5 Bridge
Leeson Mary C widow Daniel h 182 South Water
Legace Anna widow Joseph bds 321 Sisson
Lemieux Albert J rubber worker bds 47 North Water
Lemieux Andre H police h 17 Union
Lemieux Arthur J clerk 47 North Water bds 49 do
Lemieux Frank h 82 North Main
Lemieux Louis grocery and market 47 N Water h 49 do
Lemieux Martha widow Luke h 5 Wood
Lemieux Mary Mrs bds 14 Wood
Lemieux William machinist h South Main cor Baker
Lemoi Edward painter h 5 Nobert
Lemoine Lea mill emp bds f n 149 Warren av
Lemoine Paul wood chopper h f n 149 Warren av
Lenoue Eva clerk bds Liberty
Lent Joseph H (Lent & Barry) plumbers h 12 Wood
Lent Walter C cutter bds 12 Wood
Leonard Martha F school teacher bds 189 South Main
Lepucki Frank laborer h 89 Company
Lervolino Adamo barber 96 North Main bds 7 Martin
Lescault Anna bds rear 63 North Water
Lescault Cyrille clerk h 67 North Water
Lescoe Clara cloth inspector bds 46 Market
Lessard Anna mill emp bds 3 Brown
Lessard Henry second hand bds State cor Water
Lessard Lena mill emp bds 3 Brown
Lessard Louis mill emp h 3 Brown
Lessard Louis Jr laborer bds 3 Brown
Lessard Oliver clerk bds 3 Brown
Letourneau William plumber bds 70 Union
Lever John spinner h 17 Child
Levesque Alfred spinner h 6 Martin
Levesque Edward (U S A) bds 6 Martin
Levesque Wilfred (U S A) bds 6 Martin
Levin Sam tailor 137 South Main h 10 Union
Levoi Charles watchmaker h Touisset rd
Lewis George W machinist h 53 Summer
Lial Caroline bds 44 Market
Lial Manuel farmer h Kickemuit nr Handy's lane
Lial Vitramo packer h 44 Market

Liberty Stores Co The groceries (C C Cummings local mgr) Goff's block
Lightfoot Davenport & Co furniture dealers 151 Bradford
Lightfoot Edwin S (Lightfoot Davenport & Co) 151 Bradford h Fall River
Lincoln J Thayer sum res Touisset Neck
Lipshitz R tailor 77 North Water h Fall River
Liscomb Elizabeth H Miss h Union cor Liberty
Little Anna h Johnson
Little Benjamin J laborer h 38 North Water
Little John carder bds Johnson
Little Michael timekeeper bds Johnson
Littlefield Frank W C second hand h 138 South Water
Littlefield James A (U S A) bds 138 South Water
Littlefield Mildred tel operator 138 South Water
Lizak Frank carder h 96 Johnson
Lonergan Annie stenographer bds Church cor South Water
Lonergan Frank A mason bds 37 Joyce
Lonergan James H prop Hotel Warren h do
Lonergan John L clerk of court and probate judge bds 37 Joyce
Lonergan John H retired h 37 Joyce
Lonergan Mary clerk bds Church cor South Water
Lonergan Thomas F reporter bds Church cor Water
Lonergan William J restaurant 35 Joyce bds 37 do
Long Ralph G baggageman Warren depot h 6 Wood
Longpre Arthur carpenter h 26 Child
Lother Elmer jeweler h 7 Bridge
Loughran Ann widow John h 20 King
Loughran Daniel F bricklayer bds 20 King
Loughran Elizabeth W teacher High School bds 55 Child
Loughran James J student bds 55 Child
Loughran May G physical instructor bds 55 Child
Loughran Thomas J carpenter and builder 55 Child h do
Louysell Charles h 30 Market
Lowrey Robert painter bds 167 State
Lubosky Samuel freight clerk Warren h Prov
Luce Joseph A chemist h 108 Church
Lucibbla Albert shoe maker bds 282 High
Lucien J Peter rubber worker h 5 Union
Lucien Nelson bds 5 Union
Ludwig William grocery and market 28 and 32 Child h 30 do
Luther Daniel B (E M Martin Lumber Co) h Campbell
Luther Katherine E widow John E h 58 Market

WARDWELL LUMBER CO.
BRISTOL, R. I.

All Kinds of
BUILDING MATERIAL
at
LOWEST PRICES

WARREN DIRECTORY, 1917-18.

Luther Samuel H local agt Penn Oil Co h 57 Union
Luther Susan Mrs h 243 South Main cor Campbell
Luz Manuel grocery 104 South Water h do
Lynch Cornelius laborer h 65 North Main
Lynch Cornelius J second hand bds 65 North Main
Lynch Margaret J bds 65 North Main
Lyric Theater Alonzo Vail prop 3 Miller
Mabey Leon A fireman h Middle
Macara Joseph bartender 71 North Water h Croade
Macauley Frederick W Jr clerk bds 283 Wood
Macck Anna weaver bds 73 Johnson
MacDonald John J painter and paper hanger Green's Landing S W
MacDonald Mary A stenographer bds 84 Franklin
MacDonald Mildred H clerk Prov Tel Co bds 63 Burton Bristol
Macierowski Joseph laborer h 21 Arlington av
MacKenzie Herbert M R F D carrier bds 22 Child
MacKenzie Myrtle M bds W M Mackenzie
Mackenzie William M harnessmaker 24 Child h 22 do
Macomber Edward G h 88 Child
Maddox George O laborer h 120 Child
Maddox Mary bds 120 Child
Maddox William cigars confectionery etc 33 Joyce h 15 Baker
Madero Joseph farmer h Touisset rd
Maderos Manuel rubber worker h South Water cor Baker
Maderous John F farmer h Kickemuit rd
Maderous Manuel farmer h Kickemuit rd
Magee Lillian stitcher bds 29 Garfield av
Maguire Annie mill emp bds 46 Market
Maguire Edward H clerk bds 46 Market
Maguire Katherine housekeeper bds 46 Market
Maguire Mary h 46 Market
Maher Annie E h 252 Wood
Maher John spinner bds 37 North Water
Maher Mary A Miss mill emp h 10 Liberty
Mahoney Edward emp R R h 61 Child
Mahoney James carpenter bds 10 Child
Mahoney Nora h 61 Child
Main Street Garage (A J Heon prop) 105 North Main
Mainville Joseph C loomfixer h 24 Wood
Majonicz Jendrzcj laborer h Company
Majonicz Joseph carder bds Kickemuit rd
Makara Joseph bartender h Croade
MAKER ARTHUR J optician and jeweler 163 S Main h Baltimore av—see page 24
Mallory John D (U S A) bds R P Atkinson
Maloy Charles T clerk 1 and 3 N Water bds 63 N Main

Maloy John M grocer and market 1 and 3 N Water h 63 N Main
Maloy William R bookkeeper 1 and 3 N Water bds 63 N Main
Manchester Alexander D mill emp h 14 Croade
Manchester Charles E farmer bds Laura Manchester
Manchester Frank A laborer bds Bridge
Manchester Frank M hostler h 26 Warren av
Manchester Georgianna mill emp bds 26 Warren av
Manchester Harold L brakeman N Y N H & H R R h 93 Cutler
Manchester Laura widow Alfred A h Touisset Neck
Manchester Mary M bds 26 Warren av
Manchester Mary R emp Warren Mfg Co bds Bridge
Manchester William A farmer h Touisset Neck
Manley Elmer gardener h Broad Common
Mann Albert J mgr Warren Handkerchief Co h 8 Church
Mann Edward T rubber worker h 8 State
Mann Eva G handkerchief worker bds 15 Church
Mann Frederick V foreman h 15 Church
Mann Norman H foreman Warren Handkerchief Co bds 8 Church
Manquin Henry mill emp bds 74 North Water
Manquin Onesime mill emp h 74 North Water
Manville Eva mill emp bds 104 North Main
Marchand Charles rubber worker h 11 Broad
Marchand John oysterman h 82 North Water
Marchand Paul rubber worker bds 11 Broad
Marcott Almedus oyster opener h S Main cor Baker
Marhewka Valenly carder h Cutler
Marks Charles clerk bds 210 South Main
Marks David steam fitter h North Main
Marks Joseph student bds 210 South Main
Marks Nathan clothing dealer also furniture N Water and Miller h 210 S Main
Marrs Mary rubber worker bds 113 Constitution
Marshall Wilfred A engineer h 93 South Water
Marszalck Andrew weaver h 103 Company
Marszalck John weaver bds 101 Company
Marszalck John weaver h 7 Arlington av
Marszalck John spinner bds 164 Park
Marszalck Joseph mill emp bds 101 Company
Marszalck Walter weaver h 94 Company
Martin Alvertus farmer h Vernon nr Park
Martin Anna M widow Benjamin B h 12 Miller

JAMES C. GOFF CO. Sole Agents for   **ATLAS**
31 to 49 POINT ST.   **Portland Cement**
Providence, R. I.

Martin Clarence H printer bds 9 Miller
MARTIN E M LUMBER CO (Joseph W Martin Daniel B Luther) lumber ft of Church—see page 23
Martin Frank S carpenter h 57 Union
Martin Henrietta Miss h 19 Washington
Martin Howard I (U S A) h r 12 Market
Martin Joseph W (E M Martin Lumber Co) also agent Staples Coal Co h 212 South Main
Martin Mary E widow William H h 346 South Main
Martin William A printer The Warren and Barrington Gazette h 346 South Main
Mason Ambrose B farmer h Metacom av 5th south Vernon
Mason Ambrose E farmer h Reed Farm Metacom av
Mason Charles B attorney 145 Main rms 15 Baker
Mason Charles E (U S A) bds A E Mason
Mason Edson V h Birch Swamp rd
Mason Edward A carpenter h Birch Swamp rd
Mason Edward W farmer h Birch Swamp rd
Mason Elizabeth W stenographer Town Hall bds Ambrose B Mason
Mason Frank W driver h off Birch Swamp rd
Mason Frederick L dentist 92 State also Pawt h Pawt
Mason Mabel H Mrs bds William Howard
Mason Martha E bds Ambrose B Mason
Mason Oliver L bookkeeper bds A E Mason Metacom av
Massud George (U S A) bds 5 Company
Massud John mill emp h 5 Company
Masztal Casimir speed tender h 66 Sisson
Masztal Julia speed tender bds 66 Sisson
Mathos Joseph B chef h 59 Market
Mathos Mary bds 59 Market
Matteson Laura N stitcher rubber works bds 21 Broad
Matteson Margaret widow Edward H h S Water foot of Campbell
Matthiews Marguerite Mrs h 5 Barney
Mattos Miguel mill emp h Touisset rd nr R R tracks
Matula Franciszka speed tender bds 146 Warren av
Matula John weaver bds Warren av
Maxfield Arthur J fish market Coomer av h do
Maxfield Betsy C bds Child cor Asylum rd
Maxfield Charles R ice cream and variety 310 South Main bds 311 do
Maxfield Charles S grocery 310 South Main h 311 do
Maxfield Elmer C (U S A) h 18 Charles
Maxfield Frederick W farm hand bds Child cor Asylum rd
Maxfield George W longshoreman h cor Child and Asylum rd
Maxfield Julia A widow Nathaniel S ice cream 6 Federal h do
Maxfield Marion V Mrs bds 19 Child

RALPH C. WATROUS CO.
Real Estate Auctioneers
437 INDUSTRIAL TRUST BUILDING

Maxwell Ellen H bds 12 Hope
Maxwell Ellen P widow James H h 12 Hope
Maxwell Frank E clerk (Prov) h 242 South Main
Maxwell Grace E clerk bds Child cor Asylum rd
Maxwell Hannah bookkeeper (Prov) bds 12 Hope
Maxwell Mabel E bookkeeper (Prov) bds 12 Hope
Maxwell William R carpenter h 20 Church
Mayflower Store The (James H Leeson local mgr) 167 S Main
Mayhew Eli carpenter bds 29 Warren av
Mayhew Joseph A boat builder h 29 Warren av
Mayhew Peter boat builder bds 29 Warren av
Maynes Jennie bds 38 Mt Hope av
Maytum A Marie rubber worker bds 47 Cherry av
Maytum Charles G weaver bds 47 Cherry av
Maytum Thomas W student bds 47 Cherry av
Mazur Szcrepan weaver h 78 Company
Mazza Antonio shoe repairer 124 Franklin h 327 High
McAdam Ruby clerk 163 S Main bds 25 Broad
McAllister James marine engineer h 214 South Main
McCaffrey A Jennie bds 5 Church
McCaffrey Jennie E teacher (Pawt) bds 5 Church
McCaffrey Mary A bds 5 Church
McCaffrey Thomas W h 5 Church
McCann Michael F carpenter and builder Railroad av nr Depot h do
McCann Thomas J restaurant Railroad av opp R R Depot h 23 Joyce
McCanna Charles H purser steamer *Sagamore* h 11 Broad
McCanna Hugh stenographer bds 30 Wheaton
McCanna James chauffeur bds 30 Wheaton
McCanna Mary widow Charles h 30 Wheaton
McCanna see also McKenna
McCarthy Catherine widow Dennis bds 231 Wood
McCarthy F Henry engineer h 67 North Water
McCarthy Frank H (U S N) bds Frank M McCarthy
McCarthy Jerry rubber worker bds 180 Wood
McCarthy Lulle rubber worker bds Frank McCarthy
McCarthy Mary A Miss h 9 Washington
McCarty Jeremiah operative h South Water cor State
McCarty John J weaver bds 47 North Main
McCarty Margaret mill emp bds 47 North Main
McCarty Mary widow Daniel h 47 North Main
McCarty Percy J mason h 66 Charles

Blackstone Canal Nat'l Bank | **BEST FACILITIES**
20 MARKET SQ., PROVIDENCE | **Prompt Attention**

WARREN MONUMENTAL WORKS
Cor. Railroad Avenue and Croade Streets, Warren, R. I.

McCaughey William J conductor h Taylor cor King
McCaw Arthur M mgr (Bristol) h Campbell
McCaw William E ship fitter bds 123 Constitution
McComb James loomfixer h 73 Arlington av
McConnell William herdsman Colt Farm h Poppasquash
McCormick James crossing tender N h 67 Child
McCusker Alice cloth inspector bds 17 State
McCusker Anne cloth inspector h 17 State
McCusker Catherine bds 12 Luther
McDonough Bessie T Miss milliner (Prov) bds 10 Wood
McDonough Bottle Store (Russell W Pray mgr) Joyce nr Main
McDonough Bridget E widow John F h Goff's Hotel
McDonough Catherine L teacher (Fall River Mass) bds 10 Wood
McDonough James T h 21 Church cor Water
McElroy James E farmer h Market 5th bey Kickemuit rd
McElroy Mary A Mrs bds Market
McElroy Michael farmer bds Market 5th bey Kickemuit rd
McGarry Margaret Miss h South Water cor Church
McGarry Peter at rubber works h S Water cor Church
McGinn Sylvester second hand h 12 North Main
McGrath Hannah h Market
McGrath Margaret h Market
McGrath Margaret housekeeper bds 109 North Main
McGuire see Maguire
McHugh James watchman h 30 Garfield av
McKenna James A clerk bds 8 Church
McKenna Mary M widow James T h 8 Church
McKenna Veronica braider operative bds 30 Mt Hope av
McKenna William A (U S A) bds 21 Sowamsett av
McKenna William H (U S A) bds 8 Church
McKenna William Henry real estate agent h 17 Church
McKenna see also McCanna
McKenzie see Mackenzie
McLarren Arthur B gas fitter h 17 Bridge
McLaughlin William P foreman carpenter h 400 High
McLeer Johanna widow Patrick h South Water cor Miller
McLoughlin Joseph mill emp h Hope over tracks
McLoughlin Mary F widow Thomas C h 48 Market
McManus Bridget Miss mill emp h 34 North Water
McManus Katherine Miss mill emp h 34 North Water
McNeil James R laborer h Child
McQueeney James wine clerk bds Goff's Hotel
McQuilan John summer res h Metacom av
McSoley William H lawyer (406 Grosvenor bldg Prov) also 8 Child h do
Meadows John J overseer h 303 South Main

NATIONAL EXCHANGE BANK One of the Oldest and Strongest Banks
63 Westminster St., Providence   **In Rhode Island**

WARREN DIRECTORY, 1917-18.

Medeiros Jose rubber worker h Kickemuit rd
Medeiros Manuel farm hand C H Seymour bds rear do
Medeiros Toney farm hand C H Seymour bds rear do
Medley Herbert shipping clerk h Coomer av
Meiggs Ernest farmer h 188 South Water
Meiggs John R farmer h 188 South Water
Mello Manuel rubber worker h last on King
Mello Manuello farmer h Kickemuit rd
Mello Toney farmer h Child nr Touisset rd
Merchant Henry G oyster opener bds 30 Market
Merchant Joseph M physician h 125 South Main
Merchant Marcius H physician 114 North Main h do
Merchant Theophilus painter h 8 Broad
Mercier Exter clerk h 10 Martin
Mercier Hector H meat cutter 97 North Main h 10 Martin
Mercier Henry clerk 97 N Main bds 79 N Water
MERCIER JOSEPH H bakery and market 97 N Main h 79 N Water—see page 25
Mercier Leah widow Zeb h 88 Market
Mercier William Z carpenter bds 88 Market
Messier Augustus second hand h 6 Nobert
Messier Augustus Jr pool room 102 North Main h r 6 Hope
Messier Charles (U S A) bds 6 Nobert
Messier Charles O grocery Franklin also mill emp h 93 Cutler
Messier Frank (U S A) bds 6 Nobert
Meyer Eugene pattern maker bds 12 Barney
Meyhew Delia dressmaker bds 60 Child
Meyhew Eli carpenter h 29 Warren av
Meyhew Joseph A carpenter bds 29 Warren av
Michael Susan rubber worker bds 18 Bowen
Mickle Mary C widow George A h 10 Child
Mickulski Antoni laborer h Kickemuit rd
Mickulski Joseph barber 49 Metacom av h do
Midura Helena weaver bds Hampden Meadows
Miller Asahel crossing tender h 243 South Main
Miller Calvin painter h Parker av
Miller Charles L h 31 Child
Miller David F carpenter h Market
Miller Mary E Mrs bds rear 16 North Main
Miller Otis machinist h Bradford
Milligan Joseph A secy Y M C A h 78 State
Mills John B summer res h Ferry rd
Mitchell Joseph K gardener h 13 Child

Merewether & Dunn
Plumbing and Heating Contractors
31 TURNER AVENUE,   RIVERSIDE, R. I.

Modliszewski Isidor weaver bds 60 Metacom av
Modliszewski Joseph carder bds 60 Metacom av
Moffitt Mary C widow William h 103 Franklin
Molloy see Maloy
Monahan Peter driver bds 68 North Main
Monahan Thomas L clerk h 23 North Main
Monahan William ins agt h 68 North Main
MONAST WILFRED A carpenter 63 Metacom av h do—see page 24
Mondina Anna rubber worker bds 64 North Main
Mondina Georgiana rubber worker bds 64 North Main
Mondina Joseph Mrs widow bds Albert Seymour
Mondina Joseph laborer h 64 North Main
Mondina Rose mill emp bds 64 North Main
Mondina Severe barber 31 Market h 15 Child
Monroe Clara J widow Charles R h 26 State
Monroe see also Munro and Munroe
Monsell Joseph V Capt h 26 State
Moody George O reporter (Prov) h 13 Bridge
Moore Fannie H widow Ira bds 9 Bridge
Moran Della laborer h Mulberry
Morency Eugene carpenter h 11 Hope
Morey Douglass (U S A) bds 79 Union
Morgan Charles Jr clerk bds 88 Church
Morgan Mina widow Milton W bds 133 State
Morin Alfred shoe maker bds Market
Morino Arthur H confectionery 33 North Water h 33 do
Morino Moriss retired h 33 North Water
Morino Samuel M architect Prov h 33 North Water
Morisseau Simon h 8 Baker
Morisseau Theodule G physician 19 Child h do office hours 1 to 3 and 6 to 8 p m Sundays by appointment telephone
Morris Thomas painter bds H R Seymour
Morrisette Mary mill emp bds 8 Martin
Morrisette Ovid carpenter h 8 Martin
Morrison Leger carpenter h 82 North Main
Morrissey Alice R bds 76 North Main
Morrissey Daniel H attorney at law (Prov) also 76 North Main h do
Morrissey Daniel L supt Warren Mfg Co h 76 N Main
Morrissey Harry R secretary (Prov) bds 76 North Main
Morrissey Mamie Mrs h f n 203 Warren av
Morrissey Thomas M second hand bds 76 North Main
Morte P Della & Sons bakers 537 Wood h cor Franklin and Wood
Morthup Phebe cattle dept Colt's bds Allen
Morton Albert M clerk cor Child and S Main bds 18 Vernon

OUR CREDIT REPORTS TELL—Whom to trust; whom not to trust; who pay promptly; who pay slowly; who never pay their bills except under pressure. Telephone Union 1526
Western Mercantile Corporation, Providence, R. I.

WARREN DIRECTORY, 1917-18. 153

Morton Evelyn widow Albert h 18 Vernon
Moscha Nocola washer Kickemuit rd
Moulor Catherine Miss h 5 Company
Mt Hope Spinning Co (J C Smith supt) mfg of tire fabric yarn Cutler
Mowry William carder bds 37 North Water
Moy Watson teamster Colt Farm bds Allen
Muccino Dominic A grocery and market 42 N Main h 13 do
Muir Elizabeth bds 4 Federal
Muir James mill emp h 4 Federal
Muir Maxwell clerk 14 Child h 93 Child
Muir Miria L housekeeper 93 Child
Mullen Crawford teamer h 11 Washington
Mullen John P switchman h 42 Market
Mullen Margaret h 42 Market
Muller Max painter 168 S Main h 22 Manning
Mullin John P signalman Warren h 42 Market
Mumford Edmund mill emp h Kelley
Munnegle Mary E mill emp bds f n 65 North Main
Munro Alice L A laundress h 709 Constitution
Munro Elmer C crossing tender h Vernon nr Park
Munro Eugene farmer bds Vernon nr Park
Munro Joseph B veterinarian h and office Metacom av
Munro Lilla F Miss h Vernon nr Park
Munro Walter H fisherman Parker av
Munro see also Monroe and Munroe
Munroe Charles trav salesman bds Child cor Cutler
Munroe Charles E telephone inspector (Warren) h Child
Munroe Edward stable also veterinary Cutler cor Child h 35 Child
Munroe Helen A Mrs bds Child
Munroe Ida Mrs bds 35 Child
Munroe Ida D widow Henry H h Metacom av
Munroe see also Munro and Monroe
Murphy Agnes C clerk bds 222 Wood
Murphy Annie A rubber worker bls 222 Wood
Murphy Bridget widow Patrick bds Sylvester Coen
Murphy Edward F rubber worker bds 222 Wood
Murphy Hannah B clerk bds 222 Wood
Murphy Hugh J wire worker bds 222 Wood
Murphy James rubber worker h 222 Wood
Murphy James P supt Narra Rubber Co h 14 Mt Hope av
Murphy John H emp rubber works bds 26 Market
Murphy John P (U S A) bds 222 Wood

R. I. RUG WORKS
Rugs Woven from old and new carpets. Telephones {2203 2204
678 WESTMINSTER ST., PROVIDENCE

HARDWELL LUMBER CO. { **LUMBER**
YOU'LL FIND IT AT HARDWELL LUMBER CO. IF YOU FIND IT IN TOWN **LATH**
BRISTOL, R. I. { **SHINGLES**

Murphy Mary widow John h 26 Market
Murphy Mary B bds 222 Wood
Murphy Mary M bookkeeper (Prov) bds Sylvester Coen
Murphy William G mason contractor h Sowamsett av cor King
Murray Susan rubber worker bds Arthur L Kilroy
Nadeau Philip H baker 6 Nobert h do
Nans August laborer h 30 Market
Nans Edouard A chauffeur bds 30 Market
Narragansett Electric Lighting Co (Warren sub station) 1 N Main
Narragansett Rubber Co (R S Emerson pres) 228 Wood
Narragansett Worsted Co (Henry Wood agt) worsted yarns Franklin nr R R tracks
Nassar George mill emp h Arlington av
Nassar Sullivan mill emp bds Arlington av
Natel John B shoe repairer Goff Hotel blk h 1 Sowamsett av
Necka John carder bds 164 Park
Nelle Martin bds Miller cor Union
Nelle Martin T liquors 71 North Water h Miller cor Union
Nelson August R gardener h Ferry rd
Nencka Waurzynice weaver h 68 Bowen
Neveux Joseph laborer h 70 Union
Neveux Docity clerk h 18 Wood
Neveux Marie mill emp bds 70 Union
Newell Dexter E sum res Touisset Point
Newman Bradford painter h 168 High
Newman Carl (U S A) bds 40 Catherine
New York Store The (A H Morino) gents' furnishings confectionery etc 33 North Water
Nichols Elizabeth N widow Edward T h 38 Cook
Nichols Herbert carpenter h 63 King
Nichols Mary E widow William B bds 254 South Main
Niemiec Julian emp mill h 49 Union
Niepert John mill emp bds ft of Summer
Nissen Louis Peter Rev rector St Mark's Episcopal Church h Union cor Liberty
Nixon Michael crossing tender Warren h 62 Market
Nixon Sarah Mrs housekeeper 62 Market
Noima Calil canvasser h 98 Market
Nom Chin restaurant South Main h do
Noon Manuel farmer h Market
Norgaard Christian mgr Cape Ann Fish Co h 9 Sowamsett av
Norgaard Haakon bookkeeper (Prov) bds 9 Sowamsett av
Norgaard Yacobe bds 9 Sowamsett av
Northup Annie A rubber worker h 24 Cook
Northup Edwin F C h 21 Broad

| Water Supply Outfits House Pumps | Walter H. Jackson Co. 435 Industrial Trust Building Providence, - R. I. | "Dodd" System Lightning PROTECTION |

Norton Bridget mill emp bds 11 Barney
Norton Mary mill emp bds 11 Barney
Norton Michael laborer h 11 Barney
Numes Manuel S rubber worker bds 45 Catherine
Nuruszeurcy Joseph laborer h 65 Sisson
O'Brien Annie T mill emp bds 68 Market
O'Brien Ellen M Miss h 68 Market
O'Brien Johanna Miss mill emp h 78 Child
O'Brien John M spinner h 42 Market
O'Brien Mary A rubber worker bds 19 Hope
O'Brien Mary G Miss rubber worker bds 8 Church
O'Brien Thomas F laborer bds 68 Market
O'Brien Thomas Francis teamster h 88 North Water
O'Brien William crossing tender bds 100 North Main
O'Connell Dennis H mason h 30 Wood
O'Donnell James F lineman Tel Co bds 113 Constitution
O'Donnell Nora maid 112 North Main
O'Donnell Patrick mill emp bds f n 171 Bowen
Ogden Thomas retired bds 153 Child
O'Keefe Samuel J musician h 6 Broad
Olcnik Paul weaver bds 60 Metacom av
O'Leary James carpenter bds 122 Child
O'Leary Jerry (U S A) bds 122 Child
O'Leary Joseph h 122 Child
Oleh Frank owner also speed tender h Metacom av
Olive Abraham (A & A T Olive) h 72 King
Olive Alfred T (A & A T Olive) bds 72 King
Olive A & A T (Abraham and Alfred T) ice cream and confectionery South Main cor State
Olive John R musician bds 29 Lyndon cor Wheaton
Oliver Jesse fireman h South Main nr Bristol line
Oliver Manuel laborer bds Jesse Oliver
Oliveria Frances widow John h cor Handy's lane and Kickemuit rd
Olsch Frank speed tender h Metacom av
Olszonry Ignatus speed fixer bds Metacom av
Olszonry John foreman h 156 Warren av
O'Neil Bridget Miss housekeeper 117 Child
O'Neil Martin W lunch pool and bowling alley Market h Campbell
O'Neil Nora h 117 Child
O'Neil Patrick W liquors 59 North Main h 246 South Main
Orchard Carmino weaver h Kickemuit rd
Order of Divine Providence (Sister Balbina Superior) 8 Hope

WHITTEMORE & COLBURN
PRINTERS   15 Pine St., PROV.

O'Rourke William F clerk h 33 Richmond
Orrel Delvina spinner bds 10 Union
Orrel Donat mill emp bds 10 Union
Orrel John wood chopper h 10 Union
Orrel Palmelia spinner bds 10 Union
Osofsky Samuel driver h 20 Catherine
Osolinski John weaver h 84 Company
Oszajca Francis speed tender bds 19 Warren av
Oszajca Peter speed tender h 19 Warren av
Ouben Clephonse teamer h 14 Arlington av
Ouben Ovid bds 14 Arlington av
Ouben Wilfred teamer bds 14 Arlington av
Ouellette J David mill emp bds 27 Warren av
Overwood Emma Mrs h 22 Manning
Owens George W mill emp h 8 North Main
Page Eliza widow John h 7 Union
Page Frederick L Capt oyster boat h South Water
Page Ritchie pool room bds 7 Union
Page Wilfred oyster opener bds 7 Union
Palka Ignatus weaver h Sisson
Palka Stanley weaver h 85 Company
Palmieri Ernest boot and shoe repairer 98 N Main h 9 Federal
Palumbo Emily rubber worker bds 6 Bay View av
Palumbo Lena stitcher bds 6 Bay View av
Paquin Aldea organist bds 87 North Main
Paquin Annie mill emp bds 58 Child
Paquin Cordelia bds 87 North Main
Paquin Dosithe hostler h 58 Child
Paquin Hannah bds 58 Child
Paquin Henry O clerk h Franklin 2d bey the mill
Paquin Joseph N laborer bds 58 Child
Paquin Marie bookkeeper bds 87 North Main
Paquin Napoleon grocery and market 82-84 N Main h 87 do
Paquin Napoleon J roller coverer bds 12 Barney
Paquin Olavine bds 58 Child
Paquin Victor coal dealer 87 North Main bds do
Pardey Harold O plumber 10 Baker h 12 do
Pardey Lottie E bds 12 Baker
Paré Alice M cashier bds Market
Paré Elodie bds Market
Paré Onesime grocer Metacom av h Market
Parker Ella S widow Leonard h 26 Franklin
Parker George H farmer h Market
Parker Jane Mrs bds Market
Parker Mill No 2 E E Bartlett supt Metacom av (office Jefferson Fall River)
Parks James liquor dealer Metacom av h Asylum rd

Patenaude Napoleon boat builder h Washington cor Eddy
Patterson Horatio mason bds Pleasant
Patterson John J h Pleasant
Patterson Samuel B h Metacom av
Paul Emma weaver bds 27 Cole
Paul Joseph laborer h 27 Cole
Payton George E gardener h 14 Lyndon
Peabody Cyrus h 8 State
Pearce Elizabeth H h 38 North Water
Pearce see also Pierce
Peck Henry J artist bds Liberty cor Union
Peck John D hay and grain etc Cole av nr Croade h at Prov
Peck Mary J widow William H h 212 South Main
Peck Samuel L h 218 South Main
Peckham Barbara teacher Oliver School bds 262 High
Peckham George S driver h 207 South Main
Pelchat Gaudiace mill emp bds rear 91 North Main
Pelchat Joseph mill emp h f n 138 North Main
Pelland Frank bds 148 Warren av
Pelland Frank Jr clerk bds f n 148 Warren av
Pelletier Charles A carpenter bds 50 Kickemuit rd
Pelletier Eugene emp Parker Mill bds 50 Kickemuit rd
Penkala John speed tender h Kickemuit rd
Penno Susie E widow Charles N h ft of Myrtle
Pereira Antonio M h 98 Market
Pereira Francis R mgr Lightfoot Davenport & Co 151 Bradford h Fall River
Pereira Rose housekeeper 98 Market
Perkins Arthur G carpenter h 1021 Hope
Perodeau Wilhelmina J milliner for Miss Hermine Lariviere bds do
Perpall Rupert chauffeur h 190 Wood
Perrira Joseph farm hand bds J H Kemph Poppasquash
Perron Oliver bartender 29 Market h Middle
Perry Eugene carpenter h Maple
Perry Joseph S foreman h 33 Market
Perry Manuel rubber wkr h Handy's lane cor Kickemuit rd
Peters Frank rubber worker h Market
Peters John storekeeper h Metacom av
Peters John (Peters & Santos) bakers 6 Market h do
Peters Manuel mill emp bds f n 171 Bowen
Peters Roland dairy dept Colt Farm h Poppasquash
Peters & Santos (John Peters Albon Santos) bakery 6 Market
Peterson Orrin E patrolman h 26 King

Warren Monumental Works
Cor. Railroad Avenue and Croade Street,   Warren, R. I.

Peterson Orrin E foreman oyster house h 3d on left Sowamsett av
Petrello Alexander H barber 172½ South Main bds 12 Barney
Pettie Ambrose mill emp bds 5 Martin
Pettie Minnie V forelady bds 5 Martin
Pettie Philomine widow Daniel h 5 Martin
Pettie Simard G mill emp bds 5 Martin
Pettie Thomas oyster opener bds 5 Martin
Phelps Almy widow James T h 100 Franklin
Phillips Annie at rubber works bds 28 Market
Phillips Bernard hardware 80 N Water h 28 Market
Phillips Everett F machinist h 199 South Main
Phillips Grace rubber worker bds 199 South Main
Phillips Herbert weaver h 144 Child
Phillips Ida rubber worker bds 199 South Main
Phillips Sara at rubber works bds 28 Market
Phillips William loomfixer rear Parker av
Picard Alphonse upholsterer 164 South Main h 19 Church
Picard Alphonse Jr at handkerchief shop bds 19 Church
Picard Amade mill emp h 16 Union
Picard Charles h 62 Child
Picard Exilda bds 19 Church
Picard Godfried mill emp h r 47 North Water
Picard Godfried Jr variety 60 North Water bds r 47 do
Picard Joseph painter h 7 Nobert
Picard Mary mill emp bds 62 Child
Picpizowski Roman laborer bds Brown
Pictruszka Simon shoemaker h Child
Piekarnia Polska baker 28 Market h Handy
Pierce Charles L farmer h Touisset Neck
Pierce Ella H widow Frederick W h 112 S Water cor Baker
Pierce William at handkerchief shop h 85 North Main
Pierce William Jr clerk bds 85 North Main
Pierce see also Pearce
Pietruska Szymon shoemaker h 135 Child
Pigeon Alice M mill emp bds 95 Cutler
Pigeon Felix h 95 Cutler
Pimentel Otavio (Pimentel & Sousa) 217 Wood h 215 Wood
Pinkos Charles carder bds Cole opp R R station
Pinkos Stanley speed tender bds Cole opp R R station
Pis John carder h 89 Company
Pisula Joseph speed tender h 145 Warren av
Place Elizabeth W demonstrator h 214 South Main
Place Harold E periodical store (Bristol) bds 261 South Main
Place Lenius E ice cream and confectionery store (Brisol) also trav salesman h 261 South Main
Place Rachael L Miss dressmaker rms 23 State
Plante Albertina spinner h Child cor Metacom av

Plante Frederick weaver h off Kickemuit rd nr Metacom av
Podolski Alexander heel presser h 67 Child
Podolski Antonia carder bds 67 Child
Podolski Casimir weaver bds 90 Company
Poissin Arthur teamster h 81 Child
Poissin Bertha bds 81 Child
Poisson Albina mill emp bds 27 Warren av
Poisson Edward spinner bds 27 Warren av
Poisson Joseph spinner h 20 Union
Poisson Napoleon mule spinner h 50 Kickemuit rd
Poisson Oliver teamster h Warren av
Poisson Victor spinner h 27 Warren av
Poitaras Eliza widow Israel h f n 139 North Main
Poitaras Henry (U S A) bds f n 139 North Main
Poitaras Israel J (U S A) bds f n 139 North Main
Poitaras William J mill emp bds f n 139 North Main
Poja Joseph Rev pastor Our Lady Mt Carmel Church State h 141 State
Polak Mary carder bds 79 Company
Polak Simon spinner h 82 Company
Polanski Paul weaver h 55 Summer
Pollard Susan A widow James h 16 State
Porier M laborer h 12 Broad
Porthier Ecdrosse mill emp bds 7 Union
Possner Albert P h Haile
Possner Herman H mgr John D Peck grain mill h Haile
POTTER COLLAMORE & CO (D H Potter J S Collamore J P Brownell) machinists S Water cor Wheaton—see page 24
Potter D Henry (Potter Collamore & Co machinists) h 2 Haile
Pratt Cora piano teacher bds 239 South Main
Pratt Henry E dentist Main h 20 Child
Pratt Isaac N h 239 South Main
Pray Russell W mgr McDonough Bottle Store h Conimicut
Premier Bakery (Hasselin prop) 89 Market
Preterre Albert weaver h 13 Metacom av
Prevost Julius rubber worker h rear 16 North Main
Pringle Howard J painter h 59 Charles
Prior May C inspector bds 30 Mt Hope av
Proulx Desire weaver h 5 Liberty
Proulx George weaver h 61 Metacom av
Proulx Joseph engineer h 24 Warren av
Providence Telephone Co Warren Branch (S H White mgr) 11 Market

33 Canal St. CHARLES J. JAGER CO. Providence
ELECTRIC AND GASOLINE PUMPS AND PRESSURE SYSTEMS
We carry the largest stock of this kind in New England

160 WARREN DIRECTORY, 1917-18.

Provost Cecilia widow Joseph A h 11 Child
Pruneau Louis mill emp h 29 Market
Pruneau Rosalie mill emp bds 29 Market
Pryzstas Henry mill emp h Child
Pwkuska Anna rubber worker bds 66 Water
Pysz Antoni baker h Market
Pysz Frank baker 28 Market h 45 Child
Quackenbush Able dresser tender h Market
Quackenbush Agnes h Market
Quarry Richard F poultryman h Poppasquash rd
Quick Bryce W prop Hope Pharmacy h 9 Green
Quirk Bridget L widow Thomas h 59 North Water
Quirk Josephine Miss stenographer bds 59 North Water
Quirk Mary B principal Joyce Street School bds 59 N Water
Rabideau J Alfred rubber worker bds 156 Park
Rabideau John third hand bds 54 North Water
Rabideau Paul J Jr painter h 156 Park
Rabineau Joseph mill emp h 31 North Main
Raine Joseph H laborer bds f n 150 Warren av
Ramsbottom Frances widow Johnathan bds f n 141 North Main
Randell F S hog dept Colt Farm h Poppasquash
Ransom William McC civil engineer 8 Saugy bldg h cor Liberty and North Main
Rappineau Joseph 3d hand spinning h 31 North Main
Rappineau Phœbe Mrs h 37 North Water
Ratier Alfred grocer 7 Handy h do
Raycroft Jane M mill emp h 7 Warren av
Rebello John laborer h 146 Market
Rebello Marie bds 146 Market
Redfern Callas dressmaker bds James Redfern
Redfern Elizabeth F widow Daniel h 21 Sowamsett av
Redfern James farmer h off Metacom av south Vernon
Redfern James Jr (U S A) bds James Redfern
Redfern Wilfred weaver h 15 Hope
Reed House Furnishing Co (W B Child local mgr) house furnishings 14 and 16 Child
Rego Joseph V h 70 Charles
Reid see Reed
Rene Eva mill emp bds 2 Barney
Rene Frank engineer h 2 Barney
Rene Lena at rubber works bds 2 Barney
Rex George M accountant sum res Touisset Point
Reynolds John Post School High
Reynolds Virginia Miss bds 2 Lyndon
Rhoan John J bookkeeper N I R Co bds 96 Constitution
Riang Albert A rubber worker h 88 Church
Richard Emile carpenter h 10 Martin

Richardson Guy mill emp h f n 142 North Main
Ricket —— mill emp bds 23 Manning
Ridehalgh Alice folder bds Haile
Riendeau Alfred loomfixer h 54 North Water
Rinolds Madaline bookkeeper Colt Farm bds Bristol
Riopel Reme mill emp h Warren av
Riopelle Aurea at rubber works bds 8 Union
Riopelle Eva bds 8 Union
Riopelle Mary H widow Ovila h 8 Union
Ripley Leanna housekeeper 24 Lyndon
Roberts Annie P bds 16 Broad
Roberts Howard N buyer bds 16 Broad
ROBERTS OSCAR druggist 46 North Main h 38 do—see page 24
Roberts William E freight clerk h 16 Broad
Robertson Elizabeth A widow Andrew bds 93 Cutler
Robiboux Charles I telegraph opr h 8 Asselin
Robiboux Julia bds 8 Asselin
Robillard Crisologue steam fitter h 11 Liberty
Robins Charles summer res h Touisset rd
Robinson John E chemist h 188 High
Robinson Thomas spinner h r 59 North Main
Rockett Edward laborer h Avenue A
Rockett Joseph M (U S N) bds Avenue A
Rodger James florist 20 Vernon h do
Rodzen Frank painter h 146 Warren av
Rodrigues Antone farmer h Touisset rd
Rodrigues Rosa Antone farmer h off Touisset rd
Rogala Joseph carder bds 97 Johnson
Rogers Antone shoe packer bds Metacom av
Rogers Flora mill emp bds 62 North Water
Rogers Henri ice dealer 62 North Water bds do
Rogers John shoemaker bds Metacom av
Rogers Robert D A fisherman h off Metacom av
Rogers Samuel R h 62 North Water
Rooney Helen M bookkeeper bds 78 North Main
Rooney Silas foreman h 78 North Main
Rope & Braid Co (John H Estes mgr) Cutler cor Joyce
Rosa Bros grocers 129 Child
Rosa John clerk h 148 Child
Rose M Adelaide widow Walter H bds 3 Washington
ROSA MANUEL P merchant store 129 Child h 34 Arlington av—see page 25
Rosie Frank laborer bds 59 Company

Ross Alcide clerk h 158 Park
Ross George U mgr 81 North Water h Fall River
Rounds Andrew S carpenter bds 1302 Hope
Rounds Charles E salesman h 11 Baker
Rounds Hiram A confectionery store 1066 Hope h 1302 do
Roy Alfred J (U S A) bds f n 140 North Main
Roy Cordelia mill emp bds f n 140 North Main
Roy Joseph oysterman h 138 South Water
Roy Victoria mill emp bds f n 140 North Main
Rubery Albert grinder h 26 Metacom av
Rubery John D mill emp bds 148 Child
Rubery William fish and produce 7 Child h 146 Child
Russell Ellen Miss h 100 North Main
Russell Harry R rubber worker h 180 Wood
Rutkicuicz Antoni laborer h Kickemuit rd
Ryan Helen G bds f n 195 Warren av
Ryan William F second hand h f n 195 Warren av
Rybarczyk Frank piper bds 11 Warren av
Rybarczyk Frank fireman on U S *Newport* h 7 Warren av
Rybarczyk Mary widow Joseph h 14 Child
Rybarczyk P M dry goods 14 Child h over do
Rybarczyk Wicenty liquors 12 North Water h 10 do
Rymszewicz Feliks weaver bds 147 Warren av
Saczawa Mary spooler h Cutler
Sagan Jacob weaver h 162 Park
Sagan Martin laborer h 104 Company
Sahady Samuel mill emp h 73 North Water
Saillant Addie Mrs dressmaker h 12 Barney
Saillant Gaspard pianist (Prov) h 12 Market
Saillant George real estate bds 12 Market
Saillant Gideon janitor h Barney
Saillant John A painter and paper hanger 6 Barney h do
Saillant Joseph Jr clerk bds 12 Barney
Saillant Louis butcher bds 12 Market
Saindon Paul bds 8 Union
St Andre Adolph machinist h 19 North Main
St Andre Azilda mill emp bds 19 North Main
St Andre Josephine mill emp bds 19 North Main
St Andre Mary mill emp bds 19 North Main
St Lawrence Joseph spinner bds 53 Summer
St Mark's Parish House 187 South Main
St Mary's Institute 217 South Main
St Vincent Frank carpenter h Market
St Vincent George N carpenter h ft of Greene
Saitini Charles J clerk h 15 Prospect
Salamon Michael weaver bds 18 Warren av
Salisbury Alpha machinist bds 8 Vernon
Salisbury Clement chauffeur h 28 Market

Salisbury George L h 8 Vernon
Salisbury Julie M Mrs h ft of Miller
Salisbury Samuel teamster bds ft of Miller
Salisbury William A machinist h ft Miller
Salois Alfred spinner h 3 Nobert
Salois Octave mill emp h 26 Wood
Salvatore Abbie housekeeper Ellis av
Salvatore Amilinda carder bds Ellis av
Salvatore Lessio pool room 45 N Main h Ellis av
Sampson Alfred oyster opener h Franklin next to mill
Samson Ida rubber worker bds 12 Broad
Sanchas Annie emp woolen mill bds 2 Mason
Sanchas Correne bds 2 Mason
Sanchas Morris weaver h 2 Mason
Sanders Anna F B widow Nathan B h 7 Federal
Sanders Charles W clerk h 7 Federal
Sanders Lillie Mrs bds 11 Bridge
Sanford Henry L civil engineer h 173 South Main
SANITARY MARKET & HOME BAKERY (J H Mercier prop) Main cor Liberty—see page 25
Santois George H mill emp h 16 Harris av
Santos Albon (Peters & Santos) bakers 6 Market h do
Sarao Salvino hair dresser 25 North Water h do
Sarasin Adelard mill emp bds f n 197 Warren av
Sarasin Peter mill emp h f n 197 Warren av
Sarris George Capt h 24 King
Sarris John G (U S A) bds 24 King
Sarris Julia boxmaker bds 24 King
Saugy Max W prop Standard Pharmacy 1 Miller h 7 do
Saviano Gennaro boot and shoe repairer 39 North Water
Sawin Roy L pres Warren Printing & Publishing Co h 21 Washington
Sawtelle James B carpenter h 13 Hope
Sawyer Louisa spooler h Child cor Metacom av
Sayer Rebecca A widow William H h 102 Church
Schaer Elier widow Arnold h 112 North Main
Schofield Herbert E meat cutter bds 7 Barney
Scott Andrew machinist h Haile
Scott Charles E druggist and physician 27 Child h do
Scott Robert teamster Colt Farm bds Allen
Scott Walter spinner bds 37 North Water
Sealshipt Oyster System ft Baker also off S Water nr Broad
Seaton Fred mill worker bds 157 Child
Seaton James W rubber worker bds 157 Child

WHITTEMORE & COLBURN
PRINTERS 15 Pine St., PROV.

King's Fibrous Plaster Board & Hard Plaster
JAMES C. GOFF CO.
81 to 49 Point St., Prov., R. I.

Sebree Carl Capt oyster boat h 248 South Main
Seering Elisha painter h Bradford
Selden Ruth A widow Alfred P h 247 Wood
Sellen Arthur G student bds 59 Child
Sellen Gottfried A engineer h 59 Child
Sellen Hannah bds 59 Child
Severance Willard C iron molder h 5 Federal
Sevigny Alex (U S A) bds Narcisse Sevigny
Sevigny Eugene (U S A) bds rear 91 North Main
Sevigny Narcisse carpenter h rear 93 North Main
Seymour Albert oysterman h Kelley
Seymour Beatrice H at handkerchief shop bds C H Seymour 2d
Seymour Clarence H 2d machinist h Maple
SEYMOUR CLARENCE H & CO 149 S Main h 374 S Main nr Maple—see page 23
Seymour Eugene R florist 151 Child h do
Seymour Frank C plumber h 240 South Main
Seymour Frederick A sculptor bds 23 State
Seymour George E plumber h 24 Lyndon
Seymour Harry R machinist h Maple
Seymour Herbert A plumber 27 State h 23 do
Seymour Horace D physician and surgeon 140 S Main h do
Seymour James A retired bds 62 King
Seymour Louis R dentist 140 South Main bds Clarence H Seymour
Seymour Orrin S printer bds C H Seymour 2d
Seymour William J Jr carpenter h 82 State
Shakeshaft George E second hand h 65 Child
Sharky Annie widow Francis rubber worker bds 244 S Main
Shaw Halsey G crossing tender bds Metacom av
Shea Edward F jeweler bds 27 Baker
Shea Ella V maid bds 27 Baker
Shea Margaret cloth inspector bds 27 Baker
Shea Mary J mill emp bds 27 Baker
Shea William second hand h 27 Baker
Shea William Jr hairdresser bds 27 Baker
Sherman Charles E (U S A) bds 90 Union
SHERMAN GEORGE E nursery stock h 93 Child—see page 23
Sherman Samuel I (U S A) bds 90 Union
Sherry Patrick H liquors 57 N Water h 23 Manning
Sikarowicz Walter tailor 12 Child h do
Silva Anna maid 374 South Main
Silva Frank weaver h Market
Silva Frank emp Warren Mfg Co h 6 Wood
Silva Frank rubber worker h 224 Wood
Silva Frank O gardener bds 96 Constitution

Silva Joseph farm hand for E E Cole Touisset rd
Silva Joseph oysterman h rear 19 Arlington av
Silva Joseph farmer h Handy's lane
Silva Mary bds Market
Silva Mary bds South Main cor Maple
Silva Morris farmer h Metacom av next to mill
Silva Vital carpenter h Child
Silverman Jacob clothing shoes etc 6 Market
Silvia John farmer bds J Andrews Poppasquash
Simard Emil oysterman h 27 Warren av
Simister John W overseer h 98 Market
Simister John W Jr machinist bds 100 Market
Simister Mary E bds 98 Market
Simister Stanley B machinist h 92 Market
Simmons Albert J operative bds off Cole
Simmons Bertha M mill emp bds off Cole
Simmons Christopher card grinder h off Cole
Simmons Fred teamer h Birch Swamp rd
Simmons Fred R supt Staples Coal Co of R I h 271 S Main
Simmons Isaac Jr mill emp h 37 North Water
Simmons Joseph E teamer bds off Cole
Simmons Joseph N spinner bds off Cole
Simmons Rodman at Herreshoff's bds 271 South Main
Simmons Sally U bds Joseph E
Simmons Samuel C farmer h Birch Swamp rd
Simmons William mill emp h 65 North Water
Simmons William (U S A) h 21 Pierce av
Simister Mary H weaver h 100 Market
Simister Nancy L bds 98 Market
Simister Sarah A bds 92 Market
Sipple Manlove R C telegraph operator h 254 S Main
Skoldberg Ludwig spinner h 170 Brown
Skuba Joseph weaver h 164 Park
Skuce Frank laborer h Bridge
Skuce Frank J clerk h Market
Skuce James H mule spinner h r 60 Market
Skuce James T farmer bds 60 Market
Skuce Mary E bds 60 Market
Slocum Charles fisherman h r Metacom av
Slocum Henry M Capt h 23 Vernon
Slocum Henry M Jr gardener bds 23 Vernon
Slowik Albert speed tender h 86 Company
Smail James trav salesman h Maple
Smith Annie dressmaker 25 Market h do

WARREN MONUMENTAL WORKS
Cor. Railroad Avenue and Croade Streets, Warren, R. I.

Smith Annie widow William h 25 Market
Smith Annie E widow James h 10 Wood
Smith Benjamin pattern maker h 257 South Main
Smith Catherine F h 22 Miller
Smith Edith clerk Water
Smith Evelena widow William W h 161 South Water
Smith Everett J poultryman h Kickemuit rd 1st from Child
Smith Fannie clerk bds 25 Market
Smith George harnessmaker 76 State h at Prov
Smith H P hog dept Colt Farm h Poppasquash
Smith James F mason h 10 Barney
Smith James H ice cream confectionery etc 139 S Main h 111A North Main
Smith James J mill emp bds 10 Wood
Smith John (U S A) bds 36 Wheaton
Smith John C clerk Wm Smith & Co bds 25 Market
Smith John T h 6 School
Smith Joseph H teamster h 36 Wheaton
Smith Leo teamster bds 36 Wheaton
Smith Marguerite R school teacher (Prov) bds 10 Wood
Smith Richard carpenter 269 South Main h do
Smith Richard S town clerk h 343 South Main
Smith William C h South Main at Bristol line
Smith William J & Co reg phar 137 S Main h 3 Church
Smusz And laborer h 100 Company
Soais Joseph farm hand C E Gifford
Soares Frank farmer h Kickemuit rd nr Handy's lane
Sobolewska Mary widow h Brown
SOCHA JOHN M grocery and market 86 N Water h over do—see page 25
Solomon John S painter and paper hanger (Bristol) h Maple
Sousa August C grocery and market 503 Wood h 240 Franklin
Sousa Joseph (Pimentel & Sousa) 217 Wood h 27 Catherine
Sousa Joseph C mgr grocery 503 Wood bds 240 Franklin
Southworth Eliza Mrs mill emp bds 27 Market
Souza see Sousa
Sparks Charles H hardware etc 124 S Main h 21 Haile
Speakman Charles E mill emp h 17 Bridge
Spear Carlton S student bds 9 Church
Splain Mary A winder tender bds 19 Hope
Splain Michael R (U S A) h 19 Hope
Splain Patrick H laborer bds 19 Hope across R R track
Splain Sarah E winder tender bds 19 Hope
Spear Francis H Rev pastor First Meth Episcopal Church h 9 Church
Spear Waldo W student bds 9 Church
Squillant Emilio rubber worker h 53 Market

Squillant Rose bds 53 Market
Stachowiak Joseph laborer h 48 Union
Stachowiak Pelagia clerk h Child
Stagler John crossing tender h 73 North Water
Stahowiak Plasia clerk 14 Child bds Union
Standard Oil Yard (J E Johnson agt) Franklin nr R R track
STANDARD PHARMACY (M W Saugy prop) cor Main and Miller—see page 25
Stanley Edith E bds 16 State
Stanton Alice bookkeeper bds 30 Franklin
Stanton Bertha J clerk bds 30 Franklin
Stanton Catherine C clerk bds 30 Franklin
Stanton James H iceman bds 30 Franklin
Stanton James J landscape gardener h 30 Franklin
Stanton Mary M clerk P O bds 30 Franklin
STAPLES COAL CO OF R I (J W Martin pres) 137 S Water—see page 25
Staples Ethel A bookkeeper (Prov) bds 22 Manning
Staples Leroy G supt of schools Warren h 22 Manning
Staples Walter O shipping clerk bds 21 Sowamsett av
Starking Frank overseer h 207 South Main
Stebbins Harold C keeper Warren Town Farm h do
Steel A G B summer res Ferry Hill
Steen Robert shipping clerk h Vernon
Stell Mary E h Market
Stephens Samuel H physician (Prov) bds G W Adams off Metacom av
Stetson Annaleah folder bds 20 Church
Stetson William D boiler maker h 20 Church
Stevens Andrew M emp O'Bannon Corp h 112 S Water cor Baker
Stevens Henry B local agt Direct Importing Co bds Andrew M Stevens
Stevens John L tel opr Warren depot
Stevens Richard teamster h 162 South Water
Stevens Thomas C painter 24 Wheaton h do
Stevens Thomas C Jr clerk (Prov) bds 24 Wheaton
Stevens Walter L painter bds 24 Wheaton
Steward Edith C eyelet worker bds 58 Collins
Stocks George factory hand h 27 Market
Stone George P chauffeur Narragansett Elec Light Co h 113 South Water
Story Charles F farmer h off Metacom av
Strange Maude E maid Geo T Greene

Strong George electrician bds rear 10 North Main
Stuart Jennie B widow James clerk 65 N Water h Company
Stuart Lawrence W (U S A) bds rear 63 North Water
Sugden Edward fireman h 142 Child
Sugden Lilly inspector bds 142 Child
Sullings Charles H salesman bds 88 Child
Sullivan Daniel J mgr bds 60 Richmond
Sullivan Edward A emp Prov Tel Co bds 93 South Water
Sullivan John F foreman New Haven Road h 3 Franklin nr R R crossing
Sullivan John L h Parker av
Sullivan Kate bds 36 Mt Hope av
Sullivan Mary A h 60 Richmond
Sumowski Joseph laborer bds 55 Summer
Supinski Alexander owner also laborer h 51 Metacom av
Supinski Brona clerk bds 51 Metacom av
Supinski George carder h 51 Metacom av
Supinski Gregory owner also slubber tender h 51 Metacom av
Supinski Teofila weaver bds 11 Metacom av
Surgens Mary C Miss bds 235 South Main
Swan James mgr Herreshoff Mfg Co Inc h 68 Union
Swanson Oliver farmer (Pokanoket Farms) Market
Swee George A die maker h 4 Company
Swift Dora M widow Edward A h 4 Washington
Swiss Textile Co mfg of absorbent cotton and sanitary napkins Joyce Warren
Switula Peter J pastor Polish R C Church h 82 Child
Sylvia Henry J Jr clerk 173 State bds 168 Mt Hope av
Sypien Joseph carder h 150 Warren av
Sypien Sebastyan weaver h 165 Warren av
Sypier Frank driver bds 132 Main
Szercyonrcz Antoni weaver h 93 Johnson
Tanner Albert K h 19 Vernon
Tanner Albert K Jr oysterman h Metacom av
Tanner Arthur S (Tanner Bros) ice dealer h Swansea
Tanner Bertha V operative bds 5 Church
Tanner Bros (Fred M Arthur S) ice dealers
Tanner Charles A driver h 4 School
Tanner Charles E farmer h Market nr State line
Tanner Everett A stone cutter h Asylum rd
Tanner Fred M (Tanner Bros) ice dealer h Swansea
Tanner George H bookkeeper h Child
Tanner George H Jr teamster Child
Tanner Josia farmer h Kickemuit rd
Tanner Mary A bds Market near State line
Tanner Richard K driver h 3 Franklin
Tanner Samuel R chauffcur bds 5 Church

Tavares Antonio mill emp h Metacom av next mill
Tavares Antonio engineer h cor Market and Kickemuit rd
Tavares Francelina mill emp bds J M Tavares
Tavares Jesse N carpenter h 20 Wheaton
Tavares John oysterman h 28 Wheaton
Tavares Joseph M farmer h cor Market and Kickemuit rd
Taylor Edith Mrs emp Parker Mill h Child
Taylor Walter P paymaster Narragansett Worsted Co h 265 South Main
Tebeau Frank weaver h 26 Metacom av
Terio Mrs Louise bds 57 Market
Tessier Delia bds 6 Martin
Tetreault Arthur stone mason h 126 Harris av
Thereaux Diana speed tender bds 128 Bowen
Thereaux George mill emp bds f n 128 Bowen
Thereaux Rose widow George h fn 128 Bowen
Thibaudeau Eva clerk bds 61 Child
Thibaudeau Flora bds 65 Child
Thibaudeau J Alexander dry goods 143 S Main h 65 Child
Thibault Narcisse weaver bds 24 Franklin
Thibierge Joseph spinner h 18 Wood
Thomas Etta teacher bds John S Thomas
Thomlinson John W farmer h Poppasquash rd
Thompson Araline Miss sum res 186 South Main
Thompson Gilbert T agt The Warren Mfg Co h Fall River
Thornley Caroline widow Richard bds 16 State
Thuot Zephirin cabinet maker bds W A Cote
Thurber George machinist h 17 Federal
Tierney James M overseer Parker Mill h 153 Child
Tinkham George K farmer bds Touisset Neck
Tinkham Marion L school teacher bds Horace Tinkham
Tinkham Horace W farmer h Touisset Neck
Tirrell Annie G bds 18 Lyndon
Titmas Harry G 5 & 10c Store 163-165 S Main h 294 do
Titmas Jane stenographer bds 294 South Main
Titmas Margaret stenographer (Prov) bds 294 S Main
Titmas William clerk Warren P O h 5 Church
Tobey Everett N asst line foreman h 228 South Main
Tobin Catherine G chief operator Warren bds 4 Federal
Tobin Edward J janitor Joyce St School h 4 Federal
Tobin Mary h South Water cor Miller
Tomaszcwski John weaver h 78 Company
Tomaszcwski Maksymilian laborer h 155 Park
Tomlinson Thomas bds 41 North Water
Toner Fannie E widow John Jr bds 18 Broad

R. I. RUG WORKS Oriental Rugs Cleaned and Repaired.
Tels. Union 2203 and 2204
678 WESTMINSTER STREET, PROVIDENCE, R. I.

Toomey Matthew J wine clerk Goff's Hotel bds do
Torrey Fred L mfg jeweler sum res Touisset Point
Town Hall (Richard S Smith clerk) South Main
Townsend Florence L widow Joseph A bds 7 Wheaton
Trask Frank E moving picture operator h 28 Garfield av
Traverse Albert bds 23 Collins
Traverse Anthony foreman h 23 Collins
Traynor Catherine L rubber worker bds 27 Collins
Trombley Fannie C dressmaker bds 73 North Water
Trombley Celina widow Edmund h 48 North Main
Trombley Florence bds 73 North Water
Trombley George J mill hand h Metacom av
Trombley Hormidas clerk A J Heon & Co bds 48 N Main
Trombley Jennie widow Philip bds 26 Market
Trombley John B mason h Cole nr Croade
Trombley Julian mill emp h Metacom av
Trombley Laura mill emp bds 48 North Main
Trudelle Amable weaver h 6 Handy
Trudelle Amade weaver bds 13 Metacom av
Trudelle Sadie housekeeper bds 6 Handy
Trudelle William weaver bds 6 Handy
Tulley William H gardener h 370 S Main bey Maple
Tupaj John speed tender h Child
Turner Harry M rubber worker h Market
Turner Henry E weaver bds Kickemuit
Turner Joshua clerk 28 Child h Kickemuit rd 1st bey Market
Turner Nettie M widow Maxwell W h Haile
Turner Sarah A housekeeper Kickemuit rd
Twaroy John emp mill h 62 Metacom av
Union Club 161 South Main
Urban John weaver h 61 Metacom av
Urban Walter emp mill bds 61 Metacom av
Vachon Amade chauffeur h Ellis av
Vachon Ida emp French Worsted Co bds Ellis av
Vail Alonzo prop Lyric Theater h 175 South Water
Valance August E mill emp h 7 Nobert
Valance Eugene oysterman h 12 Broad
Van Sickle John T Mrs summer resident 6 Bridge
Vaughn Eugene A clerk (Prov) h 14 Miller
Veach Joseph A cutter bds 96 Constitution
Verity Thomas steward h Anthony av
Vermett Euclid driver h 97 Franklin
Vermette Rosale widow August h 79 Child
Vermette Sigfroid operative 79 Child
Verrette Joseph mill emp h 82 North Water
Viall Anna C widow William B bds 13 Washington
Viall B Willard mgr Excelsior Grocery and Market h 18 Washington

| Water Supply Outfits House Pumps | Walter H. Jackson Co. 435 Industrial Trust Building Providence, - R. I. | "Dodd" System Lightning PROTECTION |

Viall John rubber worker h Metacom av
Viall William K bank clerk (Prov) bds 18 Washington
Victory Jennie M mill emp bds 226 South Main
Victory Mary F mill emp bds 226 South Main
Victory Patrick F overseer h 226 South Main
Victory Thomas (U S A) bds 226 South Main
Victurin Manuel rubber worker h 354 Child
Viera Anthony G mill emp bds 7 Liberty
Vincent Dionis E carpenter h 16 North Water
Vincent George W rubber worker h 8 Baker
Vincent Henry carpenter h 9 Hope
Vincent Mrs weaver h Parker av
Vincent Wilfred O (U S A) bds 16 No Water
Vitullo Angelo clerk 46 North Main h 38 do
Vitullo Amanda bds 4 Ellis av
Vitullo John mill emp h Ellis av
Vitullo Joseph liquors cor N Main and N Water h over do
Vitullo Julius bartender h 18 North Water

Wagner Annie weaver bds f n 127 Bowen
Wagner Joseph J weaver h f n 127 Bowen
Wajda Faustyn grocer clerk h Water
Wajda Filip bartender bds 165 Warren av
Wallace Helen student bds 85 Union
Wallace O H Rev pastor First Baptist Church High h 85 Union
Walsh Anna Mrs h 68 North Main
Walsh Annie L at laundry bds 31 Joyce
Walsh David A soda clerk (Prov) bds 294 South Main
Walsh Jennie M widow David h 294 South Main
Walsh Robert chief police Warren h 3rd on Green
Walsh Thomas H prop Warren Hand Laundry h 53 Child
Walsh see also Welch and Welsh
Walton Sadie I mill emp bds f n 65 North Main
Ward Edward E h 15 Market
Ward Katherine T Miss dressmaker h 63 Child
Ward Mary E teacher Joyce St School bds 57 Child
Wardwell Roydon M pipe bender h 133 State
Warner Charles T clerk h 9 Federal
Warner Lucius caretaker h 50 North Water
Warner Sarah bds 50 North Water
Warren Armory Jefferson near South Main
Warren District Nursing Association (N M Jones nurse) 11 Lyndon

WHITTEMORE & COLBURN
PRINTERS   15 Pine St., PROV.

JAMES C. GOFF CO.
31 to 49 POINT ST.
Providence, R. I.

All kinds of Masons' Materials

Warren Dye Co (Francis Hoye secy) dye manuf 147 South Water
Warren Handkerchief Co 111 South Water cor Baker
Warren Hand Laundry T H Walsh prop 35 Joyce
WARREN MFG CO cotton goods manuf ft of Bowen—see page 7
WARREN MONUMENTAL WORKS 32 Railroad av—see head lines
Warren Oyster Co (Thomas S Connolly prop) off 155 South Water
Warren Post Office John M Pike postmaster South Main
WARREN PRINTING & PUBLISHING CO (R. L. Sawin pres M E Cutler treas) State nr Main—see page 22
Warren Pumping Station Bristol & Warren Works Child
Warren Railroad Station (Ambrose Feeney agt) ft of Joyce
Warren Restaurant (William J Lonergan prop) restaurant and lunch 35 Joyce
Warren Shoe Co (F C Greene) boots shoes and hosiery cor South Main and Child
Warren Town Farm H C Stebbins keeper Asylum Lane
WARREN & BARRINGTON GAZETTE (THE) Warren Printing & Publishing Co publishers State nr Main—see page 22
Waterman Byron A student bds 168 South Water
Watjen Herman W Rev pastor First Baptist Church h 8 Miller
Watjen Olive E student bds 8 Miller
Watrous Dorothy M bookkeeper Main cor Miller bds at W Barrington
Watson G Thomas mill emp h f n 141 North Main
Waterman Andrew S clerk Warren Mfg Co h 18 Broad
Waterman John O clerk Warren Mfg Co bds 168 S Water
Watson Elmer K factory and industrial broker Saugy bldg h at Nayatt
Webb Rose widow Henry C h S Water cor Bridge S W
Webster Thomas overseer Narragansett Worsted Co h Campbell
Wehby Annie h 33 North Main
Wehby George dry goods 5 Miller h 188 N Main
Wehby Mary bds 33 North Main
Wehby Sadie mill emp bds 33 North Main
Welch see also Walsh and Welsh
Wells William J painter h 166 Park
Welsh Bridget widow James h 23 Wood
Welsh Catherine V sewer bds 23 Wood
Welsh Hannah G teacher Liberty St School bds 23 Wood
Welsh Margaret A teacher bds 23 Wood

Ralph C. Watrous Co.
ESTATE MANAGERS. RENT COLLECTION A SPECIALTY
437 INDUSTRIAL TRUST BUILDING

Wennerholm Effie Mrs bds 220 South Main
West Clara Miss mill emp h 10 Luther
West John R mason and contractor 10 Lyndon h do
West John R Jr driver bds 10 Lyndon
West Marion bookkeeper bds 168 Wood
West Nellie maid bds 118 Bradford
Wharf John A carpenter bds 7 Bridge
Wheaton Adelaide M widow Francis H h 18 Lyndon
Wheaton Alice h Union cor Liberty
Wheaton Julia A widow James M sum res S Main nr Bristol town line
Wheeler Alfred P oysterman h off Metacom av
White Bessie E musician bds 9 Bridge
White Sanford C laundry agt Butman & Tucker h 9 Bridge
White Stanley H mgr Prov Telephone Co h 140 Arnold Riverside
White W Ethel stenographer Barrington bds 9 Bridge
Whitford Pearle L chauffeur h Haile
Whitman Annie H housekeeper 21 State
Whitney Elsie M forelady bds John Bryden
Whittle James gardener h Touisset road
Wightman Daniel A h off Metacom av nr Kickemuit river south side of R R
Wightman Frank A (U S A) bds Daniel A Wightman
WILBUR GEORGE M undertaker 209 S Main h do also 38 Union Bristol—see page 22
Wilbur George M Jr undertaker bds 209 South Main
Wilbur Mary P bds 209 South Main
Wilcox Delia H widow of Clayton O dressmaker h 189 S Main
Wilcox Paul (U S A) bds 189 South Main
Willard Henry G jeweler (Prov) bds 11 Croade
Willard Jerome h 11 Croade
Williams Bertha Mrs h 16 Luther
Williams Eliza bds Frank Freeman
Willis Clarence E sta engineer h 25 Market
Willis Mary A Mrs bds 33 Child
Wilmarth Anna E Miss leather goods h 11 Baker
Wilmarth Franklin E h 192 South Main
Wilmarth William S h 192 South Main
Wilson John J lineman h Campbell
Winiarska Mary weaver bds 7 Warren av
Winiarski Peter machinist bds Ward
Winn Harry E wine clerk h 124 Child

Blackstone Canal Nat'l Bank 20 Market Square PROVIDENCE, R. I.
Capital, $500,000. Surplus Profits, over $500,000

Warren Monumental Works
Cor. Railroad Avenue and Croade Street, Warren, R. I.

Winn Ozea Mrs bds 124 Child
Winn Patrick laborer h 244 South Main
Winn Thomas reporter (F R) bds 244 South Main
Winter Florence mill emp bds 224 South Main
Winter Lillian mill emp bds 224 South Main
Winter William H machinist h 224 South Main
Winters Charles E ins agt h 11 Sowamsett av
Wisnicwzki Albert carder bds 103 Company
Witze Annie bds 112 North Main
Wlodyka Adam carpenter h Company blk Sisson
Wojcick Constanty weaver h 24 Arlington av
Wojcik Jacenty weaver bds Kickemuit rd
Wojcik Mary weaver bds Kickemuit rd
Wojcik Peter farmer h Kickemuit rd
Woobleski Adolf comber h 5 Barker av
Wood Charles H carriage painter cor Market and Federal h 9 Baker
Wood Henry agent Narragansett Worsted Co h Bristol
Wood Mabel forelady h 9 Baker
Woodard Sylvanus R bds John E Johnson
Woodly Henrietta widow John bds 9 State
Woodworth Henry A loomfixer h f n 193 Park
Woodworth Kathleen shoe maker bds 6 Wood
Wroblewski Adolf carder h Child
Wujeik Kostanty weaver h 24 Arlington av
Wylie Joseph P sexton h 12 Luther
Wylie Mollie A Miss teacher of violin 12 Luther bds do
Wynn Peter J timekeeper bds 370 South Main
Wyrostck Frank laborer h 68 Sisson
Wyrostck John watchman h 55 Summer
Wysocki Joseph laborer h 87 Company

Young Edward J farmer h Metacom av
Young Elmer J auto repair man bds Metacom av

Zambik Catherine weaver bds 8 Kickemuit rd
Zambik Josephine weaver bds 8 Kickemuit rd
Zambik Michael farmer h 8 Kickemuit rd
Zbyszcnski Stephen fireman N Y N H & H R R bds 48 Union
Zbyszcwski Maryan fireman power house R R h 5 Johnson
Zicminska Kathrine weaver bds Brown
Zmuda Albert laborer h 25 Arlington av
Znamirowski Leopold shoe repairer 88 N Water h Mason
Zougaib Sadie bds 112 Market
Zougaib Solomon weaver h 112 Market

Union Publishing Co.

Directory Publishers

1013 Old South Building

BOSTON · MASS.

Publishers of Directories for Towns and Cities all over New England

For RHODE ISLAND as follows:

Bristol, Warren and Barrington Directory
Burrillville and North Smithfield Directory
Cumberland and Lincoln Directory
Jamestown and New Shoreham Directory
North Providence, Johnston and Smithfield Directory
Pawtuxet Valley Directory
Tiverton, Portsmouth and Middletown Directory
Warwick, E. Greenwich and No. Kingstown Directory

Rubber Goods
OF EVERY DESCRIPTION

Rubber Footwear Water Bottles
Rubber Coats Fountain Syringes
Garden Hose Rubber Gloves
Mill Hose Sporting Goods
Rubber Packing Rubber Collars
Rain Coats Rubber Toys

CALL AND SEE US

HOPE RUBBER CO.
93-97 Westminster Street

PROVIDENCE - R. I.

BARRINGTON
GENERAL DIRECTORY

Copyright 1918, by Union Publishing Co.

ABBREVIATIONS.—Ab., above; agt., agent; av., avenue; bds., boards; bet., between; B. H., Bristol Highlands; bldg., building; blk., block; bey., beyond; cor., corner; ct., court; do., ditto; E., East; exp., express; fr., from; ft., foot; h., house; ins., insurance; manuf., manufacturer; mfg., manufacturing; N., North; N. I. R. Co., National India Rubber Company; nr., near; opp., opposite; pl., place; P. O., Post Office; pres., president; prop., proprietor; Prov., Providence; N. Y., N. H. & H. R. R., New York, New Haven and Hartford Railroad; r., rear; rd., road; rms., rooms; R. R., Railroad; S., South; sec., secretary; sq., square; st., street; supt., superintendent; treas., treasurer; U. S. A., United States Army; U. S. N., United States Navy; W., West. After the name of the street, the word "street" is omitted.

BARRINGTON VILLAGE ABBREVIATIONS.—B., Barrington; P. O., same; H. M., Hampden Meadows; P. O., Barrington; N. P., Nayatt Point; P. O., Nayatt; W. B., West Barrington; P. O., same.

Abadiglio Andonio laborer h Swans rd
Abadillo Andonio laborer h Maple av
Abato Riga emp mill h Maple av
Aborn Clara L bookkeeper bds F B Wood H M
Aborn George L painter bds F B Wood H M
Acciardo Andonio grocer h Middle Highway N
Acciardo Pasquale emp mill bds Middle Highway N
Acciardo Pietro laborer h Middle Highway N
Aciardi Domenico laborer h Middle Highway N
Acciardi Giuseppe emp mill h Middle Highway N
Aciardi Nicola laborer h Middle Highway N
Aciardo Tomasco laborer h Middle Highway N
Adams Arthur W farmer h off Bradford W B
Adams Frank L farmer h New Meadow rd
Adams Franklin A masons' supplies h Lake
Adams Harold G carpenter bds A W Adams W B
Adams Walter R emp R I Lace Works h Richmond av W B

33 Canal St.   CHARLES J. JAGER CO.   Providence

ELECTRIC AND GASOLINE PUMPS AND PRESSURE SYSTEMS
We carry the largest stock of this kind in New England

BARRINGTON DIRECTORY, 1917-18.

Adams William H trucking h Bradford s of track W B
ADAMS WILLIAM H & SON masons supplies Bay Spring av W B—see page 27
Albana Alesandro laborer h Maple av
Albanese Francis pastor Holy Angels Church h Maple av B
Alexander Charles sum res h Rumstick rd B
Allen Chester H blacksmith off County h do B
Allen Frederick C wheelwright bds County rd B
ALLEN GEORGE E CO plumbers and steamfitters office Fourth h do W B—see page 27
Allen Hannah B h Third W B
Allen J Clifton bookkeeper bds Maple av N
Allen Joseph E provisions h Maple av N
Allen Maude C bds H C Allen
Allin Howard E trav salesman h Park av nr P O, W B
Anderson Amanda nurse bds E Anderson
Anderson Andrew farmer h County rd B
Anderson Eskil engraver h Upland Way N
Anderson Hilda M stenographer h Central av H M
Anderton Everett L weaver h Bay Spring av W B
Anderton George C textile business Pawt h Drown cor Elm W B
Andonio Luciano laborer h Roffee
Andreia Domenica emp mill h Middle Highway N
Andreozi Angelo laborer h Nayatt
Andreozi Luigi carpenter h Maple av
Andreozi Luigi laborer h Roffee
Andreozi Pepino laborer h Maple av
Andreozi Sozio laborer h Maple av
Andrews Laura P widow David Andrews bds Myra Macdonald H M
Angell Carl caretaker h Washington rd W B
Angell Emor E stone cutter h Primrose Hill W B
Angell Ernest laborer h Walsh av W B
Angelo Peter laborer h Sowams rd H M
Angelo Pio laborer h Hamilton
Annis James florist Hampden Meadows h at Cranston
Annison Frederick G clerk Rubber Co h Bradford W B
Anthony Edward bookkeeper bds with Mary Peck W B
Anthony George sum res off Nayatt av N
Anthony Harriet L widow O S Anthony cor Washington and Lincoln av W B
Anthony Harrington T Anthony Coal & Lumber Co Riverside h Lincoln av cor Washington W B
Anthony Henry A contractor h off Lincoln av cor Walnut W B
Anthony Olive Mrs housekeeper Henry Hoffman B

COLLECTIONS AND CREDIT REPORTS

Our service is as near as your telephone. We will gladly furnish names of clients whom you know, who are satisfied users of our service. Tel. Union 1526

Western Mercantile Corporation, Providence, R. I.

BARRINGTON DIRECTORY, 1917-18.   177

Arno Elmer E carpenter h County rd nr P O, B
Arnold Frank H stable (Pawt) sum res Ocean B
Arnold Leon S jeweler (Prov) h Walnut W B
Arquilla Luigi farmer h Maple av
Arzo Salvator farmer h Lincoln av
Asanti Giacomo carpenter h Maple av
Asher Franklin farmer bds Amelia Potter B
Ashley Earl H clerk bds Philip B Ashley W B
Ashley Philip B poultryman h Lincoln av side of school W B
Atazio Giovanni laborer h Prospect
Aurelio Vincenzo laborer h Middle Highway N
Austino Luigi laborer h Maple av
Austino Pasquale laborer h Maple av
Ayer Mabel E clerk bds Ernest Bay Spring W B
Azza Samuel peddler h Lincoln av
Bacon J Earle emp Prov bds Mathewson rd
Beattie Robert farmer Ferry lane N
Beattie Robert G gardener h Rumstick rd B
Bagaglia Michele laborer h County rd
Bagar Michel weaver h County rd H M
Baggs Laura bds William Martin
Bailey Walter S sum res h Appian Way Annawomscott (Prov) W B
Baker George T real estate (Prov) h cor Washington and Drown rd W B
Baker Nathaniel C h Broadway cor Fourth W B
Baker William sum res h Blanding av Bay Spring W B
Baldwin Carrie F housekeeper W H Fales B
Ballou Frederick A sum res h Nayatt av N P
Ballou Henry C (Ballou Johnson & Nichols Co Prov) h "Dreamwold" Annawomscott W B
Ballou Henry C sum res h Appian Way Annawomscott (Prov) W B
Ballou John farmer h Maple av N
Bantevenca Vincenzo oyster opener Madison av N P rd B
Barber Frank M (sec Prov) sum res h Mathewson av B
Barker William B bds Rumstick rd B
Barnes George W farmer bds Ann E Barnes W B
Barnes Levi A farmer bds Ann E Barnes W B
Barney Jonathan retired h County rd B
Barnum Edna A Mrs bds I T Barnum Maple av N
Barnum Isaac T retired h Maple av N
Barnum Lottie Mrs bds I T Barnum Maple av N
Barrington Post Office County rd

R. I. RUG WORKS RUG CLEANING, CARPET CLEANING AND LAYING
678 WESTMINSTER ST., PROVIDENCE. Telephones Union 2203 and 2904

Barrington R R Depot (Ovide Belanger agt) County rd at R R
Barrington Steam Brick Co off Maple av across tracks B Prov office 304 Grosvenor bldg
Barrington Yacht Club Mathewson rd nr bridge B
Barrows Ester A jeweler bds H L Barrows W B
Barrows Howard L jeweler h Washington
Barrows Mabel L jeweler bds H L Barrows W B
Bartlett Mary E Mrs sum res at Walter S Bailey's W B
Barton Maria widow Robert h County rd B
Batchelder Frank sum res h Blanding av Bay Spring W B
Bates Alice W bds Mrs Emma Bates
Bates Clifford L farm hand bds with Mrs Emma Bates B
Bates Emma A widow Watson h 77 County rd B
Bates Wendell R farm hand bds Mrs Emma Bates B
Baxter Adelaide h Sowams rd
BAY SPRING PUBLIC MARKET cor Bay Spring and Narragansett av W B—see page 26
Bay Spring Shoe Repair Shop (Peter Marcello prop) Bay Spring av W B
Beard Findley machinist bds Mary Peck
Beard Findley B engineer bds Pecks Corner B
Beattie R rubber worker h Ferry lane
Beattie Robert G gardener h Rumstick rd B
Beecher Louis h Walnut W B
Belanger Ovid station agent Barrington bds 26 Child W
Bell Thomas clerk h Ferry lane
Bell Thomas H sum res (Prov) h Bay Spring at shore W B
Bellefratte Sozio laborer h Maple av
Bellemer Charles M contractor h New Meadow rd H M
Benedetto Montacquila laborer h Roffee
Benedetto Rocco laborer h Hamilton
Bennett Etta A Mrs bds L G Fisher Jennys lane B
Bennett John H sum res h Clark av
Berard Charles A tinsmith h Washington rd W B
Berossi August mill emp h Maple av
Berry Manetta widow Ed H h Narragansett rd W B
Berube Wilfred chauffeur h Ocean B
Bestwick Lewis emp R I Lace Works h Narragansett rd W B
Bianche Vincenzo h Anoka av
Bianco Gerrard laborer h Wusica av
Bianco Luigi laborer h Wusica av
Bigelow Charles F mgr (Prov) h off Lincoln av cor Walnut W B
Billedeau Yvonne Miss teacher High School bds The Gables
Birchell George janitor bds J H Cutting

WALTER H. JACKSON CO. 435 Industrial Trust Building
PROVIDENCE, R. I.
"DELCO" ELECTRIC LIGHTING & PUMPING PLANTS
WINDMILLS, GASOLINE ENGINES AND TRACTORS

Bird John summer res h Bay Spring on Point W B
Bishop Henry L sum res Bay rd B
Bishop John J What Cheer Wire Works h Spring nr R R track W B
Bishop Marie L Miss h West rd B
Blackmar Amanda A bds Amelia Potter B
Blackmar Charles electrician bds Amelia Potter B
Blake Irving L inspector (B & S Mfg Co Prov) h Broadway and Fourth W B
Blake Mertis teacher (Prov) bds Mabel Black New Meadow rd H M
Blisdell Byron G teamer h 32 Park av W B
Bliss Harold B bds I W Bliss B
Bliss Ida G widow Elliott L bds Joseph W Gardiner W B
Bliss Irving W carpenter and builder h Rumstick rd bey schoolhouse B
Bogman James R farmer h Walnut W B
Bond Carl T bds Irving E Noyes W B
Booth Ernest lacemaker h Alfred Drown rd W B
Bortoni Gelardi laborer h Maple av
Bosworth Albert L clerk L P Bosworth B bds over do
Bosworth Ellen Miss h New Meadow rd
BOSWORTH LEONARD P coal and wood hay and grain lumber also grocery Broad at R R crossing h do B—see page 26
Bosworth Miriam L bds L P Bosworth B
BOURASSA THOMAS F tin and sheet metal works Bay Spring av h do W B—see page 27
Bourne R Marjorie Mrs h Bay Point av B
Bourne Willard A poultry h Bay Point av B
Boutwell George S janitor h Jennys lane
Bovee Frederick contractor h Walnut W B
Bowden Alfred B oyster dealer h 22 Bowden av B
Bowden Charles H state inspector of roads h Massasoit av E bey river B
Bowden Clarence L bds W B Bowden H M
Bowden Cora corsetier bds W B Bowden H M
Bowden Elmer F grocer h Blanding av Bay Spring W B
Bowden John F oyster dealer h 33 Bowden av B
Bowden John J sum res h Blanding av Bay Spring W B
Bowden M Isabell widow W B Bowden h Massasoit av E bey river B
Bowden Philip K chemist bds Samuel F Bowden B
Bowden Samuel F retired h County rd Princes Hill B

WHITTEMORE & COLBURN
PRINTERS   15 Pine St., PROV.

JAMES C. GOFF CO. Sole Agents for **ATLAS**
31 to 49 POINT ST. Providence, R. I. **Portland Cement**

Bowen Harry M gardener for LeRoy Fales bds do B
Bowen Richard LeBaron general mgr O'Bannon Corp W B h Prov
Bowen Sylvanus gardener h New Meadow rd H M
Bowles Betsey A widow Silas h Bay Spring W B
Bowles Herbert E sum res Bay Spring W B
Bowser Clifford chauffeur h Ocean cor Narragansett av B
Boyden Charles F trav salesman h 86 County rd bey Cong Church B
Boylan Bernard summer res (Prov) h Blanding av Bay Spring W B
Boylan James clerk h Spring av W B
Bradford Frank J collector (Prov) h County rd opp Town Hall B
Bradley John fireman bds E J Gonyea W B
Braley Anna Miss school teacher bds The Gables
Brannigan John H sum res h Buckingham Beach nr ft Shore av (Pawt) W B
Briggs Grace G h New Meadow rd H M
Briggs Nathaniel P carpenter h New Meadow rd H M
Briggs Walter B crossing tender bds C Butman W B
Briggs William F crossing tender h Washington rd W B
Brigham Edward M sum res h Drown nr Fifth (Florida) W B
Brochu Romeo J machinist h Narragansett rd W B
Broomhead Fred C caterer (Prov) h Drown rd W B
Broomhead George C clerk (Prov) h Pleasant W B
Brovino Dalfino laborer h Hamilton
Brown Caroline S widow Wilson O h First W B
Brown Charles H brick layer h Second W B
Brown Harold L emp Brown & Sharpe h Mathewson rd
Brown John T h Mathewson av B
Brown Mildred D teacher (N Y State) bds Caroline S Brown W B
Brown Wilbur D clerk (Prov) h Drown opp Second W B
Brown William A farmer h junc Middle High & County rd W B
Brown William F trucking bds W A Brown W B
Brown William L sum res h Drown (Everett Mass) W B
Bryant Samuel baker R A Gibbs h Washington opp P O, W B
Bryden Albert fireman h County rd H M
Bryden Fenton farmer h County rd H M
Bryden Fenton Jr mill emp bds Fenton Bryden H M
Bryden James Jr electrician bds County rd H M
Bryden James C electrician h Sowams rd H M
Bryden John W longshoreman bds R W Bryden B
Bryden Robert longshoreman h County rd B

RALPH C. WATROUS CO.
Real Estate Auctioneers
437 INDUSTRIAL TRUST BUILDING

BARRINGTON DIRECTORY, 1917-18.

Bucklin Bessie F Miss sum res off Ocean B
Bullock Albert farmer h Love lane B
Bullock Eben G sum res h Love lane B
Bullock Lydia C housekeeper bds Albert Bullock H M
Burgess William R fireman Narragansett rd h Bay Spring W B
Burke John sum res (Prov) h Narragansett av Bay Spring W B
Burke John Jr sum res (Prov) with John Burke W B
Burrows Charles John George Leo Walter summer res at James Radigan W B
Burrows Mary clerk h Richmond av W B
Butler Joseph H farmer bds Wm Butler
Butler William farmer h Upland Way N
Butman Charles W watchman h off Shore av W B
Butterworth Arthur A engineer h Bay Spring av W B
Cady Edith W bds H L Cady County rd B
Cady Hamilton L prop garage h County rd nr Town Hall B
Cady Louise M bds H L Cady h County rd B
Calella Domenico mill emp h Maple av
Caletro Michele laborer h Anoka av
Campanelli Lionardi laborer h Middle Highway N
Campbell Cyril H crossing tender B h off County rd B
Campbell William D furniture repairer h Howard off Fountain av W B
Canada Katherine teacher B H S bds cor County rd and Federal rd B
Canada Rev Prentice A pastor Cong Church B h cor County rd and Federal rd B
Cangiani Nicola laborer h Whipple
Caporali Paolo emp mill h Anoka av
Carbona Lucia laborer B
Carboni Luciano mason h Anoka av
Card Harry E mason h County rd at Warren Bridge B
Cardende Cesere emp mill h Anoka av
Carlo Tomaso emp mill h Middle Highway N
Carlone Domenico emp mill h Maple av
Carlone Luca laborer h Wusica av
Carlone Pasquale laborer h Maple av
Carlone Pietro mill emp h Maple av
Carolan John J foreman h Drown nr Elm W B
Carpenter Angelia A widow Jesse L h Drown nr Third W B
Carpenter Blanche E bds Mrs Angelia A Carpenter W B
Carpenter Mary E bds Mrs Angelia A Carpenter W B

Blackstone Canal Nat'l Bank | BEST FACILITIES
20 MARKET SQ., PROVIDENCE | Prompt Attention

WARREN MONUMENTAL WORKS
Cor. Railroad Avenue and Croade Streets, Warren, R. I.

Carpenter William E carpenter h Bay Spring av W B
Carr Della Mrs bds B F Bucklin B
Carrott Ernest summer res Upland Way N
Casale Luigi laborer h Anoka av
Casalo Tomasco laborer h Anoka av
Cavanaugh Andrew B asst foreman h Orchard av H M
Cavanaugh Michael C polisher h Bay Spring av W B
Cavanaugh Richard polisher h Bay Spring av W B
Cazone Pietro driver h Princes Hill
Cazzone Andonio laborer h Princes Hill
Cazzone Angelo farmer h Princes Hill
Cazzone Francesco farmer h Middle Highway W B
Cazonne Frank farmer h at Nayatt Switch off Lincoln av W B
Ceirchia Michele grocer h Maple av
Chaffee Alfred sum res h Nayatt av N
Chaffee William H bookkeeper h West rd H M
Chapin H Mildred teacher bds W M Chapin
Chapin Walcott clerk (Prov) bds W M Chapin
Chapin William M Rev rector St John's Episcopal Church also warden St Andrew's Industrial School h do B
Chapman Robert J farmer h Ferry lane B
Chase Charles B engineer h Spring W B
Chase Henry G farmer h Sowams rd
Chase Margaret E housekeeper Sowams rd
Chase Mary A h New Meadow rd H M
Child Emily widow Charles E bds J Maxfield B
Child Harry S bank clerk R I Hospital Trust (Prov) h West rd H M
Child Ruth C widow James M with S J Waterman B
Christ Carl Jr chauffeur bds Nellie Christ B
Christ Nellie widow of Carl h Old River rd B
Church Frederick P town clerk h Rumstick rd ¼ m south R R tracks B
Church Lorenzo laborer h off County rd nr cor Church B
Cialella Angelo laborer h Anoka av
Cialella Francesco emp mill bds Anoka av
Cialella Giuseppe driver h County rd
Cicerchia Andimiegli laborer h Maple av
Cicerchia Giovanni laborer h Maple av
Cicerchia Pepino carpenter h Maple av
Ciol Luigi laborer h Anoka av
Ciol Rocco laborer h Hamilton
Citrone Gaitano laborer h Anoka av
Clark Agnes A widow Robert Martin av H M
Clark Charles A emp Texas Oil Co (Prov) bds G Edwin Clark
Clark Cora R dressmaker bds Robert K Clark H M

Clark G Edwin trav salesman h Old River rd
Clark Herbert J jeweler h Martin av H M
Clark Ida Mrs bds Mathewson rd
Clark Robert K jeweler h Martin av H M
Cleland Almon W farmer h Maple av B
Cleland Howard A teamer bds Maple av B
Cleland Lucy A Mrs h Rumstick rd south of tracks B
Cloutier William G farmer h off Sowams rd H M
Cochrene Robert farmer h Mathewson rd N
Cocoran Mary Mrs widow Dennis bds County rd
Cocoza Giuseppe laborer h Maple av
Codega Pietro laborer h Bay View av
Colasanti Domenico carpenter h Maple av
Cole Edmund sum res Bay Spring W B
Cole Grace E bookkeeper J F Grant also asst postmaster Barrington bds Warren
Cole Mabel Mrs housekpr bds Willis G Hutchinson W B
Coleman Eda school teacher B bds The Gables
Coleman Thomas supt B A Jackson estate h off Nayatt av N
Colley William E banker (Prov) h Watson N P
Collins Joseph W sum res off Beach av B
Colwell Paul A insurance adjuster h Lincoln av W B
Companelli Lionardi laborer h Middle Highway N
Congdon Cora E widow Frank H bds H R Congdon B
Congdon Henry R h Rumstick rd south of tracks B
Connolly Thomas H retired h Mathewson av B
Connor Sara bds B F Bucklin B
Conte Alberto laborer h Anoka av
Conti Luigi h Maple av
Conti Silvio emp brick yard h Middle Highway N
Conti Silvonio laborer h Maple av
Conto Andonio laborer h Cottage
Conto Criscianzo laborer h Wusica av
Conyers Marion teacher (B) bds Mason
Cook Cecil chauffeur h Primrose Hill B
Corcoran Margaret T bds M Corcoran County rd
Corcoran Stephen J brick layer h County lane
Corey Walter E meat cutter h Washington rd W B
Cornell Howard P sum res h Rumstick rd B
Corvo Domenico emp mill h Hamilton
Cosbarro Luigi laborer h Hamilton
Cotico Pietro laborer h Hampden Meadows
Coughlin Anna M clerk (Prov) bds Thomas Coughlin B
Coughlin Catherine bds Thomas Coughlin

Coughlin John chauffeur bds Thomas Coughlin
Coughlin Mary bds Thomas Coughlin
Coughlin Thomas gateman h County rd B
Couter Armand sum res h Buckingham Beach (Woon) W B
Covell Arthur F clerk (Prov) h Sowams rd nr tracks H M
Covell Louis E clerk (Prov) h Sowams rd nr tracks H M
Covell Sarah A widow Arnaldo E h Sowams rd H M
Cozzone Angelo farmer h Maple av nr R R tracks B
Crawshaw James florist Upland Way N
Cristofano Andonio emp mill h Anoka av
Cristofano Giuseppe laborer h Cottage
Cross Dorothy teacher Warren High School, bds W P Cross B
Cross Ellen M widow William J bds W P Cross B
Cross Mary L widow of William P h Mathewson rd
Cross William L emp Wanskuck Mills h Mathewson rd B
Crossey Mary B widow Michael h Rumstick rd cor Nayatt av B C
Crossman E A expressman Washington nr P O, W B h do
Crossman Luther C bookkeeper bds E A Crossman W B
Crowell Charles A silversmith (Prov) h West rd H M
Crowell Frank V draughtsman h West rd H M
Crowell Hiram B mason bds C A Crowell H M
Cuciarillo Amadio laborer h Maple av
Cuicci Lorenzo laborer h White Church
Curtelessa Andonio laborer h Maple av
Curtelessa Giuseppe laborer h Maple av
Cushman Elton G lawyer (Prov) h Bay rd
Cutbertson Rachel widow James H h Ferry lane B
Cutting Bessie L office clerk bds J H Cutting W B
Cutting Julia H widow R S Cutting h Walnut cor Bradford W B
Dabraccio Pasquale emp mill h Maple av
Daley Cornelius F bookkeeper O'Bannon Corp W B
Dalozio Angelo machinist h County rd
Daniels William W foreman oyster house h Church W B
Daniels Winslow W engraver (Prov) h Drown cor Third W B
Darezzo Charles A gardener h 16 County rd
Darling Waldo E h Shore av nr Buckingham Beach W B
Darling W Arthur stenog bds Waldo E Darling W B
Davenport Joseph laborer h Ferry lane B
Davis Abial F Mrs sum res h Rumstick rd B
Davis Earl R broker bds Mrs A F Davis B
Davis Foster B broker (Prov) bds Mrs A F Davis B
Davis George F foreman farmer h Washington opp P O, W B
Davis Henry N inspector h Fourth W B

OUR CREDIT REPORTS TELL—Whom to trust; whom not to trust; who pay promptly; who pay slowly; who never pay their bills except under pressure. Telephone Union 1526

Western Mercantile Corporation, Providence, R. I.

Davis Lillian H Mrs corsetier bds John A Ward H M
Davis Ruth A widow Albert S bds Mrs H L Anthony W B
Dawson William millwright h Bay Spring av W B
Dea Mary A widow James K h Spring W B
Deangelis Sozio laborer h Hamilton
Delaney George W mgr Household Loan Co (Prov) h Third W B
Delano Thomas S bookkeeper sum res h Jennys lane
Delefratte Pio laborer h Hamilton
Delsando Michele laborer h Anoka av
Delsanto Francisco constable h 220 Middle Highway N
Delsanto Luigi driver h Hamilton
Delse Domenico laborer h Maple av
Denam Harry jeweler (Prov) h Pleasant W B
De Pasquale Mariano emp mill h Maple av
Deprise John carpenter h Ernest Bay Spring W B
Devlin Joseph J station agent Nayatt Depot also postmaster h Maple av N P
Dexter Charles S tool maker h Bay Spring W B
Dexter Fanny O bds L B Dexter Martin av B
Dexter Lewis B blockmaker (Prov) h Martin av B
Dexter Mary H teacher (piano) bds L B Dexter H M
Diangelo Giuseppe laborer h Hamilton
Diangelo Tomaso laborer h Hamilton
Dicica Gaietano laborer h Cottage
Disisto Andonio laborer h Anoka av
Ditomaso Domenico laborer h Middle Highway N
Doane Maria F widow Jonathan F bds Wilbur D Brown W B
Doane Sarah H Mrs bds The Gables
Dodge Arthur H oysterman bds John W Dodge Bay Spring W B
Dodge Charles J oysterman h Bay Spring W B
Dodge John W oyster grower and shipper h Bay Spring W B
Dodge Samuel R oysterman h Bay Spring W B
Dodge Samuel R Jr oysterman bds Samuel R Dodge Sr
Dole Stephen h Bay Spring W B
Draper Harriet L Miss h off Nayatt av N
Drew Willis A clerk (Prov) h Massasoit av E bey river B
Dube Israel variety County rd at Warren river B h opp do
Dubois Russell C C real estate agt h County rd bey Cong Church B
Dunbar Julia F Mrs h Alfred Drown rd W B

R. I. RUG WORKS
Rugs Woven from old and new carpets. Telephones { 2203 / 2204
678 WESTMINSTER ST., PROVIDENCE

Dunbar Lincoln gardener h Drown W B
Dundas Alexander optician h Fountain av W B
Dunn James M gardener h Mathewson rd B
Dupirito Andonio laborer h Middle Highway N
Durand Eva M bds O T Sherman Walnut W B
Easton N Howard sum res h Town Beach off Narragansett av B
Eccleston John W farmer h Old River rd nr the river W B
Eccleston Rosco farmer bds John Eccleston
Eldridge Franklin M carpenter h Lincoln cor Walnut W B
Ellis Martha A widow James M bds John J Bishop W B
Elmore Frank H prop F H Elmore Co h Nayatt av N P
Elsbree Hattie A widow Fred H h New Meadow rd B
England John J lace weaver h Bay Spring av B
Ernst Reuben R laborer h Narragansett av Bay Spring W B
Evans George W (Prov) office mgr O'Bannon Corp sum res h Nayatt
Evans William E fruit dealer h Church W B
Fairbrother Harry A lace maker h Leslie av Bay Spring W B
Fairbrother Thomas H lace weaver Bay Spring av W B
Fales J Richmond (Pawt) sum res Jennys lane B
Fales LeRoy manufacturer (Pawt) h Narragansett av B
Fales William H retired h Massasoit rd
Farina Alfredo carpenter h Anoka av
Farquhar George gardener Osamequin Farm h Old River rd near River B
Farrell John J sum res h Shore Drive Bay Spring W B
Ferra Arduino laborer h Princes Hill
Ferrazano Benedetta greenhouse h Maple av
Ferrucci Sisto laborer h Anoka av B
Ferucci Andonio emp mill h Anoka av
Ferucci Luigo laborer h Maple av
Fessenden Abbie W widow Robert bds Rumstick rd B C
Fidanza Michele laborer h Maple av
Field Frank O wholesale grocer (Prov) h West rd B
Field Russell clerk h New Meadow rd
Fielding William chauffeur bds A W Adams W B
Fillmore Clarence J silk mfr h cor Drown and Spring W B
Fisher Anna B bds L G Fisher Jennys lane B
Fisher Lewis G cer acct (Prov) h Jennys lane
Fisher Lewis G Jr electric engineer bds L G Fisher B
Fisk William farmer h off County rd nr Cong Church B
Fiske Charles W summer res (Prov) h Blanding av Bay Spring W B
Fiske Wayland E summer res (Prov) h r Blanding av Bay Spring W B
Fitzmaurice Myles gardener h County rd

Flanagan Charles Dr osteopath (Prov) h Drown W B
Fletcher Albert F lacemaker h Drown W B
Foley Joseph P machinist h Bay Springs W B
Fortier Walter chauffeur h Ocean opp Narragansett av B
Fortin Elzea laborer h County rd
Foster Isaac F manuf jeweler (Prov) h County rd nr Broad B' C
Foster Thomas summer res New Meadow rd H M
Fowler Henry E lawyer h Walnut W B
Fox John emp O'Bannon Carp bds M Gonyea W B
Frances Clovis V lacemaker h Spring W B
Frazee Victor grammar school principal h Fremont N P
Frey Martha weaver h Sowams rd
Furnaro Gaietano laborer h Maple av
Fusco Tomaso emp mill h Middle Highway N
GABLES (THE) (Mrs John S Thompson prop) Mathewson rd B—see page 26
Galitri Pietro laborer h Cottage
Gardiner Abbott L h Jenneys lane B
Gardiner Florence M wid Walter G Gardiner h off County rd nr Town Hall B
Gardiner Harriet H rubber worker bds Florence M
Gardiner Herbert N painter bds Mrs J Q A Gardiner B
Gardiner John Q A Mrs h ft of Rumstick rd B
Gardiner Joseph W h Lincoln av W B
Gardiner Minnie L forelady bds Florence M Gardiner B
Gauntlett Septemus machinist h Sowams rd
Gee James h Lake av W B
Geremia Michele mill emp h Maple av
Germelli Sarafino emp mill h Middle Highway N
Giardini Giovanni laborer h Cottage
Gibbs Francis B clerk bds R A Gibbs W B
Gibbs Harold N clerk h Sowams rd B
Gibbs Reuben A grocer and baker Washington cor Broadway also postmaster West Barrington h nr do W B
Gilbert George A clerk bds George H Gilbert W B
Gilbert George H machinist h Washington W B
Gill Marcus lace maker h First W B
Gillespie Thomas crossing tender bds Bay Spring av W B
Giorgi Andonio laborer h Maple av
Giorgi Nicola laborer h Maple av
Giorgi Pietro laborer h Anoka av
Giuliano Cosimo laborer h Anoka av
Gladding Alverin M boss carpenter h Jennys lane B

WHITTEMORE & COLBURN
PRINTERS   15 Pine St., PROV.

Gladding Carrie F Mrs h Jennys lane B
Gladding George D sum res (Prov) h Jennys lane B
Gladding Howard E bookkeeper bds Mrs C F Gladding B
Gladding Laura R Mrs bds Mrs C F Gladding Jennys la B
Glen John M insurance engineer h Third W B
Godin Victor chauffeur h Beach av B
Goff Jerry W mason h Washington cor Fountain W B
Goggin David T real estate h Orchard av and Sowams rd H M
Gonyea Edward J electrician h Narragansett rd W B
Gonyea Margaret boarding house Narragansett rd W B
Goodreau George mason h Church Annawomscott W B
Goodrow George mason h Broadway W B
Gosling Elizabeth A Mrs sum res h Clark av B
Graepen Frederick W receiver h Washington nr P O, W B
Graham John J farmer h Old River rd nr the river
Grande Gughirmo gardener h Middle Highway N
Granger C Edward Capt h South lane
Grant Annie bookkeeper (Prov) bds Wm Grant N P
Grant Charles crossing tender bds Willard H Grant H M
Grant Herbert M farmer h Sowams rd B
GRANT JAMES F postmaster B and news dealer County rd and Rumstick rd bds William Grant N P—see page 27
Grant John L farmer h Sowams rd nr town line H M
Grant Orrin mechanic h Sowams rd nr town line H M
Grant Willard H farmer h Sowams rd nr town line B
Grant William farmer h County rd B
Gray Robert B lawyer h County rd
Gray Robert B Jr emp R I Co freight dept bds County rd
Greene Bessie H bds F Greene B
Greene E Frederick bookkeeper (Prov) h West rd H M
Greene Elizabeth Mrs h Mathewson rd B
Greene Frederick salesman h Mathewson rd B
Greene Frederick D retired h Rumstick rd B
Greene Howard N clerk h Bay Spring W B
Greene John C trav salesman h County rd B
Greene Sarah P widow Benjamin h Sowams rd H M
Griffith Benjamin student bds J H Griffith B
Griffith James H h Rumstick rd B
Griffith Robert clerk bds J H Griffith B
Griffiths James lace maker h Bay Spring av W B
Griswold Walter H sum res h Annawomscott av (E Prov) W B
Gughietto Giuseppe mill emp h Maple av
Gughietto Norato mill emp h Maple av
Guido Domenico emp mill h Maple av
Guido Francesco laborer h Maple av

RALPH C. WATROUS CO.
RESIDENTIAL and INVESTMENT PROPERTY
Of All Kinds For Sale
487 Industrial Trust Building

BARRINGTON DIRECTORY, 1917-18.

Guild Williams machinist h Allen W B
Haldane H Clair asst treas O'Bannon Corp W B h W B
Haldane Henry C leather h Drown rd cor Spring W B
Hall Albert hoisting engineer h Narragansett rd W B
Hall Bertha A h Bay Spring W B
Hall Frank rubber worker h County rd nr Cong Church B
Hames John W laborer h Martin av
Hamilton William A gardener h Ferry lane B
Hamlin Edward B Jr N Y Express Co (Prov) h First W B
Hanley Amy F dressmaker bds M D Hanley B
Hanley John W jeweler (Prov) h Sowams rd
Hanley Margaret H stenographer bds M Hanley H M
Hanley Mary I stenographer (Prov) bds H M Hanley H M
Hanley Michael D salesman h Sowams rd H M
Hanson Frederick laborer h Martin av H M
Hanson Horace lace weaver bds Martin av
Hanson Louise H organized charities bds Mathewson rd
Hargreaves Bert shoemaker h Martin av
Hargreaves Julia h 16 County rd
Hargreaves Percy machinist h 16 County rd
Harkins Charles E bds with Owen Harkins Bay Spring WB
Harkins Fred O oysterman h Bay Spring av W B
Harkins John M bds Owen Harkins W B
Harkins Mary A bds Owen Harkins W B
Harkins Owen foreman oyster house (Warren) h Bay Spring W B
Harkins Sadie A bds Owen Harkins W B
Harkins William F machinist bds Owen Harkins W B
Harrington Thomas operative bds E Metz W B
Harris Louisa A widow Otis G h County rd B
Harris William A electrician (R I Co power house B) h East Providence
Harrower Peter carpenter h Walnut W B
Hart John M chemist bds Green av W B
Hartshorn Catherine h County rd
Hartshorn Daniel L lineman h County rd
Haskell Dorothy E student bds G H Haskell W B
Haskell George H Capt oyster dealer (Warren) h Alfred Drown rd nr track W B
Hathaway Charles H poultryman h County rd nr Cong Church B
Hathaway Frank P sum res Park av W B
Hathaway Isabel E housekeeper h County rd near Cong Church B

Blackstone Canal Nat'l Bank | A Progressive Bank
20 Market Sq., Prov. R. I. | Fully Equipped for Service

Warren Monumental Works
Cor. Railroad Avenue and Croade Street, Warren, R. I.

Hawes Charles E retired h Lincoln av cor Washington W B
Hayes Mae L tel op bds G Edwin Clark B
Hayes Mary widow William h County rd B
Head John F carpenter h Bay Spring av W B
Healy Fernando B carpenter Blanding av Bay Spring W B h do
Heath Annie bds W C Heath B
Heath William C Mrs h Rumstick rd nr schoolhouse B
Hedenborg George A head master St Andrew's School
Hempstead William R money clerk h Jennys lane B
Henley John C h Orchard av H M
Hewitt Arthur R sum res (Attle) h Bay Spring W B
Hewitt Ella M bds A R Hewitt W B
Hewitt Lillian dressmaker (Prov) bds Wm S Hewitt W B
Hickey Edwin E master mechanic h Narragansett rd W B
Hill Alton dairyman h on Osamequin Farm B
Hill Edward K sum res h Appian Way Annawomscott (Worcester) W B
Himmelman Sarah M Miss house mother St Andrew's Industrial School h do B
Hinkel Frederick C clerk O'Bannon Corp W B
Hinkel Frederick W clerk h Spring W B
Hoar Charles A clerk (Prov) h West rd B
Hoar Fred carpenter bds Lucy Hoar Sowams rd
Hoar John carpenter bds with Lucy Hoar Sowams rd
Hoar Lucy h Sowams rd near town line
Hoffman Henry A (Arnold Hoffman & Co Prov) h Rumstick rd south of tracks B
Hoffman William H Mrs h Rumstick rd B
Holden Ella M widow Michael h Primrose Hill
Holden Edwin W mfg jeweler (Prov) h Drown cor First W B
Holmes Charles W asst treas (Prov) bds T D Holmes
Holmes Thomas D Mrs County rd nr Cong Church B
Honan John farmer h Sowams rd
Hornby Philip traffic mgr h Walnut W B
Howard John I emp O'Bannon Corp h Howard W B
Hudson Elizabeth F stenographer bds E Arno B
Hughes Lida school teacher bds The Gables
Hunt Lucian barber h Washington rd W B
Hunt Reuben T Mrs h Drown nr Fifth W B
Hurley James H h County rd B
Huston Frederick mason h Blanding av Bay Spring W B
Hutcheson Peter D gardener bds G A Hutton B
Hutchinson Willis G carpenter h Drown bey Fifth W B
Hutton George A supt h Rumstick rd B
Ingraham Howard B retired h County rd B
International Rubber Cloth div O'Bannon Corp Park av R R track W B

Jackson Benjamin A sum res h Nayatt av N P
Jackson Donald sum res h Nayatt av N P
Jackson Eugene sum res Bay Point av B
Jacobs Harold C bds William Jacobs
Jacobs William (supt Atlantic Mills Prov) h County rd nr Broad B
Jacobs William DeL paying teller Union Trust (Prov) bds W Jacobs
Jacobson Frank sea captain h County rd
Jacobson Harold rubber worker bds County rd
Jacovelle Mary widow Rocci h County rd B
James Harry (Pawt) sum res County rd B
Jansson A painter and paper hanger Washington opp P O West Barrington h 29 Hoppin av Riverside
Jeffreys James farmer h Fifth W B
Jenckes John h Washington south Grove N P
Jenckes Stephen W h Town Beach off Narragansett av B
Jencks Charles W clerk International Rubber Cloth Co W B
Jenks Frederic T market gardener h Lincoln av 2d south Grammar School W B
Jenks George W carpenter h Narragansett av Bay Spring W B
Jennison Charles fisherman h Ferry la cor Mathewson rd B
Jennison Charles H fisherman h off Ferry lane
Jennison Joseph E fisherman bds C Jennison B
Jennison William fisherman h Ferry lane
Johnson Alvin rubber worker h 18 County rd
Johnson Charles chauffeur h County rd W B
Johnson Franklin J boss farmer h off Nayatt av N
Johnson Henry carder bds 18 County rd
Johnson Joseph salesman h Bay Spring av
Johnson Pheling G oysterman h Bay Spring W B
Jollie Annie E bds Charles F Boyden B
Jollie Louis G tool maker h Narragansett av W B
Jones Ernest G clerk R A Gibbs h Drown cor First
Jordon Charles E machinist bds W R Burgess W B
Jordon Ethel L lace worker bds W R Burgess W B
Joynes Walter lace weaver h Spring W B
Keiser John B asst supt O'Bannon Corp h Riverside
Keiser William B supt O'Bannon Corp h Riverside
Kelly Robert L h Rumstick rd B
Kenny John P laborer bds Marcella M Sharples W B
Kent Ira A farmer h New Meadow rd H M

Kenyon Annie Mrs h Jennys lane B
Kenyon Elizabeth Miss h Clark av N P
Kenyon John F sum res h Bluff av B
Kenyon William J trav salesman h Jennys lane B C
Kirby Alice Miss h Maple av B
Kirby Kate W bds The Gables
Kirby Margaret school teacher bds Maple av B
Kirby Mary bds Maple av B
Kirk Saukis grocery opp R R depot B h Providence
Knight Albert insurance h Lincoln av W B
Knott Alfred J retired bds Percy Townsend W B
Lama Pietro laborer h Maple av
Lamb Manuel S carpenter h Lincoln av nr Grammar School W B
Lamson Norton J contractor and builder h New Meadow rd B
Langlois Hypolite R night watchman h Bridge av B
Larisa Carlo laborer h Anoka av
Lavin James E machinist bds Narragansett rd W B
Lavin Matthew M machinist h Bay Spring W B
Lavin Thomas B enginer bds Narragansett rd
Lemoi Thomas laborer h County rd
Lenox William emp B & S (Prov) h Church W B
Leonard Augustus B ice dealer Drown nr Elm h do W B
Leonard William A ice dealer also road surveyor Spring nr Elm h do W B
Lerose Gabriele barber h Maple av
Lester Grace T supervisor of music B bds The Gables
Leverton John C gardener bds W H Adams W B
Lewandoski Joseph laborer h off Sowams rd
Lewis Arthur electroplater (Prov) h 46 Drown W B
Lewis Clinton D with R I Hospital Trust Co (Prov) h Drown W B
Lewis Hope H bds Arthur Lewis W B
Lewis Joseph W treas Henry W Cooke Co (Prov) h Nayatt Point B
Lewis Loren R machinist h Narragansett av W B
Lewis William T Jr electroplater (Prov) h Drown nr Elm W B
Lincoln Marston h Jennys lane B
Lisseto Nicola emp brick yard h Anoka av
Livingstone Archibald summer res (Pawt) Bay Spring at shore W B
Lloyd John W brick maker bds County rd
Lobardi Sozio laborer h Anoka av
Lomas Holmes sum res Nayatt Clark av
Lombardi Giovani laborer h Hamilton
Lombardi Pietro laborer h Maple av

LIVE WIRE collectors of BAD BILLS
"No Collection—No Charge"
WESTERN MERCANTILE CORPORATION
420-421 Grosvenor Building. Tel. Union 1526 Providence, R. I.

BARRINGTON DIRECTORY, 1917-18. 193

Lombardi Salvatore laborer h Hamilton
LORD THOMAS A contractor and builder First h do W B
—see page 27
Luciani Lurenzo laborer h Maple av
Luciano Sozio laborer h Roffee
Lumbardi Luigi laborer Maple av
Lumbardi Nicola grocery h Maple av
Luther Frederick scale builder h 20 County rd
Lyman Harold C trav salesman Mathewson B
Lyman Hertha Mrs h Mathewson rd
Lyon Lawrence A bds First W B
Lyons Cornelius J retired h Green av W B
Macdonald George A machinist h Leslie av Bay Spring W B
Macdonald Jane emp Int Rubber Co bds N Swindell Lincoln av W B
Macdonald Myra S widow Arthur W h Sowams rd H M
Macdonald Robert B sum res (Attle) h ft Blanding av Bay Spring W B
Macdonald Robert B Jr bds Robert Macdonald Bay Spring W B
MacDougall Howard painter h County rd
MacDowell Daisy student bds W A Bourne B
MacKennon Edward machinist bds New Meadow rd H M
MacKennon Mary h New Meadow rd H M
MacKennon William H machinist bds New Meadow rd H M
Madigan John clerk h New Meadow rd
Madigan Nellie milliner bds New Meadow rd
Mailhot J Gideon grocer Bay Spring av h do
Main Leland H shipping clerk h Fourth W B
Maiura Piucci emp mill h Maple av
Manchester Horace L wholesale jeweler (Prov) h Jennys lane B
Manchester James Mrs bds H L Manchester B
Manchester Mary E Mrs h County rd B
Manchester Nellie F Mrs h Jennys lane B
Mancino Fonzo barber h 36 Maple av
Mancino Pambano laborer h Anoka av
Mancino Placido grocer h 36 Maple av
Mandsley Edwin wood turner bds W J Mandsley
Mandsley William J R R mail clerk h Lincoln av B
Mangianti Luigi emp mill h Cottage
Mansfield Edward B clerk Lincoln av B
Marcello Andonio laborer h Anoka av

R. I. RUG WORKS
Furniture Repaired and Repolished, Chairs Reseated
678 Westminster Street, Providence. Telephone Union 2903 and also Union 2204

Marcello Luigi emp mill h Anoka av
Marcello Peter shoe repair shop Bay Spring rd h Nayatt
Marcello Pietro shoe maker h Middle Highway N
Marcello Pippino laborer h Anoka av
Marcillo Tomaso laborer h Anoka av
Mariani Giovanni emp mill h Maple av
Mariano John h Maple av
Marlon Minnie h New Meadow rd H M
Marotte Amedee carpenter h Church W B
Marshall Edwin P engraver (Prov) h Third W B
Marshall John E pur agt (Prov) h Jennys lane B
Martin Caroline H Mrs h Broad south of tracks B
Martin Charles H wire tester h Ferry lane B
Martin Edgar W sum res h Rumstick Point B
Martin Gertrude M bds Ferry lane
Martin Henry A farmer h Massasoit rd E bey the river B
Martin Marshall H, R F D driver bds C H Martin
Martin Mary E bds H A Martin B
Martin Mary T widow Walter E h Washington W B
Martin S Annie bds Ferry lane
Martin Sidney A clerk h County rd B
Martin William R mason New Meadow rd h do B
Martin William S carpenter h off Ocean rd B
Martini Luigi laborer h Maple av
Martini Pambano laborer h Maple av
Martini Sazio laborer h Hamilton
Martino Vincenzo laborer h Hamilton
Martone Michelo laborer h Maple av
Martone Pasquale farmer h County rd
Masello Rafael laborer h Anoka av
Mason Charles H carpenter h South lane
Massey Peter carpenter h New Meadow rd H M
Masteriano Gugliermo emp mill h Maple av
Mathews Alfred W metal worker h Fountain av W B
Mathewson Grace H h Jennys lane B
Mathewson House (Mrs W F Thompson prop) Mathewson
    av B
Mathewson Olive student bds Jennys lane B
Mathewson William A real estate (Prov) h Jennys lane B
Mattio Alfonzo laborer h Cottage
Mauro Clemende laborer h South
Maxfield Dorothy T school teacher bds W Maxfield
Maxfield Ina stenographer bds W Maxfield B
Maxfield James jeweler (Prov) h County rd B
Maxfield William silversmith h County rd B
MAYOTT & OGDEN grocery and meat market Bay Spring
    av W B—see page 26
McAnespic Thomas farmer h Washington W B
McArdle Thomas S engineer (Prov) h Narragansett rd WB

WALTER H. JACKSON CO. 435 Industrial Trust Building
PROVIDENCE, R. I.
"DELCO" ELECTRIC LIGHTING & PUMPING PLANTS
WINDMILLS, GASOLINE ENGINES AND TRACTORS

McBriar Samuel calendar hand h cor Fifth and Drown W B
McBride John gardener h Rumstick rd B
McCandless John H leather worker h ft Broadway W B
McCann Elizabeth housekeeper bds Sowams rd
McCann Michael farmer h Sowams rd
McCanna Eunice M bds County rd B
McCardel Thomas engineer lace works h Narragansett av Bay Spring W B
McCoy James C summer res h Nayatt Point N P
McDowell William T chauffeur h Rumstick rd B
McFarland James laborer h Ferry lane
McFectears James gardener h Washington W B
McGinn Catherine G widow John C McGinn bds W V McGinn W B
McGinn Walter P sum res h Buckingham Beach near ft Shore av (Prov) W B
McGowan John B jewelry tool maker bds George C Anderton W B
McGuy Lottie bds L E Cleland B
McHugh Michele J summer res h Shore av (Prov) W B
McKenna Charles H lawyer (Prov) h County rd B
McKenna Frank caretaker h Nayatt rd nr Watson N
McKenna Walter summer res (Prov) h Blanding av Bay Spring W B
McKnight William Ervma Weaving Co (Pawt) h Narragansett rd W B
McManus Peter B sum res Beach near Town Beach B
McRae Arthur A summer res h Watson N P
Mead Edgar jeweler h Third W B
Medbery Frank I emp Lace Works h Bay Spring W B
Medbury Annie W Miss bds Ann E Medbury B
Medbury Charles carpenter bds Mrs A E Medbury B
Medbury Lucy C nurse bds Ann E Medbury
Medici Casamino laborer h Middle Highway N
Medicio Andonio laborer h Maple av
Mendall George C trav salesman h Bay Spring W B
Merchant George B sum res h Appian Way Annawomscott (Prov) W B
Merriman Charles H Jr sum res h Nayatt Point N P
Merriman Isaac B sum res N P
Metz Edward W painter h Bay Spring av cor Lake av W B
Metz Frederick emp Pawt h Welsh av W B
Midwood Edith E bds G A Midwood W B
Midwood George A wholesale grocer (Prov) h Alfred Drown rd nr track W B

WHITTEMORE & COLBURN
PRINTERS   15 Pine St., PROV.

King's Fibrous Plaster Board & Hard Plaster
JAMES C. GOFF CO.
31 to 49 Point St., Prov., R. I.

Midwood George A Jr student bds G A Midwood W B
Miller Benjamin S jeweler bds B T Medbury W B
Miller Charles M h County rd B
Miller Clifford F jeweler h Washington rd W B
Miller Elizabeth Mrs rubber worker h Ferry lane
Miller Joseph A patent attorney (Prov) h Lincoln av cor Howard W B
Miller Louis farmer h New Meadow rd H M
Miller Olga rubber worker bds Ferry lane
Miller William H farmer h New Meadow rd H M
Modliszewski Walter weaver bds off Sowams rd
Morrison Charles H carpenter h Drown rd W B
Morrissey Edmond J farmer h Sowams rd H M
Morteletto Domenico laborer h Anoka av
Morton Josephine C h County rd B
Moscaro Giovanni laborer h Maple av
Mumford Benjamin sum res h Appian Way Annawomscott (Prov) W B
Musca Luca laborer h Wusica av
Musca Silvio emp mill h County rd
Needam John fireman h Martin av H M
Newcomb Arthur M engraver h Crossways
New England Steam Brick Co (Firth Marsden supt) off Maple av across R R track B
Nichols Daniel A Capt Prov F D h County rd nr Cong Church B
Nichols Gladys stenographer (Prov) bds D A Nichols B
Nichols Leon machinist bds D A Nichols B
Nichols Parker rubber worker h County rd B
Nickerson Harley L fisherman h Drown W B
Nightingale Oscar farmer h Washington rd W B
Noble Mary Emma Miss h Washington nr Grove W B
Noble Sarah A Miss h Washington nr Grove W B
Norris Thomas E summer res h off Drown W B
Norton Annie P bds B Norton B C
Norton Benjamin carpenter h County rd nr Broad B
Norton Lyra M Mrs h Crossways
Noyes Irving E butcher h Fountain av W B
O'BANNON CORPORATION (R LeB Bowen vice-pres and genl mgr) imitation leather Park av W B— see page 5
O'Brien John T driver bds William A Leonard W B
O'Connor Charles B paymaster O'Bannon Corp h Upland Way B
Ogden Laura M grocer Bay Spring av h do
Oliva Michele laborer h County rd B
O'Neil Clara L rubber worker bds W E Winterbottom W B
O'Neil Dennis bleacher h Bay Spring av W B

Ralph C. Watrous Co. FARMS and SUBURBAN PROPERTY For Sale
437 INDUSTRIAL TRUST BUILDING

BARRINGTON DIRECTORY, 1917-18. 197

O'Neil Michael laborer h Watch W B
Owen Charles D sum res h Nayatt Point N P
Owens Frederick sum res h Blanding av Bay Spring W B
Paine Charles W butcher h Drown cor Fifth W B
Paine Franklin D fisherman bds Green av W B
Paine George sum res off Watson N
Paine Joshua A butcher h Lincoln av cor Walnut W B
Paine William E sum res off Watson N
Pallumbo Giuseppe emp mill h Lincoln av
Palmieri Michael A prop Bay Spring Market h do
Palumbo Andonio emp mill h Maple av
Palumbo Andonio laborer h Maple av
Palumbo Augusta laborer h Maple av
Palumbo Francesco emp mill h Maple av
Palumbo Francesco emp mill h Lincoln av
Palumbo Giovanni emp mill h Maple av
Palumbo Micelangelo laborer h Maple av
Palumbo Pietro laborer h Maple av
Palumbo Rapaielo laborer h Nayatt
Panarillo Giuseppe laborer h Maple av
Pandozzi Pasquale barber h Bay Spring av W B
Panorelli Giovanni laborer h Maple av
Panorello Sabatino laborer h Maple av
Paolella Stepane laborer h County rd
Paolino Fonzo laborer h Wusica av
Paolino Gilardo emp mill h Hamilton
Paolino Giuseppe dyer h Maple av
Papa Andonio laborer h Wusica av
Pare Fortunat carpenter h rear Bartons County rd
Parish Charles painter h Third W B
Parker Alice R sum res at Charles W Paine (Worcester) W B
Parker Grace C teacher B H S bds J Crawshaw
Parker John W draughtsman (Prov) h Massasoit av B
Parmelee Harold V electrician h County rd B
Parmelee Leander M h County rd B
Parotti Giovanni laborer h Sowams rd
Pary Alfred W blacksmith h off County rd B
Patterson Francis Mrs bds The Gables
Patton William G tester h Martin av
Peace Christopher sum res h Annawomscott nr ft Shore av (Prov) W B
Pease Emerson E awning maker sum res Barrington av B
Peck Charles C grocer (Prov) sum res Jennys lane B

Blackstone Canal Nat'l Bank	Established 1831
20 MARKET SQ. PROVIDENCE	STRONG AND CONSERVATIVE

Peck Clara Mrs bds C C Peck Jennys lane B
Peck Clarence I market gardener h at Peck's Corner W B
Peck Frederick S wool h Primrose Hill nr river W B
Peck George F farmer h Willard av W B
Peck Mary E widow Albert h Peck's Corner W B
Peck Sarah widow Leander h Old River rd nr the river WB
Peck Sarah F widow Alpheus F Peck bds Geo Baker W B
Peck William retired bds G Edwin Clark B
Pelegrino Carafino laborer h Maple av
Pelland Samuel rubber worker h Bay Spring W B
Pendlebury Ella W Mrs bds Ballou Maple av N
Pendlebury Frederick W clerk bds Ballou Maple av N
Perelto Frederick mill emp bds John Perelto H M
Perelto John mill emp h off Sowams rd H M
Perry Clarence L boss express (Pawt) h Bay Spring av at shore B
Perry Frederick D sum res (Pawt) h Bay Spring at shore W B
Perry Hiram F Rumstick rd B
Perry John Jr sum res (Pawt) h Bay Spring at shore W B
Perry Warren H bds C L Perry B
Peterman Albert florist bds Otto Peterman
Peterman Otto farmer h Broad bey Cong Church B
Petit Peter h Bay Spring W B
Petrucci Andonio emp mill h Maple av
Petrucci Francesco laborer h Anoka av
Pezullo Giovanni emp mill h Maple av
Pezullo Giuseppe laborer h Maple av
Pezullo Giuseppe emp mill h Hamilton
Pezullo Luigi laborer h Maple av
Pezullo Pasquale emp mill h Hamilton
Phillips George lace worker bds T H Phillips Bay Spring W B
Phillips James J foreman (Prov) h Bay Spring W B
Phillips Thomas H compositor (Prov) h Bay Spring W B
Phillips Vincent F foreman h Bay Spring W B
Picard Ovida chauffeur bds Myra Macdonald H M
Piccirilli Andonio laborer h Anoka av
Piccirilli Gramatista laborer h South
Piccirilli Gusueto laborer h Anoka av
Piccirilli Pietro emp mill h Anoka av
Piccirillo Luigi laborer h Anoka av
Picerilli Rafaiele laborer h Anoka av
Picirilli Alberto laborer h Wusica av
Picirrelli Giovanni emp mill h Anoka av
Picker Henry lace worker h Bay Spring av W B
Picurilli Giuseppe laborer h South
Pietruszka Felix weaver h off Sowams rd

National Exchange Bank
63 Westminster St., Prov.
Established 1801
If you think of changing your bank, there is
None better than this

Pietruszka John loomfixer bds off Sowams rd
Pirmeo Edith C Miss farmer h Old River rd
Place John farm laborer h rear of Graham B
Pombeio Giuseppe laborer h Roffee
Pombeio Rocco laborer h Maple av
Porrotti Giovanni laborer h Swansea rd
Potter Amelia widow Stephen h Old River rd nr the river
Potter Charlotte M Miss h off Shore av W B
Potter Grace F Miss enameler h off Shore av W B
Potter S J Miss h Rumstick rd B
Powers Thomas R janitor h Walnut W B
Powers William sum res h Rumstick Point B
Pratt Henry A wire chief h Spring W B
Preston Albert L poultry man h New Meadow rd H M
Preston Albert R farmer bds New Meadow rd H M
Preston Annie L house mother St Andrew's School
Preston Frederick S stone setter (Prov) bds New Meadow rd H M
Prey Martha E widow Alfred Prey bds Willis A Drew H M
Price Walter fisherman bds County rd
Prthel Irwin trav salesman h Massasoit av B
Prthel Olga saleswoman (Prov) bds Massasoit av B
Purvere Clarence J sum res (E Prov) Blanding av Bay Spring W B
Puzzullo Vincenzo laborer h Nayatt
Raccabello Riciardo laborer h Nayatt
Radigan James H sum res (Prov) h ft Drown W B
Ramsbottom Phebe bds Mrs M R Smith W B
Rapone Giovanni carpenter h Hamilton
Rea Emma L bds Harriet A Smith
Rea Harriet A Miss bds Harriet A Smith B
Rea Rafaille laborer h Maple av
Rea Tomaso laborer h Maple av
Read Charles H machinist h Old River rd nr the river
Reynolds T R Mrs h Mathewson rd
Rhode Island Country Club Nayatt av N
Rhode Island Lace Works (Arthur Smith supt) lace makers Park av south of tracks W B
Rhode Island Suburban Co's Sub Station County rd next to river B
Rhodes Augustus S retired h Third W B
Ricci Andonio laborer h Anoka av
Ricci Giovanni emp brick yard h Anoka av
Richards George coachman h Middle Highway

Merewether & Dunn
Plumbing and Heating Contractors
51 TURNER AVENUE,   RIVERSIDE, R. I.

Richardson Preston clerk h Adams Pt off Ferry lane B
Richardson Robert gardener h Church W B
Richmond Leroy J grocer (E Prov) h First W B
Rines Charles A h Third (Prov) W B
Ritondo Pasquale laborer h Anoka av
Robbins George W poultry dealer bds New Meadow rd H M
Robbins Olive Mrs h Lincoln av W B
Robbins Thomas E chief police B h New Meadow rd bey school H M
Robinson Adele h New Meadow rd
Robinson Annie widow Walter h Sowams rd H M
Robinson Edwin D electrician h New Meadow rd
Robinson Harry D stock clerk bds Annie Robinson Sowams rd
Robinson Henry S (treas Prov Tel Co) h Jennys lane B
Robinson William farmer bds Annie Robinson H M
Roe Ellery T chemist h Washington rd W B
Romanelli Giovianni laborer h Maple' av
Ross John greenhouse worker bds George Farquhar
Rossi Pietro farmer h Maple av
Rossi Salvatore emp mill h Maple av
Russell George W Jr electrician h Washington rd W B
Russell Harold h Bradford W B
Russo Andonio laborer h Cottage
Russo Rafaiele laborer h Cottage
Rutledge James A overseer h Ferry lane nr Water B
Rutledge Rebecca h Ferry lane
St Joseph's Hospital Retreat for Sisters Appian Way Annawomscott W B
Salisbury George A crossing tender Park av h Welch av nr R R, W B
Sammis Chester bds New Meadow rd H M
Sammis Frederick E at rubber works h West rd nr County rd B
Sampson Mabel h Bay Spring W B
Sandiglio Luigi laborer h Maple av
Sang Anna E widow William V h County rd nr Peck's Corner B
Santini Luigi laborer h Cottage
Santois John operative h Sowams rd H M
Santois Leona operative bds J Santois H M
Santois Mary operative bds J Santois H M
Saracino Luigi laborer h County rd
Sarcini Carmino laborer h Anoka av
Sargent William P sum res Rumstick rd B
Sayles Clarence G Miller Mfg Co (Prov) bds Mathewson rd
Scaleia Giuseppe laborer h Hampden Meadows

Schauble Frank laborer h Sowams rd H M
Sciotti Michael A restaurant Narragansett rd h do W B
Senft Joseph musician bds Julius Senft B
Senft Julius loomfixer h Sowams rd B
Serveny Edward carpenter h County rd
Sessions Henry W mgr (Prov) h Crossways H M
Seymour Augusta widow James DeW h Rumstick rd south R R track B
Seymour Edward D bds A Seymour B
Seymour George S sign writer h Rumstick rd next school house B
Seymour M F Mrs h Rumstick rd and Nayatt rd B
Sharpe Ellen D Miss sum res h Nayatt av N P
Sharpe Henry D sum res h Nayatt av N P
Sharples Marcella M widow William B h Washington W B
Shaw Chester R supt of schools (B) h South lane
Shepard Albina bds Charles Read B
Shepard Arthur F vice warden St Andrew's Industrial School h do B
Shepperton Alfred H steel worker h Sowams rd B
Sherman Oscar T teller R I H Trust Co h Walnut W B
Shore Henry yard clerk h Green av W B
Silva Anthony laborer h Walnut W B
Simmons Edward emp Prov bds Maple av
Simmons Frank electrician bds Maple rd B
Simmons Frank W ice dealer bds L J Richmond
Simmons George blacksmith h Maple av B
Simonette Samuel machinist h Maple av
Simonetti Andonio mill emp h Maple av
Simoni Andonio laborer h Roffee
Simpson Grace bds R Simpson
Simpson Robert millwright h Spring W B
Sisson Alfred P retired h New Meadow rd H M
Sives Thomas V mason h Pleasant W B
Smith Adelaide widow George L h Nayatt av N P
Smith Alerbo jeweler h County rd nr Cong Church
Smith Angelica T widow Nathan J h Mathewson av near County rd
Smith Arthur supt R I Lace Works h County rd W B
Smith Arthur L wholesale paints etc (Prov) h Mathewson rd nr County rd B
Smith Bertha school teacher bds W Maxwell
Smith Charles A bds Joseph S Smith W B
Smith Charles E sum res h Broad north Cong Church B

Smith Charles J h Rumstick rd B
Smith Cristena S jeweler bds Joseph T Smith W B
Smith E Augusta bookkeeper bds Ella A Smith W B
Smith Edward P gardener h Washington nr Nayatt av N P
Smith Ella A widow Charles E h Washington cor Grove av W B
Smith Eva N Narragansett rd W B
Smith Ezra sum res h Shore Drive Bay Spring W B
Smith George F gardener H D Sharpe h off Washington Nayatt Point N P
Smith George H (Asa Peck & Co Prov) h Washington cor Drown W B
Smith George R machinist h Richmond av W B
Smith Harriet A widow Rufus B h County rd bey Cong Church B
Smith Isabelle widow Albert h Washington nr tracks W B
Smith Joseph T machinist h Broadway W B
Smith Lewis B mechanic bds M S Smith B
Smith Marion B teacher (Prov) bds New Meadow rd H M
Smith Marion K bds Harriet Smith
Smith Mary Mrs bds E E Hickey W B
Smith Mary R Mrs grocery Bay Spring av cor Lake av WB
Smith May S widow Benjamin K h Narragansett av cor Rumstick rd B
Smith Olive M Susan T and Mary E Misses bds Mrs S K Smith B
Smith Paul S chemist O'Bannon Corp h Washington W B
Smith Richard E pres Flint & Co (Prov) h New Meadow rd H M
Smith Richard W retired bds New Meadow rd H M
Smith Sarah h Washington nr P O, W B
Smith Thomas H lace weaver h Bay Spring W B
Smith William E h Clarke av N P
Smyth William E sum res ft Shore av (E Prov) W B
Soriani Nicola laborer h Maple av
Soule Harry B piano tuner h Broad nr Cong Church B
Spaulding C Eugene real estate (Prov) bds G E Whaley
Spaulding Mabel teacher St Andrew's School
Spear William A sum res h Annawomscott nr ft Shore av (Attleboro) W B
Spencer Daniel E mechanical drawing h off County rd nr Peck's Corner W B
Spencer E L sum res h Rumstick rd B
Spencer Frank G sum res h Appian Way Annawomscott (Prov) W B
Sposito Andonio laborer h Anoka av
Sposito Domenico emp mill h Anoka av
Spray Samuel lacemaker h Bay Spring av B

Water Supply Outfits House Pumps	Walter H. Jackson Co. 435 Industrial Trust Building Providence, - R. I.	"Dodd" System Lightning PROTECTION

Stafford Mary L house mother St Andrew's School
Stanley Eliza L Mrs h off Mathewson rd B
Stanley Viall farmer bds Sowams rd H M
Stanley William E farmer h Sowams rd H M
Stanton Eliza J widow Horace D h Pleasant av W B
Staples Levi janitor Town Hall h County rd opp do B
Starkweather Joseph U wholesale drugs and chemicals (Prov) h Nayatt Point N P
Staton John A mfg silk hosiery (Prov) h Lincoln av W B
Stefano Luca laborer h Maple av
Steinacker Jacob emp H A Hoffman h Rumstick rd B
Stonaker Walter W knitter h Washington rd W B
Stone Abram rubber worker h rear of Wallace County rd
Stone C Moulton sum res h New Meadow rd H M
Stone Henry M market gardener h Old River rd junction County rd B
Stone Henry P real estate (Prov) h New Meadow rd H M
Struthers Clara J Miss h Third W B
Suddard Frederick S silversmith bds G A Salisbury W B
Suliano Michele baker h Maple av
Sullivan Dennis R sum res h Buckingham Beach near ft Shore av (Prov) W B
Sullivan John J gardener h off County rd Princess Hill B
Sullivan Timothy T gardener h County rd
Sutcliffe George C brakeman h Ernest Bay Spring W B
Swan Samuel B electric engineer h Mathewson av B
Sweet Bryan D sum res (Prov) with G E Jenks Bay Spring W B
Sweet Emery P physician Mathewson av h do B
Sweet Henry E sum res (Mansfield) h on point Bay Spring W B
Sweetland Edward R Rev retired h Massasoit av B
Sweetland Mary social service (Prov) bds Massasoit av B
Swenson John farmer h New Meadow rd nr town line B
Swindell George machinist bds Lincoln av W B
Swindell John machinist bds Lincoln av W B
Swindell Nellie h off Lincoln av W B
Syner Jacob carpenter h New Meadow rd H M
Tallman Harry B engraver h Massasoit av E B
Tattersall Eleanor F h Ernest Bay Spring W B
Terrell Hubert N school teacher h Lincoln av W B
Tester Albert driver h County rd B
Testo Alberto laborer h County rd
Thatcher Ronald sum res Bay Spring W B

WHITTEMORE & COLBURN
PRINTERS   15 Pine St., PROV.

JAMES C. GOFF CO.
31 to 49 POINT ST.
Providence, R. I.

All kinds of Masons' Materials

Thomlinson John W farmer h Middle rd B
Thompson Anna M Mrs h Bay Spring W B
Thompson Benjamin G oysterman h Bay Spring W B
Thompson Ernest R bds The Gables
Thompson Florence bds W F Thompson B
Thompson Fred D summer res (Prov) h ft Blanding av at shore Bay Spring W B
Thompson Frederick C longshoreman bds W B
Thompson George B oyster opener h Bay Spring W B
Thompson Harriet P Mrs bds Mrs W F Thompson B
Thompson John S emp Anthony Furniture Co (Prov) h Mathewson rd
Thompson Mary A prop The Gables Mathewson rd
Thompson Walter F prop Mathewson House h do B
Thorpe Caroline widow Luke Thorpe sum res (Prov) h Bay Spring W B
Thorpe Thomas sum res (Pawt) h Bay Spring W B
Thurber William H sum res h Nayatt av N P
Thurston Samuel L electrician h Old River rd
Tiffany Ebenezer town treasurer Barrington h County rd nr Cong Church B
Tiffany Harriet L widow Ebenezer h County rd nr Cong Church B
Timmans William foreman machinist h Lake av W B
Tingley A Brintnall with Henry W Cooke Co (Prov) h Jennys lane B
Tingley Alice E Mrs h Jennys lane B
Tingley Arthur D office 171 Westminster (Prov) h Jennys lane
Tingley Henry F bds A D Tingley B
Townend Percy clerk (Prov) also variety store Shore av h nr do W B
Tracy Edith bds Frank S G Sowams rd H M
Track Frank S G jeweler h Sowams rd H M
Trifiletti Filippo laborer on R R h County rd nr R R
Tripletto Filippo h County rd
Tryan Estella clerk bds G R Smith Richmond av W B
Tucker Atwell gardener h Ferry lane
Tyler S Mason bookkeeper (Riverside) h Massasoit av E bey river B
Ulmschneider Joseph laborer h Sowams rd H M
Urquhart Robert salesman h Drowne rd W B
Varone Carmella spinner bds County rd
Varone Pimgipio h County rd
Vellone Andonio laborer h Maple av
Venditulo Tony shipping clerk O'Bannon Corp W B h Maple av B
Vendituolo Michael emp Outlet (Prov) h Walnut W B

Ralph C. Watrous Co.
ESTATE MANAGERS.   RENT COLLECTION A SPECIALTY
437 INDUSTRIAL TRUST BUILDING

Verry Elisha carpenter h off County rd W B
Viall Frances V bds I Viall Upland Way N
Viall Frederick h Upland Way N
Viall Grace widow Arthur dressmaker h Narragansett av cor Rumstick rd B C
Viall Grace E widow Everett V bds Mrs Helen Whiting B
Viall Henry I bookkeeper bds I Viall Upland Way N
Viall Isaac F farmer h Upland Way N
Viall Nettie M Mrs h Maple av N
Viall Sarah A Mrs h Upland Way N
Viau Leon J prop Leon's Express h Martin av B
Vieth George A clerk Arnold & Hoffman (Prov) h New Meadow rd W B
Virgilia Luigi laborer h Maple av
Vitulso Domonicka farmer New Meadow rd H M
Waite William H (Prov) h Rumstick rd B
Walker W Howard sum res h Appian Way Annawomscott (Prov) W B
Wallace James E carpenter h Sowams rd H M
Wallis Eugene F wholesale meats h County rd at Warren river B
Walsh John greenhouse worker bds George Farquhar
Walsh John retired bds L Williams W B
Walsh Julia A bds Charles Walsh W B
Ward Alice L singing teacher bds J A Ward B
Ward A P accountant h Drown rd W B
Ward John A foreman pattern maker h New Meadow rd B
Waterman Nicholas Mrs h Rumstick rd south of tracks B
Watrous Augustus B watchman h Shore av cor Appian Way W B
Watrous Dorothy M bookkeeper bds A B Watrous W B
Watrous Luman P trav salesman bds Augustus P Watrous W B
Watson Elmer K gen contractor Warren h Bluff av N P
Watson Joseph H h Mathewson rd B
Watson Thomas lace weaver h off Blanding av W B
Watson Walter J ins clerk bds Mrs W H J Watson B
Watson William H J Mrs sum res h Mathewson av B
Waugh William machinist h Narragansett rd W B
Weaver Alvah G boatman h Rumstick rd B
Webb Alfred J sum res (Pawt) h Bay Spring at shore W B
Webb George sum res bds Alfred J Webb Bay Spring at shore W B
Weeden Samuel S laborer h off Washington rd W B

Blackstone Canal Nat'l Bank 20 Market Square PROVIDENCE, R. I.
Capital, $500,000.   Surplus Profits, over $500,000

Warren Monumental Works
Cor. Railroad Avenue and Croade Street, Warren, R. I.

Weir Benjamin carpenter bds Mrs Eliza J Stanton W B
Welchman Charles emp Bristol Rubber Co h Sowams rd
Welcome Harriet h Bay Spring W B
West Barrington Post Office Washington rd
West J Leonard poultry farm h Crossways B
West Leonard E teaming Sowams rd h do H M
West Stella E bds L E West H M
Whaley George E trav salesman h Drown rd W B
White Ethel bookkeeper L P Bosworth B C bds Warren
Whitehead William lace worker h Pleasant W B
Whiting Edna M teacher (Cranston) bds Mrs Helen Whiting B
Whiting Helen Mrs h Jennys lane B
Whitney Martha P housekeeper bds Green av W B
Wickes Elizabeth comb winder h 16 County rd
Wickes Harry clerk h 16 County rd
Wilbur Martin B retired bds Mrs T D Holmes County rd nr Cong Church B
Willard Andrew F tool maker h 7 Shore av W B
Williams John R emp R I Lace Works bds L Williams WB
Williams Llewellyn emp R I Lace Works h Bradford W B
Williamson Leonard machinist h Fountain av W B
Wilson Clifford electrician h Washington rd W B
Wilson Volney M broker (Prov) h Rumstick rd B
Winchester James M farmer h ft Broadway W B
Windsor Lila house mother St Andrew's School
Wing Isabel Mrs h Lincoln av W B
Winterbottom Mary drawing-in hand bds Mary E Winterbottom W B
Winterbottom Mary E forelady h Narragansett W B
Wood Emma F widow George R h Bay Spring av
Wood Frederick B mechanic County rd bds G L Aborn
Wood Kenneth F sum res h Nayatt av N P
Wood Lorenzo packer emp Bristol h Lake av W B
Woodward George E gen agent N Y N H & H R R h Drown nr Spring av W B
Woodward Harriet clerk (Prov) bds Martin av H M
Woodward Ida M artist bds Woodward B
Woodward Joseph H inspector h Martin av B
Yager Anna widow Henry h Massasoit av E bey river B
Yager Henry L farmer h Massasoit av bey river B
Young Francis A clerk h County rd nr Cong Church B
Zimfro Longo laborer h Maple av
Zinni Giovanni emp mill h Maple av
Zizarelli Camillo driver h Princes Hill
Zomba Antonio loomfixer h County rd B
Zomba Luigi laborer h County rd
Zomba Nuzio laborer bds Sanarella Sabatino

NATIONAL EXCHANGE BANK 63 WESTMINSTER ST. PROVIDENCE
IF YOU ARE LOOKING FOR A STRONG BANK, WHERE A FRIENDLY Welcome Always Awaits You, Open an Account With Us

BRISTOL COUNTY
BUSINESS DIRECTORY

Agricultural Implements

WARDWELL LUMBER CO Thames ft of Bradford—see head lines — Bristol

Apothecaries (see Druggists)

Artists

Woodward Ida M Abbie Woodward H M — Barrington
Cady Henry N Union cor Liberty — Warren
Peck Henry J Liberty cor Union — Warren

Auctioneers

Straight Clark H 329 Hope — Bristol
Brown John H 34 North Water — Warren

Auto Painter

TORREY E F 1039 Hope—see page 21 — Bristol

Automobile Repairing

Bristol Auto Shop 750 Hope — Bristol
CENTRAL GARAGE 41 Church—see page 21 — Bristol
FRANKLIN ST GARAGE (THE) cor Thames and Franklin—see page 18 — Bristol
COLE GEORGE R 27 Baker—see page 23 — Warren
POTTER COLLAMORE & CO South Water opp Wheaton—see page 24 — Warren

Automobile Storage

FRANKLIN ST GARAGE (THE) cor Thames and Franklin—see page 18 — Bristol

---

Merewether & Dunn
Plumbing and Heating Contractors
31 TURNER AVENUE, RIVERSIDE, R. I.

33 Canal St.   CHARLES J. JAGER CO.   Providence
ELECTRIC AND GASOLINE PUMPS AND PRESSURE SYSTEMS
We carry the largest stock of this kind in New England

Automobile Supplies

Bristol Auto Shop 750 Hope	Bristol
FRANKLIN ST GARAGE (THE) cor Thames and Franklin—see page 18	Bristol
Main St Garage 105 Main	Warren

Autos to Let

FRANKLIN ST GARAGE (THE) cor Thames and Franklin—see page 18	Bristol

Bakers

Gibbs Reuben A Washington W B	Barrington
MALAFRONTE BROTHERS 264 Wood—see page 19	Bristol
Morte P Della & Sons 537 Wood	Bristol
Nelle Charles F 184 Thames	Bristol
Sodini & Guesti 51 State	Bristol
Nadeau Philip H 127 Child	Warren
Peters & Santos 6 Market	Warren
Piekarnia Polska 28 Market	Warren
Premier Bakery 89 Market	Warren
SANITARY MARKET & HOME BAKERY cor Main and Liberty—see page 25	Warren

Banks

INDUSTRIAL TRUST CO Bristol Branch 525 Hope—see front cover also insert in centre of book	Bristol
INDUSTRIAL TRUST CO Warren Branch Main cor Market—see front cover also insert in centre of book	Warren

Barbers

Baker Herbert W 99 Bradford	Bristol
De Federico Aniello 495 Wood	Bristol
De Felice & Gennaro 433 Wood	Bristol
De Palmer Joseph 125 Franklin	Bristol
Ferraro Vincenzo 446 Hope	Bristol
Ferreira Adolph 155 Bradford	Bristol
Guinta Joseph 475 Hope	Bristol
Langello Frank 237 State	Bristol
Millemaggi Paul C 148 Bradford	Bristol
Pearce Frank K 559 Hope	Bristol
Riccardi Carlo 359 Wood	Bristol
Santulli Nicholas 57 State	Bristol
Calcagno Joseph 8 Market	Warren
Capuccilli Michele cor N Main and N Water	Warren
Gennaro Gallucci 61 N Main	Warren

COLLECTIONS AND CREDIT REPORTS
Our service is as near as your telephone. We will gladly furnish names of clients whom you know, who are satisfied users of our service. Tel. Union 1526

Western Mercantile Corporation, Providence, R. I.

BRISTOL COUNTY BUSINESS DIRECTORY. 209

Guli Stanley 65 N Water	Warren
Healey Charles H 141 S Main	Warren
Healey Joseph E 5 Child	Warren
Iervolino Michele 54 N Water	Warren
Lervolino Adamo 96 N Main	Warren
Mondina Severe 31 Market	Warren
Petrella Alexandro 172½ S Main	Warren
Sarao Silvino 25 N Water	Warren

Belting, Hose and Packing

National India Rubber Co Wood nr Bradford	Bristol

Bicycle Dealer

Burgess William A 20 Miller cor N Water	Warren

Bicycle Dealers and Repairers

Glancy Frederick 70 N Water	Warren
MacKenzie William M 24 Child	Warren

Blacksmiths

Pary Alfred W B	Barrington
DAGENAIS JOSEPH A rear 281 Thames—see page 21	Bristol
STUART RICHARD S ft of State—see page 21	Bristol
Burke James W ft of Church	Warren
Cole William R Market	Warren

Boarding and Livery Stable

WOOD O L 23 Court—see page 21	Bristol

Boarding House (Summer)

GRAND VIEW HOUSE Prudence Island—see page 16	Bristol

Boarding Houses

THE GABLES (Mary L Precourt prop) Mathewson rd—see page 26	Barrington
Mathewson House (W F Thompson prop) Mathewson av	Barrington
Brown Alice C 399 Hope	Bristol
Church Street House 5 Church	Bristol
Gearns Mary A Mrs 96 Thames	Bristol
Revere House 9 Church	Bristol
Lafrance Wilhelmina Mrs ft of Summer	Warren

R. I. RUG WORKS RUG CLEANING, CARPET CLEANING AND LAYING
678 WESTMINSTER ST., PROVIDENCE. Telephones Union 2203 and 2204

WARDWELL LUMBER CO.
YOU'LL FIND IT AT WARDWELL LUMBER CO., IF YOU FIND IT IN TOWN.
BRISTOL, R. I.

All Kinds of
BUILDING MATERIAL
at LOWEST PRICES

Boat Builders and Repairers

HERRESHOFF MFG CO INC Hope opp Burnside and 20 Burnside—see page 5	Bristol
Maxwell & Goddard Poppasquash rd	Bristol
Moore George F 7 Howe	Bristol
Covo George H rear 121 S Water	Warren

Boat Storage

HERRESHOFF MFG CO INC Hope opp Burnside and 20 Burnside—see page 5	Bristol

Book and Job Printers

WARREN PRINTING & PUBLISHING CO State nr Main—see page 22	Warren

Boot and Shoe Dealers

Butler's Shoe Store 452 Hope	Bristol
Naroditzky Samuel 302 Hope	Bristol
Nerone Augustine P 561 Hope	Bristol
PANZARELLA A C 401 Wood—see page 19	Bristol
Turrillo Michael 346 Wood	Bristol
Bander Joseph M 135 S Main	Warren
Silverman Jacob 6 Market	Warren
Warren Shoe Co cor S Main and Child	Warren

Boot and Shoe Repairers

Capocchiano John 572 Wood	Bristol
Levy Louis 35 State	Bristol
Mazza Antonio 124 Franklin	Bristol
Millemaggi Carmel 148 Bradford	Bristol
Naroditzky Samuel 302 Hope	Bristol
Tammaro Carlo 419 Wood	Bristol
Varolo Peter 43 Bradford	Bristol
Bacon Oliver 100 S Water	Warren
Daniel Angelo 29 N Water	Warren
Kozik Sebastian 12 West	Warren
Natel John B Goff's Hotel blk	Warren
Palmieri Ernesto 98 N Main	Warren
Saviano Gennara 39 N Water	Warren
Warren Shoe Co cor S Main and Child	Warren
Znamirowski Leopold 88 N Water	Warren

Bottlers

Morris Bros 300 Thames	Bristol
McDonough Bottle Store Joyce nr Main	Warren

Bowling Alley

O'Neil Martin W Market	Warren

WALTER H. JACKSON CO. 435 Industrial Trust Building
PROVIDENCE, R. I.
"DELCO" ELECTRIC LIGHTING & PUMPING PLANTS
WINDMILLS, GASOLINE ENGINES AND TRACTORS

Brick, Lime and Cement

ADAMS WM H & SON Bay Spring av—see
    page 27   West Barrington
WARDWELL LUMBER CO Thames ft Bradford—see head lines   Bristol

Brick Manufacturers

Barrington Steam Brick Co off Maple av across
    R R tracks   Barrington

Broker

Watson Elmer K (factory and industrial) Saugy
    bldg   Warren

Building Materials

BOSWORTH L P Broad at R R crossing—see
    page 26   Barrington
WARDWELL LUMBER CO Thames ft of Bradford—see head lines   Bristol
MARTIN E M LUMBER CO ft of Church—see
    page 23   Warren

Building Mover

ROUNDS SPENCER 17 Pierce av—see page 21   Bristol

Butcher

Paine Joshua A Lincoln av cor Walnut W B   Barrington

Cabinet Maker

Dunbar Howard B 361 Hope   Bristol

Cameras and Supplies

SHERMAN HAROLD G 399 Wood—see page 19   Bristol

Carpets and Rugs

BELL WILLIAM H 361-365 Hope—see page 20   Bristol

Carpenters and Builders

Bliss Irving W Rumstick rd   Barrington
LORD THOMAS A First—see page 27   West Barrington
Ball Sumner A   Bristol
Buffum Joseph L Gooding av   Bristol
Doran Dennis J 99 Franklin   Bristol
ROUNDS SPENCER 17 Pierce av—see page 21   Bristol

WHITTEMORE & COLBURN
PRINTERS   15 Pine St., PROV.

JAMES C. GOFF CO. Sole Agents for   **ATLAS**
31 to 49 POINT ST.   **Portland Cement**
Providence, R. I.

BRISTOL COUNTY BUSINESS DIRECTORY.

Wall Charles W 278 Hope — Bristol
Lapane A J Cornell av — Warren
Loughran Thomas J rear 55 Child — Warren
McCann Michael F Railroad av — Warren
Mercier William Z 88 Market — Warren
MONAST WILFRED A 63 Metacom av—see page 24 — Warren
Smith Richard 269 S Main — Warren

Carriage Painter

TORREY E F 1039 Hope—see page 21 — Bristol

Caterers

Maxfield Julia A 6 Federal — Warren

Cigar Manufacturer

Gardner David V 8 Market — Warren

Cigars and Tobacco

GRANT JAMES F County rd cor Rumstick—see page 27 — Barrington
BUFFINGTON WILLIAM H 458 Hope—see page 20 — Bristol
SHERMAN HAROLD G 399 Wood—see page 19 — Bristol
YOUNG J H & CO 479 Hope—see page 20 — Bristol
Bedard Delphice L 96½ N Main — Warren
BENNETT W S & CO cor Main and Joyce—see page 27 — Warren
BLISS CHARLES C Goff's Hotel—see page 25 — Warren
Family Drug Store The (Dr C E Scott) 27 Child — Warren
Maddox William 33 Joyce — Warren
New York Store The (A H Morino) 33 N Water — Warren
ROBERTS OSCAR 46 N Main—see page 24 — Warren
STANDARD PHARMACY cor Main and Miller—see page 25 — Warren

Circulating Library

DARLING HENRY M 444 Hope—see page 20 — Bristol

Civil Engineers

PERRY WILLIAM W 814 Hope—see page 21 — Bristol
ESTES CHARLES Touisset rd—see page 24 — Warren
Estes Joseph C 111 N Main — Warren

Clergymen

Albanese Francis Maple av — Barrington
Chapin William M (Episcopal) B — Barrington
Prentice A Canada (Cong) County rd — Barrington

RALPH C. WATROUS CO.
Real Estate Auctioneers
437 INDUSTRIAL TRUST BUILDING

BRISTOL COUNTY BUSINESS DIRECTORY.

Allen Annie S (P) 154 Wood — Bristol
Cahill Albert L (R C) 330 Wood — Bristol
Constance Mary G (P) 154 Wood — Bristol
Gillan Thomas J (R C) 330 Wood — Bristol
Howard Anson B (E) 15 Church — Bristol
Locke George L (E) 45 Woodlawn av — Bristol
McGilton Adam Clark (M E) 129 State — Bristol
Poja Joseph (R C) 141 State — Bristol
Rebbelo Antonio P (R C) 577 Wood — Bristol
Wallace O H (B) 85 Union — Bristol
Whitley John E (Cong) 35 Church — Bristol
Caron Elfhege (R C) cor Main and Hope — Warren
Colgan Edward J Rev (R C) 215 S Main — Warren
Nissen Louis Peters (E) Union cor Liberty — Warren
Spear Francis H (M E) 9 Church — Warren
Watjen Herman W Rev (B) 8 Miller — Warren

Clothing Dealers

CONNERY WILLIAM M 491 Hope—see page 18 — Bristol
Dimond Frank 462-4 Hope — Bristol
Makowsky Max 55 State — Bristol
Suzman Fred E 533 Hope — Bristol
Bander Joseph M 135 S Main — Warren
Marks Nathan N Water and Miller — Warren
Silverman Jacob 6 Market — Warren

Coal Dealers

BOSWORTH L P Broad at R R crossing—see page 26 — Barrington
Paull Seth Co 267 Thames — Bristol
STAPLES COAL CO OF R I 239 Thames—see page 5 — Bristol
Paguin Victor 87 N Main — Warren
STAPLES COAL CO OF R I 137 S Water—see page 5 — Warren

Coated Fabrics

O'BANNON CORPORATION Park av—see page 5 — West Barrington

Combed and Carded Yarns

WARREN MFG CO ft of Bowen—see page 7 — Warren

Concreting

CALLAN L H COL 237 Franklin—see page 4 — Bristol

Blackstone Canal Nat'l Bank | **BEST FACILITIES**
20 MARKET SQ., PROVIDENCE | **Prompt Attention**

WARREN MONUMENTAL WORKS
Cor. Railroad Avenue and Croade Streets, Warren, R. I.

Confectionery

GRANT JAMES F County rd cor Rumstick—see page 27	Barrington
BUFFINGTON WILLIAM H 458 Hope—see page 20	Bristol
DARLING HENRY M 444 Hope—see page 20	Bristol
Dracoules Bros 473 Hope	Bristol
Goglia Luigi 374 Wood	Bristol
Hope Drug Co 297 Hope	Bristol
King Joseph L 467 Hope	Bristol
NORTHUP BROS 539 Hope—see page 16	Bristol
Rounds Hiram A 1066 Hope	Bristol
SHERMAN HAROLD G 399 Wood—see page 19	Bristol
YOUNG J H & CO 479 Hope—see page 20	Bristol
Bedard Delphice L 96½ N Main	Warren
BENNETT W S & CO cor Main and Joyce—see page 27	Warren
BLISS CHARLES C Goff's Hotel—see page 25	Warren
Family Drug Store The (Dr C E Scott) 27 Child	Warren
New York Store The (A H Morino) 33 N Water	Warren
Olive A & A T South Main cor State	Warren
STANDARD PHARMACY cor Main and Miller —see page 25	Warren

Contractors

Lamson Morton G West rd B C	Barrington
LORD THOMAS A First—see page 27	W Barrington
Buffum Joseph L Gooding av	Bristol
CALLAN L H COL 237 Franklin—see page 4	Bristol
CARD PELEG & SON 10 Washington—see page 21	Bristol
Le Clair Eugene (mason) 19 Thames	Bristol
Dube E J 30 Franklin	Warren
Lawson William 118 Child	Warren
McCann Michael F Railroad av	Warren
MONAST WILFRED A 63 Metacom av—see page 24	Warren
West John R (mason) 10 Lyndon	Warren

Convalescent Home

Rockwell Martha B S Convalescent Home 41 Usher place	Bristol

Cottage Lots for Sale

ALDRICH CHARLES A Prudence Island—see page 16	Bristol

NATIONAL EXCHANGE BANK One of the Oldest and Strongest Banks
63 Westminster St., Providence   In Rhode Island

BRISTOL COUNTY BUSINESS DIRECTORY.

Cotton Goods
Parker Mill No 2 100 Metacom av — Warren

Crockery and Glassware
BELL WILLIAM H 361-365 Hope—see page 20 — Bristol

Cut Flowers
Congdon Giles S 69 Court — Bristol
KINDER SAMUEL & BRO 317 Hope — see page 18 — Bristol
BARKER LOUIS F Barker av—see page 25 — Warren

Cut Glass, etc.
KUNZ EDWARD D 469 Hope—see page 20 — Bristol

Dentists
Church Howard W 471 Hope — Bristol
Gallup Jennie H Miss 617 Hope — Bristol
Gallup Julius C 617 Hope — Bristol
Mason Frederick L 92 State — Bristol
O'Brien Michael J 497 Hope — Bristol
Tobin William J 101 Bradford — Bristol
Denby John 172 S Main — Warren
Gilleran Lawrence F Saugy bldg — Warren
Pratt Henry E Main — Warren
Seymour Louis R 140 S Main — Warren

Doors, Sash and Blinds
BOSWORTH L P Broad at R R crossing—see page 26 — Barrington
WARDWELL LUMBER CO ft of Bradford—see head lines — Bristol
MARTIN E M LUMBER CO ft of Church—see page 23 — Warren

Dressmakers
Hanley Amy F B — Barrington
Balfour Elizabeth C 409 Hope — Bristol
Carter Annie C Mrs 736 Hope — Bristol
Cole Elizabeth Mrs 108 Union — Bristol
DeWolf Florence E 31 Catherine — Bristol
Eaton Ida 329 Hope — Bristol
Gardner Mabel L 145 High — Bristol
Ingraham Mary M 1059 Hope — Bristol

Merewether & Dunn
Plumbing and Heating Contractors
31 TURNER AVENUE,   RIVERSIDE, R. I.

| Gasoline Engines Pumps Wind Mills Tanks, Towers Irrigation Spray Goods | **Established 1876** **CHARLES J. JAGER CO.** 33 Canal St., Providence, R. I. | Automatic Pressure Systems Electric Pumps Well Supplies Repairs And Accessories |

Lee James Mrs 21 Cook — Bristol
Luther Elizabeth B 31 Constitution — Bristol
Paull Seraphine B 42 Franklin — Bristol
Pearse Mabel R 115 High — Bristol
Peckham Harriet L 702 Hope — Bristol
Simmons Hattie L 27 Cook — Bristol
Slade Cecelia G 103 Bay View av — Bristol
Whittemore Alfratta M Miss 201 High — Bristol
Bowen Mary S 189 S Main — Warren
Donohue Mary 27 Broad — Warren
Place Rachael Miss 23 State — Warren
Redfern Elizabeth F Mrs Sowamsett av — Warren
Saillant Addie Mrs 12 Barney — Warren
Smith Annie 25 Market — Warren
Twombley Fannie C 73 N Water — Warren
Ward Katherine T Miss 63 Child — Warren
Wilcox Delia H 189 S Main — Warren

Druggists

BUFFINGTON WILLIAM H 458 Hope—see page 20 — Bristol
Hope Drug Co 297 Hope — Bristol
SHERMAN HAROLD G 399 Wood—see page 19 — Bristol
YOUNG J H & CO 479 Hope—see page 20 — Bristol
BENNETT W S & CO cor Main and Joyce—see page 27 — Warren
Family Drug Store The (Dr C E Scott) 27 Child — Warren
Hope Pharmacy 127 S Main — Warren
ROBERTS OSCAR 46 N Main—see page 24 — Warren
Smith William J & Co 137 S Main — Warren
STANDARD PHARMACY cor Main and Miller —see page 25 — Warren

Dry Goods

Dimond Frank M 462 and 464 Hope — Bristol
Eisenstadt Abraham 419 Hope — Bristol
Goldstein Israel 31 State — Bristol
Hamill Dry Goods Store 499 Hope — Bristol
Jamial George & Son 45 State — Bristol
MALAFRONTE BROS 264 Wood—see page 19 — Bristol
Molasky Jacob 44 State — Bristol
PANZARELLA A C 401 Wood—see page 19 — Bristol
Besaw Charles Saugy bldg — Warren
Gildert Peter 140 Child — Warren
Heon Edward F 63 N Water — Warren
Jamial George & Son Miller cor Water — Warren
Rybarczyk P M 14 Child — Warren
Thibaudeau J Alexander 143 S Main — Warren
Wehby George 5 Miller — Warren

OUR CREDIT REPORTS TELL—Whom to trust; whom not to trust; who pay promptly; who pay slowly; who never pay their bills except under pressure.   Telephone Union 1526
Western Mercantile Corporation, Providence, R. I.

BRISTOL COUNTY BUSINESS DIRECTORY. 217

Dye Manufacturers
Warren Dye Co 147 S Water   Warren

Electrical Appliances
TALBOT & HOPKINS 53 Bradford—see page 4   Bristol
BLACKMAR C R JR 2 Church—see page 22   Warren

Electric Light Companies
Bristol County Gas & Electric Co 327 Hope   Bristol
Bristol County Gas & Electric Co 124 S Main   Warren

Electrical Contractors
TALBOT & HOPKINS 53 Bradford—see page 4   Bristol
BLACKMAR C R JR 2 Church—see page 22   Warren
JOHNSON FREDERICK I 7 Lyndon—see page 24   Warren

Electricians
TALBOT & HOPKINS 53 Bradford—see page 4   Bristol
BLACKMAR C R JR 2 Church—see page 22   Warren
JOHNSON FREDERICK I 7 Lyndon — see page 24   Warren

Embalmers
Simmons George W (est of) 104 Constitution   Bristol
WILBUR GEORGE M 38 Union—see page 22   Bristol
WILBUR GEORGE M 209 S Main—see page 22   Warren

Emigration Agent
MALAFRONTE LUIGI 270 Wood—see page 19   Bristol

Expresses
Crossman E A Washington P O, W B   Barrington
Adams Express Co 563 Hope   Bristol
Adams Express Co (F J Conley agt) S Main cor Joyce   Warren

Fancy Yarns
CRANSTON WORSTED MILLS Thames near Church—see page 5   Bristol

Farming Implements
WARDWELL LUMBER CO Thames ft of Bradford—see head lines   Bristol

---

R. I. RUG WORKS
Rugs Woven from old and new carpets.   Telephones { 2203 / 2204
678 WESTMINSTER ST.,   PROVIDENCE

WARDWELL LUMBER CO. (You'll find it at Wardwell Lumber Co. if you find it in town) **LUMBER**
BRISTOL, R. I. **LATH SHINGLES**

BRISTOL COUNTY BUSINESS DIRECTORY.

Ferry

Prudence Island Transportation Co (H Chase)
    Church St dock   Bristol

Fire Insurance

SKINNER P JR 259 Hope—see page 28   Bristol

Fish Markets

Burke William 13 State   Bristol
Gladding Theodore O 219 Thames   Bristol
Shepard W Mrs 205 Thames   Bristol
Brown Edward V r 183 S Water   Warren
Cape Ann Fish Co (wholesale) Green's landing   Warren
Maxfield Arthur J Coomer av   Warren
Rubery William 7 Child   Warren

Five and Ten Cent Stores

Ideal 5 & 10c Store Saugy bldg   Warren
Titmas Harry G 163-165 Main   Warren

Floral Designs

Congdon Giles S 69 Court   Bristol
GEISLER FREDERICK A 122 Mt Hope av—
    see page 4   Bristol
KINDER SAMUEL & BRO 317 Hope — see
    page 18   Bristol
BARKER LOUIS F Barker av—see page 25   Warren

Florists

Crawshaw James Upland Way N   Barrington
Hampden Meadows Greenhouses   Barrington
Black Robert A Sherry av   Bristol
Booth Starr L rear 202 High   Bristol
Congdon Giles S 69 Court   Bristol
GEISLER FREDERICK A 122 Mt Hope av—
    see page 18   Bristol
Barker Francis P Middle off Child   Warren
BARKER LOUIS F Barker av—see page 25   Warren
Barney Bros Metacom av and Parker av   Warren
Rodgers James 20 Vernon   Warren
Seymour Eugene R 151 Child   Warren

Ford Service

COLE GEORGE R 27 Baker—see page 23   Warren

Fruit and Confectionery

Felson Joseph 376 Hope   Bristol

| Water Supply Outfits House Pumps | **Walter H. Jackson Co.** 435 Industrial Trust Building Providence, - R. I. | "Dodd" System Lightning PROTECTION |

Funeral Directors

Simmons George W (est of) 104 Constitution — Bristol
WILBUR GEORGE M 38 Union—see page 22 — Bristol
WILBUR GEORGE M 209 S Main—see page 22 — Warren

Furniture Dealers

BELL WILLIAM H 361-365 Hope—see page 20 — Bristol
Lightfoot Davenport & Co 151 Bradford — Bristol
Reed House Furnishing Co 30 Bradford — Bristol
Marks Nathan North Water and Miller — Warren
Reed House Furnishing Co 14 and 16 Child — Warren

Furniture Mover

Roderick Antonio 20 State — Bristol

Garages

Bristol Auto Shop 750 Hope — Bristol
CENTRAL GARAGE 41 Church—see page 21 — Bristol
FRANKLIN ST GARAGE THE cor Thames and Franklin—see page 18 — Bristol
Ryone & Farr Constitution nr Hope — Bristol
COLE GEORGE R 27 Baker—see page 23 — Warren
Gagnon Henry C Market — Warren
Main St Garage 105 Main — Warren

Gardeners

Bristol Floral Co (F C F Geisler mgr) 583 Hope — Bristol
GEISLER FREDERICK A 122 Mt Hope av—see page 4 — Bristol
KINDER SAMUEL & BRO 317 Hope — see page 18 — Bristol

Gas Companies

Bristol County Gas & Electric Co 327 Hope — Bristol
Bristol County Gas & Electric Co 124 S Main — Warren

Gasoline and Oil

GRANT JAMES F County rd cor Rumstick—see page 27 — Barrington
CENTRAL GARAGE 41 Church—see page 21 — Bristol
FRANKLIN ST GARAGE THE cor Thames and Franklin—see page 18 — Bristol
COLE GEORGE R 27 Baker—see page 23 — Warren
Standard Oil Yard Franklin nr R R tracks — Warren

WHITTEMORE & COLBURN
PRINTERS   15 Pine St., PROV.

Gents' Furnishings

CONNERY WILLIAM M 491 Hope—see page 18 Bristol
David Abraham 301 Hope Bristol
Goldstein & Schwartz 581 Hope Bristol
PANZARELLA A C 401 Wood—see page 19 Bristol
Besaw Charles J Saugy bldg Warren
Marks Nathan North Water and Miller Warren

Granite Dealers

WARREN MONUMENTAL WORKS 32 Railroad av—see head lines Warren

Grocers

BAY SPRING PUBLIC MARKET cor Bay Spring av and Narragansett—see page 26 West Barrington
BOSWORTH LEONARD P Broad B C—see page 26 Barrington
Bowden Elmer F Blanding av Bay Spring W B Barrington
Gibbs Reuben A Washington W B Barrington
MAYOTT & OGDEN Bay Spring av—see page 26 West Barrington
Smith Mary R Mrs Bay Spring av cor Lake av W B Barrington
Townend Percy Shore av W B Barrington
Bassing Samuel I 178 Thames Bristol
Benjamin Lewis 254 Wood Bristol
Biagio Del Toro 23 Catherine Bristol
Campenello Bros 219 Wood Bristol
Carreia Almeida E 281 Thames Bristol
Castroitto John 431 Wood Bristol
Castriotto L 324 High Bristol
Clarke & Manchester 96 High Bristol
Clerico Alfred 257 Wood Bristol
De Federico Francesco Wood Bristol
Dimond Charles F 174 High Bristol
Eisenstadt Maurice 1 State Bristol
Frederico Frank 215 Wood Bristol
Furtado Joseph M 421 Wood Bristol
FURTADO J ROSA 229 State—see page 19 Bristol
Gambardella Luigi 26 Mt Hope av Bristol
Gilroy John F 75 Franklin Bristol
GIUSTIANY PETER 247 Thames—see page 19 Bristol
GOFF'S MARKET cor High and Lincoln av—see page 20 Bristol
Great A & P Tea Co The 583 Hope Bristol
Janson's Market 22 State Bristol
Johnson Charles A 678 Hope Bristol

RALPH C. WATROUS CO.
RESIDENTIAL and INVESTMENT PROPERTY
Of All Kinds For Sale
487 Industrial Trust Building

BRISTOL COUNTY BUSINESS DIRECTORY.   221

Kebrek Pauline Mrs 255 Wood	Bristol
Kirk Saukis opp R R depot	Bristol
Liberty Market 217 High	Bristol
Lombardi Gaetano 174 Bradford	Bristol
Lopes Francisco 149 Bradford	Bristol
MALAFRONTE DOMINIC 264 Wood — see page 19	Bristol
Malafronte Tony 239 State	Bristol
Mayflower Store The 541 Hope	Bristol
McCaw Samuel 179 High	Bristol
Miller Archibald M 557 Hope	Bristol
Molasky Louis M 238 Thames	Bristol
Montagna Antonio Wood and Roma	Bristol
Nelle Charles F 184 Thames	Bristol
Newman Bros 296-300 Hope	Bristol
Nussenfeld Samuel 237 Thames	Bristol
O'Reilly Vincent A 52 Mt Hope av	Bristol
Paull Marion H Mrs cor Hope and Franklin	Bristol
Pepe Francesco 429 Wood	Bristol
Perry William Court	Bristol
Pozzi Giovanni 139 Bradford	Bristol
Quirk Bros (Edward J Quirk) 173 State	Bristol
Romano Pasquale 220 State	Bristol
Sansone Pasquale 117 Bradford	Bristol
Sarra Michael 213 State	Bristol
Sousa A C 503 Wood	Bristol
SOUSA ANTONY J 157 Bradford—see page 19	Bristol
Troiano Matteio 570 Wood	Bristol
Vargas Antonio 198 Thames	Bristol
Xavier Julius F Franklin cor Wood	Bristol
Batchelor John B S Main cor Child	Warren
Brown Mary Mrs 211 S Main	Warren
Burke Martin 45 Market	Warren
COLE GEORGE R 27 Baker—see page 23	Warren
De Bease Vincenzo 25 N Main	Warren
DIONNE CHARLES 140 Child—see page 25	Warren
Excelsior Grocery & Market 191-193 S Main	Warren
Gildert Peter 140 Child	Warren
Great A & P Tea Co 135 Main	Warren
Grzbian Zygmund 69 N Water	Warren
HAWTHORNE HUGH 174 S Main—see page 25	Warren
Jannetti Angelo 41 N Water	Warren
Janson Alphonse 79-81 N Water	Warren
Krawczyk John 66 N Water	Warren

Blackstone Canal Nat'l Bank
20 Market Sq., Prov. R. I.

A Progressive Bank
Fully Equipped for
Service

Warren Monumental Works
Cor. Railroad Avenue and Croade Street, Warren, R. I.

Lemieux Louis 47 N Water — Warren
Liberty Store Co The Goff's block — Warren
Ludwig William 32 Child — Warren
Luz Manuel 104 S Water — Warren
Maloy John M 1-3 N Water — Warren
Maxfield Charles S 308 S Main — Warren
Mayflower Store The 167 S Main — Warren
Messier Charles O Franklin nr Cutler — Warren
Muccino Dominic A 42 N Main — Warren
Paquin Napoleon 80 and 84 N Main — Warren
Para L Onesime Metacom av nr Child — Warren
Ratier Alfred 7 Handy — Warren
ROSA MANUEL P 129 Child—see page 25 — Warren
Rubery William 7 Child — Warren
SANITARY MARKET & HOME BAKERY cor Main and Liberty—see page 25 — Warren
SOCHA JOHN M 86 N Water—see page 25 — Warren

Hacks to Let

WOOD O L 23 Court—see page 21 — Bristol

Handkerchief Manufacturers

Duitt Mfg Co 197 S Main — Warren
Warren Handkerchief Co 111 S Water cor Baker — Warren

Hardware, Cutlery, Tools etc.

Miller Archibald M 557 Hope — Bristol
Remieres Frank T 573 Hope — Bristol
WALDRON CO (THE) 49 Bradford—see page 2 — Bristol
WARDWELL LUMBER CO Thames ft of Bradford—see head lines — Bristol
Angell W H Hardware Co S Main — Warren
Phillips Bernard 80 N Water — Warren
Sparks Charles H 124 S Main — Warren

Harness Maker

Smith George 76 State — Bristol
Mackenzie William M 24 Child — Warren

Hats and Caps

CONNERY WILLIAM M 491 Hope—see page 18 — Bristol

Hay and Grain

BOSWORTH L P Broad at R R crossing—see page 26 — Barrington
Peck John D Thames nr Franklin — Bristol
Peck John D Cole nr Croade — Warren

NATIONAL EXCHANGE BANK, 63 Westminster St., Providence
Stands First on "ROLL of HONOR" Among R. I. Banks. We respectfully ask for Your Account

BRISTOL COUNTY BUSINESS DIRECTORY. 223

Heating (Hot Water and Steam)
ALLEN GEORGE E CO Fourth—see page 27
    West Barrington

Horseshoers (see also Blacksmiths)
DAGENAIS JOSEPH A rear 281 Thames—see
  page 21   Bristol
STUART RICHARD S ft of State—see page 21   Bristol

Hotel (Summer)
GRAND VIEW HOUSE Prudence Island—see
  page 16   Bristol

Hotels
BRISTOL HOTEL (J F McLaughlin prop) 24
  State—see page 20   Bristol
DeWolf Inn (private) 173 Thames   Bristol
HOTEL BELVEDERE Hope opp Post Office—
  see page 18   Bristol
Ye Anchor Inn (H J Allen prop) 190 Hope   Bristol
Goff's Hotel (formerly Cole's Hotel) (John F Mc-
  Donough prop) S Main cor Joyce   Warren
Lonergan James H S Main cor Joyce   Warren

House Furnishings
BELL WILLIAM H 361-365 Hope—see page 20   Bristol

Ice Cream Dealers
Dracoules Bros 473 Hope   Bristol
Maxfield Julia A Mrs 6 Federal   Warren
Olive A & A T South Main cor State   Warren
Smith James H 139 S Main   Warren

Ice Cream Manufacturers
NORTHUP BROS 539 Hope—see page 16   Bristol
Maxfield Julia A Mrs 6 Federal   Warren

Ice Dealers
Leonard Augustus B Drown W B   Barrington
Leahy John Metacom av nr Chestnut   Bristol
Morris Bros 300 Thames   Bristol
Vermette Alphonse 410 Thames   Bristol
Tanner Bros 10 Child   Warren

Merewether & Dunn
Plumbing and Heating Contractors
31 TURNER AVENUE,   RIVERSIDE, R. L.

33 Canal St. CHARLES J. JAGER CO. Providence

ELECTRIC AND GASOLINE PUMPS AND PRESSURE SYSTEMS
We carry the largest stock of this kind in New England

BRISTOL COUNTY BUSINESS DIRECTORY.

India Rubber Goods Manufacturers
NATIONAL INDIA RUBBER CO Wood opp
    Bradford—see page 6   Bristol

Insurance Agents
Drury John Temple Drury blk   Bristol
SKINNER P JR 259 Hope—see page 28   Bristol
Straight Clark H 329 Hope   Bristol
Fielding John nr 151 Warren   Warren
MARTIN E M LUMBER CO ft of Church—see
    page 23   Warren

Investment Securities
SKINNER P JR 259 Hope—see page 28   Bristol

Jewelers and Watch Repairers
Cohen Louis F Church cor Hope   Bristol
Markoff Aaron E 657 Hope   Bristol
KUNZ EDWARD D 469 Hope—see page 20   Bristol
MAKER ARTHUR J 163 S Main—see page 24   Warren

Jewelers' Tools
Bosworth E B & Son Manning   Warren

Job Printers
FARRALLY BROS 547 Hope—see page 17   Bristol
WARREN PRINTING & PUBLISHING CO
    State nr Main—see page 22   Warren

Junk Dealer
Brown Jacob State   Bristol

Kitchen Furnishings
WALDRON CO THE 49 Bradford—see page 2   Bristol
WARDWELL LUMBER CO Thames ft of Bradford—see head lines   Bristol

Lace Manufacturers
Rhode Island Lace Works Park av south track
    W B   Barrington

Ladies' Tailor
DAVID ABRAHAM 301 Hope—see opp page 45   Bristol

Laundries
Chin Charlie 577 Hope   Bristol
Wah Sam 577 Hope   Bristol
Wing Moy 33 State   Bristol
Gee Chin 6 Baker   Warren
Warren Hand Laundry 35 Joyce   Warren
White Sanford C (agent) 9 Bridge   Warren

LIVE WIRE collectors of BAD BILLS
"No Collection—No Charge"
WESTERN MERCANTILE CORPORATION
420-421 Grosvenor Building. Tel. Union 1526 Providence, R. I.

BRISTOL COUNTY BUSINESS DIRECTORY. 225

Lawyers
Bosworth Orrin L 652 Hope (also Prov)	Bristol
Hammill Frank H 54 State	Bristol
Lavender James F 54 State	Bristol
Leahy Edward L 18 High (also Prov)	Bristol
Lindemuth Benjamin F G 471 Hope (also Prov)	Bristol
O'Donnell William T 471 Hope	Bristol
Cooke George L 145 S Main (also Prov)	Warren
Mason Charles B 145 S Main	Warren
McSoley William H 8 Child (also Prov)	Warren
Morrissey Daniel H 76 N Main	Warren

Leather Goods Dealer
Wilmarth Anna E 11 Baker	Warren

Leather Manufacturers (Imitation)
O'BANNON CORPORATION Park av—see page 5
West Barrington

Liquor Dealers
Breen Bernard 5 John	Bristol
BRISTOL HOTEL 24 State—see page 20	Bristol
Bruno Bros 157 Bradford	Bristol
De Felice Bros 164 Bradford	Bristol
MALAFRONTE LUIGI 270 Wood—see page 19	Bristol
Manchester Henry R 206 Thames	Bristol
Morris Bros 300 Thames	Bristol
Murphy Hugh 171 Bradford	Bristol
Peterson Robert H 18 State	Bristol
Puggino Alfonso 410 Wood	Bristol
Quinn Edward A 220 Thames	Bristol
Silva Joseph 162 Bradford	Bristol
Asselin Napoleon 29 Market	Warren
Bliss & Co (wholesale) 105 Child	Warren
Buff Luigi 42 N Main	Warren
Hotel Warren S Main cor Joyce	Warren
Nelle Martin T 71 S Water	Warren
O'Neil Patrick W 59 N Main	Warren
Parks James Metacom av	Warren
Rybarczyk Wicenty 12 N Water	Warren
Sherry Patrick W 57 N Water	Warren
Vitullo Joseph North Main cor North Water	Warren

Livery Stables
WOOD O L 23 Court—see page 21	Bristol
Munroe Edward Cutler and Child	Warren

R. I. RUG WORKS
Furniture Repaired and Repolished, Chairs Reseated
678 Westminster Street, Providence. Telephone Union 2306 and also Union 2304

WARDWELL LUMBER CO.
BRISTOL, R. I.

WINDOWS
WINDOW FRAMES
DOORS AND BLINDS
At Lowest Prices

226   BRISTOL COUNTY BUSINESS DIRECTORY.

Lubricating Saddles

Dixon Lubricating Saddle Co 182 High   Bristol

Lumber Dealers

BOSWORTH L P Broad at R R crossing—see
    page 26-   Barrington
Paull Seth Co 267 Thames   Bristol
WARDWELL LUMBER CO Thames ft of Brad-
    ford—see head lines   Bristol
MARTIN E M LUMBER CO ft of Church—see
    page 23   Warren

Lunch Rooms

BROWN GEORGE 5 Bradford—see page 20   Bristol
Lindley Benjamin I Thames cor Constitution   Bristol
NORTHUP BROS 539 Hope—see page 16   Bristol
Murphy John E Child cor Metacom av   Warren
O'Neil Martin W Market   Warren
Warren Restaurant (W J Lonergan prop) 35 Joyce   Warren

Machine Forging

DAGENAIS JOSEPH A rear 281 Thames—see
    page 21   Bristol

Machinists

Bosworth E B & Son Manning   Warren
POTTER COLLAMORE & CO cor Wheaton and
    S Water—see page 24   Warren

Manufacturing Companies

Barrington Steam Brick Co off Maple av across
    R R tracks   Barrington
O'BANNON CORPORATION Part av West
    Barrington—see page 5   Barrington
Rhode Island Lace Works Park av W B   Barrington
CRANSTON WORSTED MILLS Thames near
    Church—see page 5   Bristol
HERRESHOFF MFG CO INC 20 Burnside—see
    page 5   Bristol
NATIONAL INDIA RUBBER CO Wood opp
    Bradford—see page 5   Bristol
U S RUBBER CO Wood opp Bradford—see page 6   Bristol
Arnold George B (tag) 341 S Main   Warren
Duitt Mfg Co (handkerchief) 197 S Main   Warren
Mt Hope Spinning Co (tire fabric yarns) Cutler   Warren
Narragansett Worsted Co (worsted yarns) Frank-
    lin   Warren
Parker Mill Metacom av   Warren

WALTER H. JACKSON CO. 435 Industrial Trust Building
PROVIDENCE, R. I.
"DELCO" ELECTRIC LIGHTING & PUMPING PLANTS
WINDMILLS, GASOLINE ENGINES AND TRACTORS

BRISTOL COUNTY BUSINESS DIRECTORY. 227

Rope Braid Co Cutler cor Joyce — Warren
Swiss Textile Co Joyce — Warren
Warren Dye Co (dyes) 147 S Water — Warren
Warren Handkerchief Co 111 S Water cor Baker — Warren
WARREN MFG CO ft of Bowen—see page 7. — Warren

Marble and Granite Workers
WARREN MONUMENTAL WORKS 32 Railroad av—see head lines — Warren

Market Gardeners
Stone Henry M River rd junc Warren rd B — Barrington

Masons
Martin William R West rd H M — Barrington
CARD PELEG & SON 10 Washington — see page 21 — Bristol
Le Clair Eugene 19 Thames — Bristol
Murphy William G Sowamsett av — Warren
West John R 10 Lyndon — Warren

Masons' Supplies
ADAMS WILLIAM H & SON Bay Spring av—see page 27 — West Barrington

Meat Markets
BAY SPRING PUBLIC MARKET cor Bay Spring av and Narragansett—see page 26 — West Barrington
MAYOTT & OGDEN Bay Spring av—see page 26 — West Barrington
Viall Isaac F Washington nr P O, W B — Barrington
Wallis E F (wholesale) Bridge av B — Barrington
Bassing Samuel I 178 Thames — Bristol
Benjamin Lewis 254 Wood — Bristol
Dimond Charles F High — Bristol
Gilroy John F 75 Franklin — Bristol
GOFF'S MARKET cor High and Lincoln av—see page 20 — Bristol
GUISTIANY PETER 247 Thames—see page 19 — Bristol
Janson's Market 22 State — Bristol
Johnson Charles A 678 Hope — Bristol
Liberty Market 217 High — Bristol
Lopes Francisco 149 Bradford — Bristol

WHITTEMORE & COLBURN
PRINTERS   15 Pine St., PROV.

King's Fibrous Plaster Board & Hard Plaster
JAMES C. GOFF CO.
81 to 49 Point St., Prov., R. I.

McCaw Samuel 176 High	Bristol
Newman Bros 296-300 Hope	Bristol
Nussenfeld Samuel 237 Thames	Bristol
Paull Marion H Mrs cor Hope and Franklin	Bristol
PIMENTAL & SOUSA 217 Wood—see page 19	Bristol
Rawson & Easterbrooks 186 Wood	Bristol
Romio N 162½ Bradford	Bristol
Sansone Joseph 121 Bradford	Bristol
Sousa A C 503 Wood	Bristol
SOUSA ANTONY J 157 Bradford—see page 19	Bristol
Tani Alfred 12 State	Bristol
Batchelor John B Main cor Child	Warren
COLE GEORGE R 27 Baker—see page 23	Warren
De Bease Vincenzo 25 N Main	Warren
DIONNE CHARLES 140 Child—see page 25	Warren
Excelsior Grocery & Market 191 S Main	Warren
Grzbian Zygmund 69 N Water	Warren
Janson Alphonse 79-81 N Water	Warren
Kiawczyk John 66 N Water	Warren
Lemieux Louis 47 N Water	Warren
Ludwig William 28 Child	Warren
Maloy John M 1 and 3 N Water	Warren
Muccino Dominic A 42 N Main	Warren
Paquin Napoleon 80-84 N Main	Warren
ROSA MANUEL P 129 Child—see page 25	Warren
SANITARY MARKET & HOME BAKERY cor Main and Liberty—see page 25	Warren
SOCHA JOHN M 86 N Water—see page 25	Warren

Milk Dealers

Gilroy William Metacom av	Bristol
Smith William F Kickemuit av	Bristol
Wood Moses Metacom av	Bristol
Cole Elmer E Touisset rd	Warren
Gifford Charles E South Main at Bristol line	Warren
SHERMAN GEO E 93 Child—see page 23	Warren

Milliners

Bunn M S & Co 450 Hope	Bristol
Hughes Theresa 535 Hope	Bristol
Newman Irene M 295 Hope	Bristol
Rawson Susan D 41 Franklin	Bristol
Stanley Grace A Mrs 70 State	Bristol
Wilson Lillian T 450 Hope	Bristol
Bergeron Marie Mrs 63 Metacom av	Warren
Lariviere Hermine 159 S Main	Warren

Ralph C. Watrous Co. FARMS and SUBURBAN PROPERTY For Sale
437 INDUSTRIAL TRUST BUILDING

BRISTOL COUNTY BUSINESS DIRECTORY. 229

Mill Supplies
Dixon Lubricating Saddle Co 182 High   Bristol

Monuments and Monumental Works
WARREN MONUMENTAL WORKS 32 Railroad av—see head lines   Warren

Newsdealers
GRANT JAMES F County rd cor Rumstick—see page 27   Barrington
DARLING HENRY M 444 Hope—see page 20   Bristol
BLISS CHARLES C Goff's Hotel block—see page 25   Warren

Newspapers
BRISTOL PHOENIX (Farrally Bros props) 547 Hope—see page 17   Bristol
WARREN & BARRINGTON GAZETTE State nr Main—see page 22   Warren

Notaries Public (see Contents)
SHERMAN GEO E 93 Child—see page 23   Warren

Nurses
Medbury Lucy C   Barrington
Condon Ellen L 11 Franklin   Bristol
Graham Martha 68 Bay View av   Bristol
Lake Elizabeth 85 Union   Bristol
McCaughey Annie 849 Hope   Bristol
McCaughey Margaret 849 Hope   Bristol
Cole Frank B Mrs 7 Miller   Warren
Jones Nellie M 11 Lyndon   Warren
Warren District Nursing Association (N M Jones nurse) 11 Lyndon   Warren

Opticians
KUNZ EDWARD D 469 Hope—see page 20   Bristol
MAKER ARTHUR J 163 S Main—see page 24   Warren

Optometrist
MAKER ARTHUR J 163 S Main—see page 24   Warren

Oyster Growers and Shippers
Dodge John W Bay Spring W B   Barrington
Gladding Theodore O 219 Thames   Bristol

Blackstone Canal Nat'l Bank | Established 1831
20 MARKET SQ. PROVIDENCE | STRONG AND CONSERVATIVE

WARREN MONUMENTAL WORKS
Cor. Railroad Avenue and Croade Streets, Warren, R. I.

230   BRISTOL COUNTY BUSINESS DIRECTORY.

Atwood H & R ft of Washington	Warren
Blount Eddie B South Water bey Wheaton	Warren
Buckingham's Son B ft of Miller	Warren
Cape Ann Fish Co Greene's Landing	Warren
Greene George T Jr Greene's Landing	Warren
Sealshipt Oyster System ft of Baker also off S Water nr Broad	Warren
Warren Oyster Co off 155 S Water	Warren

Painters and Paper Hangers

Gardiner Herbert (house) Broad B	Barrington
Jansson A Washington W B	Barrington
Bush George H 142 High	Bristol
Coggeshall LeRoy B 733 Hope	Bristol
Coggeshall Walter H 30 Constitution	Bristol
Macauley Frederick W 283 Wood	Bristol
Smith Raymond P 31 High	Bristol
TORREY E F 1039 Hope—see page 21	Bristol
Warner Thomas H 270 High	Bristol
Burtis Hiram O 250 S Main	Warren
Conrick Thomas Market cor Main	Warren
MacDonald John J Greene's Landing	Warren
Muller Max 168 S Main	Warren
Saillant John A 6 Barney	Warren
Stevens Thomas C 24 Wheaton	Warren
Wood Charles H (carriage) Market cor Federal	Warren

Paints, Oils and Glass

BOSWORTH L P Broad at R R crossing—see page 26	Barrington

Periodicals

GRANT JAMES F County rd cor Rumstick—see page 27	Barrington
DARLING HENRY M 444 Hope—see page 20	Bristol
BLISS CHARLES C Goff's Hotel block—see page 25	Warren

Photographic Supplies

Burgess William N 276 Hope	Bristol
Church Gordon B 145 S Main	Warren

Photographs

Posytan Henry H 56 State	Bristol
Church Gordon B 145 S Main	Warren

National Exchange Bank
63 Westminster St., Prov.

Established 1801
If you think of
changing your
bank, there is
None better than this

BRISTOL COUNTY BUSINESS DIRECTORY. 231

Physicians

Sweet Emery P Mathewson av B	Barrington
DeWolf Harold 132 High	Bristol
Duffy William F 322 Wood	Bristol
Dyer William H 271 Hope	Bristol
Hasbrouck Cornelius J 115 State	Bristol
Merriman Alfred M 597 Hope	Bristol
Siegel Oswald R 159 High	Bristol
Teller Henry L Jr 118 Bradford	Bristol
Williams W Frederick 249 Hope	Bristol
Barney Milton E Manning cor Washington	Warren
Bergeron G Gernon 230 S Main	Warren
Church Gilbert L 87 N Water	Warren
Conway John J 93 N Main	Warren
Hall Nelson R 9 Wood	Warren
Hopkins Henry W Miller cor Union	Warren
Merchant Joseph M 125 S Main	Warren
Merchant Marcius H 114 Main	Warren
Morisseau Theodule G 19 Child	Warren
Scott Charles E 27 Child	Warren
Seymour Horace D 140 S Main	Warren

Piano Tuner

Soule Harry B Broad nr Cong Church B   Barrington

Plain and Fancy Goods Manufacturers

WARREN MFG CO ft of Bowen—see page 7   Warren

Plumbers

ALLEN GEORGE E CO Fourth—see page 27
 West Barrington
BOURASSA T F Bay Spring av—see page 27
 West Barrington
McGann George W 278 Hope   Bristol
Morrissey Edward C 39 State   Bristol
WALDRON CO THE 49 Bradford—see page 2   Bristol
Brochu Felix 4 Martin   Warren
Brownell John P South Water cor Wheaton   Warren
Gauthier & Dallaire Co 78 N Water   Warren
Pardy Harold O 10 Baker   Warren
SEYMOUR C H & CO 149 S Main—see page 23   Warren
Seymour Herbert A 27 State   Warren

Merewether & Dunn
Plumbing and Heating Contractors
31 TURNER AVENUE,   RIVERSIDE, R. I.

Gasoline Engines · Pumps · Wind Mills · Tanks, Towers · Irrigation · Spray Goods

Established 1876
CHARLES J. JAGER CO.
33 Canal St., Providence, R. I.

Automatic Pressure Systems · Electric Pumps · Well Supplies · Repairs And Accessories

Pool Rooms

Battaglio Alfonso 172 Bradford	Bristol
Messier Augustus Jr 102 N Main	Warren
O'Neil Martin W Market	Warren
Salvatore Lessio 45 N Main	Warren

Poultry Supplies

BOSWORTH L P Broad at R R crossing—see page 26 — Barrington

Printers

FARRALLY BROS 547 Hope—see page 17	Bristol
WARREN PRINTING & PUBLISHING CO State nr Main—see page 22	Warren

Private Boarding House

GABLES THE (Mrs John S Thompson prop) Mathewson rd—see page 26 — Barrington

Private School

Bache Private School rear 86 State — Bristol

Provision Dealers (see also Grocers)

BAY SPRING PUBLIC MARKET cor Bay Spring av and Narragansett—see page 26 — West Barrington
BOSWORTH L P Broad at R R crossing—see page 26 — Barrington
MAYOTT & OGDEN Bay Spring av—see page 26 — West Barrington

FURTADO J ROSA 229 State—see page 19	Bristol
GOFF'S MARKET cor High and Lincoln av—see page 20	Bristol
GUISTIANY PETER 247 Thames—see page 19	Bristol
Janson's Market 22 State	Bristol
Nelle Charles F 184 Thames	Bristol
Paull Marion H Mrs cor Hope and Franklin	Bristol
PIMENTAL & SOUSA 217 Wood—see page 19	Bristol
SOUSA ANTONY J 157 Bradford—see page 19	Bristol
COLE GEORGE R 27 Baker—see page 23	Warren
DIONNE CHARLES 140 Child—see page 25	Warren
Excelsior Grocery and Market 191 S Main	Warren
HAWTHORNE HUGH 174 S Main—see page 25	Warren
ROSA MANUEL P 129 Child—see page 25	Warren
SANITARY MARKET AND HOME BAKERY cor Main and Liberty—see page 25	Warren
SOCHA JOHN M 86 N Water—see page 25	Warren

A Scientific Collection Service Based On The Principle of
HONESTY.
Western Mercantile Corporation. 420-421 Grosvenor Building Prov. R. I. Tel. Union 1526

BRISTOL COUNTY BUSINESS DIRECTORY.

Publishers

FARRALLY BROS 547 Hope—see page 17	Bristol
WARREN PRINTING & PUBLISHING CO State nr Main—see page 22	Warren

Real Estate Agents

Drury John Temple Drury blk	Bristol
Hammill Charles L 149 State	Bristol
Straight Clark H 329 Hope	Bristol
Brown John H 34 N Water	Warren

Registered Pharmacists

BUFFINGTON WILLIAM H 458 Hope—see page 20	Bristol
Hope Drug Co 297 Hope	Bristol
SHERMAN HAROLD G 399 Wood—see page 19	Bristol
YOUNG J H & CO 479 Hope—see page 20	Bristol
BENNETT W S & CO cor Main and Joyce—see page 27	Warren
Family Drug Store The Dr C E Scott 27 Child	Warren
Hope Pharmacy 127 South Main	Warren
ROBERTS OSCAR 46 N Main—see page 24	Warren
Smith William J & Co 137 South Main	Warren
STANDARD PHARMACY cor Main and Miller —see page 25	Warren

Restaurants

BROWN GEORGE 5 Bradford—see page 20	Bristol
Kemlick William 141 Bradford and 1 Franklin	Bristol
Bella Napoli 175 Bradford	Bristol
Ciniglio Luigi 47 North Water	Warren
McCann Thomas J Railroad av opp R R Depot	Warren
Nom Chin South Main	Warren
Warren Restaurant (W J Lonergan prop) 35 Joyce	Warren

Road Builder

CALLAN L H COL 237 Franklin—see page 4	Bristol

Roofer

CALLAN L H COL 237 Franklin—see page 4	Bristol

Roofing Material

ADAMS WILLIAM H & SON Bay Spring av— see page 27	West Barrington

R. I. RUG WORKS Oriental Rugs Cleaned and Repaired.
Tels. Union 2203 and 2204
678 WESTMINSTER STREET, PROVIDENCE, R. I.

HARDWELL LUMBER CO.
BRISTOL, R. I.
Builders' Hardware
Paints, Glass
Masons & Carpenters'
TOOLS

BRISTOL COUNTY BUSINESS DIRECTORY.

Rubber Goods Manufacturers
International Rubber Co at R R crossing   West Barrington
Narragansett Rubber Co 228 Wood   Bristol
NATIONAL INDIA RUBBER CO Wood opp Bradford—see page 6   Bristol
U S RUBBER CO Wood opp Bradford—see page 6   Bristol

Sand and Gravel
ADAMS WILLIAM H & SON Bay Spring av—see page 27   West Barrington

Sateens and Twills Manufacturers
WARREN MFG CO ft of Bowen—see page 7   Warren

Schools
Bache Private School rear 86 State   Bristol

Second-hand Furniture
Hochman William 25 State   Bristol

Second-hand Goods
Hochman Louis North Water   Warren

Sewer Pipe
ADAMS WILLIAM H & SON Bay Spring av—see page 27   West Barrington

Sewing Machine Agent
Diniz Jacintho F 141 South Main   Warren

Sheet Iron Workers
SEYMOUR C H & CO 149 S Main—see page 23   Warren
Seymour Herbert A 27 State   Warren

Shoe Polishing Parlor
Anastas & Kerrias 489 Hope   Bristol
Shoe Repairers (see Boot and Shoe Repairers)

Sign Painter
Mullen Max 168 South Main   Warren

Stables
WOOD O L 23 Court—see page 21   Bristol
Munroe Edward Cutler near Child   Warren

Water Supply Outfits | Walter H. Jackson Co. 435 Industrial Trust Building | "Dodd" System Lightning
House Pumps | Providence, - R. I. | PROTECTION

Stationery

BUFFINGTON WILLIAM H 458 Hope—see page 20 — Bristol
DARLING HENRY M 444 Hope—see page 20 — Bristol
Hope Drug Co 297 Hope — Bristol
SHERMAN HAROLD G 399 Wood—see page 19 — Bristol
YOUNG J H & CO 497 Hope—see page 20 — Bristol
BENNETT W S & CO cor Main and Joyce—see page 27 — Warren
BLISS CHARLES C Goff's Hotel block—see page 25 — Warren
Family Drug Store The Dr C E Scott 27 Child — Warren
Lavigueur Herbert South Main — Warren
ROBERTS OSCAR 46 N Main—see page 24 — Warren
STANDARD PHARMACY cor Main and Miller —see page 25 — Warren

Steam and Gas Fitters

ALLEN GEORGE E CO Fourth—see page 27 — West Barrington
WALDRON CO THE 49 Bradford—see page 2 — Bristol

Steam and Hot Water Heating

McGann George W 278 Hope — Bristol
WALDRON CO THE 49 Bradford—see page 2 — Bristol
SEYMOUR C H & CO 149 S Main—see page 23 — Warren
Seymour Herbert A 27 State — Warren

Steamship Company

Dyer Transportation Line ft of State — Bristol

Storage Warehouse

PERRY CO (THE) (W W Perry mgr) Perry—see page 21 — Bristol

Stoves and Ranges

BELL WILLIAM H 361-365 Hope—see page 20 — Bristol
WALDRON CO (THE) 49 Bradford—see page 2 — Bristol

Surveyors

PERRY WILLIAM W 814 Hope—see page 21 — Bristol
ESTES CHARLES Touisset rd—see page 24 — Warren

WHITTEMORE & COLBURN
PRINTERS   15 Pine St., PROV.

JAMES C. GOFF CO. | **All kinds of Masons' Materials**
31 to 49 POINT ST.
Providence, R. I.

Tag Manufacturer

Arnold George B 341 South Main	Warren

Tailors

Aiello Vincent 374 Wood	Bristol
DAVID ABRAHAM 301 Hope—see opp page 45	Bristol
DeFelice Alfonso 355 Wood	Bristol
DeLauro Alfredo 372 Hope	Bristol
Lollo Albert D 483 Hope	Bristol
Phenes Isaac 17 State	Bristol
Wilkinson John J 481 Hope	Bristol
Faulkner William 147 South Main	Warren
Katt William 31 North Water	Warren
Levin Sam 137 South Main	Warren
Lipshitz R 77 North Water	Warren
Sikorowicz Walter 12 Child	Warren

Tea, Coffee and Spices

Direct Importing Co 139 S Main	Warren
Fahey Edward J South Main nr Maple	Warren
Great A & P Tea Co 135 Main	Warren

Teachers

Dexter Mary H (piano) Martin av H M	Barrington
Ward Alice L (vocal) bds J A Ward H M	Barrington
Blaisdell Myra F (designing) Bay View nr Sherry	Bristol
Church Reba Howe (piano) 281 Hope	Bristol
Connery Catherine E 110 Church	Bristol
Salisbury Mabel B 96 Burton	Bristol
Asselin Diana (piano) opp 29 Market	Warren
Campbell Ella M (drawing) 119 Child	Warren
Coyle Matilda Mrs 6 Broad	Warren
Green Maude M 36 Child	Warren
Koechling A G (violin) Saugy bldg	Warren
Pratt Cora Miss (drawing and music) 239 S Main	Warren
Wylie Mollie A Miss (violin) 12 Luther	Warren

Teamsters

ADAMS WILLIAM H & SON Bay Spring av— see page 27	West Barrington
West Leonard E East av B	Barrington
Cole Freeborn R 64 Constitution	Bristol
Connors James T 380 Thames	Bristol

Telephone Companies

Providence Telephone Co 565 Hope	Bristol
Providence Telephone Co 11 Market nr Main	Warren

Ralph C. Watrous Co.
ESTATE MANAGERS.   RENT COLLECTION A SPECIALTY
437 INDUSTRIAL TRUST BUILDING

Textile Machinery Dealers
Fyans Fraser & Blackway Cole cor Croade — Warren

Theaters
Pastime Theater 85 State — Bristol
Star Theater Hasbroucks block 537 Hope — Bristol
Lyric Theater 3 Miller — Warren

Tin and Sheet Metal Worker
BOURASSA T F Bay Spring av—see page 27 — West Barrington

Tinsmiths
WALDRON CO THE 49 Bradford—see page 2 — Bristol

Tire Fabric Yarn Manufacturers
Mt Hope Spinning Co Cutler — Warren

Trading Stamp Company
Sperry & Hutchinson Co The 495 Hope — Bristol

Transportation Lines
DYER TRANSPORTATION LINE (185 S Water Prov) ft of State—see page 11 — Bristol
Prudence Island Transportation Co (H Chase) Church st dock — Bristol

Undertakers
Duffy Augustus P 322 Wood — Bristol
Simmons George W (est of) 104 Constitution — Bristol
Tobin Michael J 66 Franklin — Bristol
WILBUR GEORGE M 38 Union—see page 22 — Bristol
WILBUR GEORGE M 209 S Main—see page 22 — Warren

Upholsterers
Mackenzie William M 24 Child — Warren
Picard Alphonse 164 South Main — Warren

Variety
Dube Isreal Bridge av — Barrington
Briggs William F 213 High — Bristol
Dio Henry 439 Hope — Bristol
Kempf Herman J Jr 681 Hope — Bristol
Palumbo Dominik 467 Wood — Bristol

Blackstone Canal Nat'l Bank 20 Market Square PROVIDENCE, R. I.
Capital, $500,000.   Surplus Profits, over $500,000

Warren Monumental Works
Cor. Railroad Avenue and Croade Street,   Warren, R. I.

Place Lenius E 485 Hope	Bristol
Conrick Thomas Market cor Main	Warren
Maxfield Charles R 310 South Main	Warren
Picard Godfried 60 North Main	Warren

Veterinary Surgeons

Conklin H R Dr Maple nr South Main	Warren
Munroe Edward Cutler cor Child	Warren

Watchmakers and Repairers (see also Jewelers)

KUNZ EDWARD D 469 Hope—see page 20	Bristol
Markoff Aaron E 657 Hope	Bristol
Krevolin Jacob P 139 South Main	Warren
MAKER ARTHUR J 163 S Main—see page 24	Warren
Munro Joseph B Metacom av	Warren

Water Works

Bristol & Warren Water Works 553 Hope	Bristol
Bristol & Warren Water Works State	Warren

Wheelwrights

DEGENAIS JOSEPH A rear 281 Thames—see page 21	Bristol
STUART RICHARD S ft of State—see page 21	Bristol

Woman's Exchange

Bristol Woman's Exchange 331 Hope	Bristol

Wood Dealers

BOSWORTH L P Broad at R R crossing—see page 26	Barrington
Grangere Moses 43 North Water	Warren

Worsted Goods

CRANSTON WORSTED MILLS 83 Thames—(yarns)—see page 5	Bristol

Worsted Yarns

CRANSTON WORSTED MILLS 83 Thames—see page 5	Bristol
Narragansett Worsted Co Franklin	Warren

Yacht and Boat Builders (see also Boat Builders)

HERRESHOFF MFG CO INC Hope opp Burnside and 20 Burnside—see page 5	Bristol

Yacht Supplies

WARDWELL LUMBER CO Thames ft of Bradford—see head lines	Bristol

NATIONAL EXCHANGE BANK 63 WESTMINSTER ST. PROVIDENCE
IF YOU ARE LOOKING FOR A STRONG BANK, WHERE A FRIENDLY Welcome Always Awaits You, Open an Account With Us

BUSINESS DIRECTORY
OUT-OF-TOWN PATRONS

Agricultural Implements
BARRETT W E CO Canal and Waterman Prov—see opp page 77

Asphalt Dealers
BARRETT CO (THE) 35 Wendell Boston Mass—see back cover

Asphalt Shingles
BARRETT CO (THE) 35 Wendell Boston Mass—see back cover

Attorney at Law
ARMINGTON ARTHUR A 530 Industrial Trust Bldg Providence—see outside front cover

Automobile Agency
PUGH BROS CO 49 Mathewson Providence and 532 South Main Fall River—see page 14

Automobile Trimmings
WEBSTER & CO 270 Pearl Providence—see page 15

Badges, Plates, etc.
WHITE A A CO 114 Westminster Providence—see page 15

Banks
BLACKSTONE CANAL NATIONAL BANK 20 Market Square Providence—see foot lines
CITIZENS' SAVINGS BANK 846 Westminster Providence—see page 9
INDUSTRIAL TRUST CO 49 Westminster Providence —see front cover and insert opp Warren Directory

Merewether & Dunn
Plumbing and Heating Contractors
31 TURNER AVENUE, RIVERSIDE, R. I.

33 Canal St. CHARLES J. JAGER CO. Providence

ELECTRIC AND GASOLINE PUMPS AND PRESSURE SYSTEMS
We carry the largest stock of this kind in New England

240   OUT-OF-TOWN BUSINESS DIRECTORY.

MECHANICS' NATIONAL BANK 34 Dorrance Providence—see page 8
NATIONAL EXCHANGE BANK 63 Westminster Providence—see head lines
PEOPLES SAVINGS BANK IN PROVIDENCE 27 Market Sq Providence—see page 12

Binders
LOOSE LEAF MFG CO 257 West Exchange Providence—see page 2

Boat Builders and Repairers
NOCK FREDERIC S ft of Division East Greenwich—see page 3

Boiler Makers
PROVIDENCE BOILER CO cor Dyer and Ship Providence—see page 10

Book and Job Printing
LOOSE LEAF MFG CO 257 West Exchange Providence—see page 2

Brick, Lime, Cement and Sand
GOFF JAMES C CO 31 to 49 Point Providence—see head lines
MANCHESTER & HUDSON CO 55 Point Providence—see page 28

Builders' Materials
BARRETT CO (THE) 35 Wendell Boston Mass—see back cover
GOFF JAMES C CO 31 to 49 Point Providence—see head lines
MANCHESTER & HUDSON CO 55 Point Providence—see page 28

Building Contractors
BOWEN CONSTRUCTION CO (THE) 180 Greenwood av Rumford—see front cover

Building Papers
BARRETT CO (THE) 35 Wendell Boston Mass—see back cover

Business College
CHILDS BUSINESS COLLEGE 290 Westminster Providence—see page 28

COLLECTIONS AND CREDIT REPORTS
Our service is as near as your telephone. We will gladly furnish names of clients whom you know, who are satisfied users of our service. Tel. Union 1526

Western Mercantile Corporation, Providence, R. I.

OUT-OF-TOWN BUSINESS DIRECTORY. 241

Carpets and Rugs
BROWN E S CO 166-188 N Main Fall River Mass—see opp page 92

Cement Blocks
BOWEN CONSTRUCTION CO (THE) 180 Greenwood av Rumford—see front cover

Cement Drain Pipes
BOWEN CONSTRUCTION CO (THE) 180 Greenwood av Rumford—see front cover
GOFF JAMES C CO 31 to 49 Point Providence—see head lines

Chemicals
ARNOLD HOFFMAN & CO INC 55-61 Canal Providence —see page 12

Civil Engineer
LATHAM JOSEPH A 87 Weybosset Providence—see insert opp Barrington Directory

Coal Tar Products
BARRETT CO (THE) 35 Wendell Boston Mass—see back cover

Collecting Agencies
LISABELLES COLLECTING AGENCY 76 Dorrance Providence—see page 14
WESTERN MERCANTILE CORP 420 Grosvenor bldg Providence—see head lines

Commercial School
CHILDS BUSINESS COLLEGE 290 Westminster Providence—see page 28

Contractors
BOWEN CONSTRUCTION CO (THE) 180 Greenwood av Rumford—see front cover
FAMIGLIETTI ROCCO M 539 Charles Providence—see page 14
PIERCE FREDERIC L 74 Weybosset Providence—see page 13

R. I. RUG WORKS RUG CLEANING, CARPET CLEANING AND LAYING
678 WESTMINSTER ST., PROVIDENCE. Telephones Union 2203 and 2204

Contractors' Supplies
BARRETT CO (THE) 35 Wendell Boston Mass—see back cover

Credit Reports
WESTERN MERCANTILE CORP 420 Grosvenor bldg Providence—see head lines

Creosote Oil
BARRETT CO (THE) 35 Wendell Boston Mass—see back cover

Department Store
BROWN E S CO 166-188 N Main Fall River Mass—see opp page 92

Detective Agency
NATIONAL DETECTIVE AGENCY (THE) 330 Industrial Trust bldg Providence—see page 15

Disinfectant Manufacturers
BARRETT CO (THE) 35 Wendell Boston Mass—see back cover

Doors, Sash and Blinds
HAWKINS LUMBER CO 1 Washington av East Providence—see page 11

Drain Pipe
GOFF JAMES C CO 31 to 40 Point Providence—see head lines
MANCHESTER & HUDSON CO 55 Point Providence—see page 28

Druggists
ARNOLD HOFFMAN & CO INC 55-61 Canal Providence —see page 12

Druggists' Supplies
HOPE RUBBER CO 93-97 Westminster Providence—see page opp Barrington Directory

Drugs and Dye Stuffs
ARNOLD HOFFMAN & CO INC 55-61 Canal Providence —see page 12

Dry Goods
BROWN E S CO 166-188 N Main Fall River Mass—see opp page 92

WALTER H. JACKSON CO. 435 Industrial Trust Building
PROVIDENCE, R. I.
"DELCO" ELECTRIC LIGHTING & PUMPING PLANTS
WINDMILLS, GASOLINE ENGINES AND TRACTORS

OUT-OF-TOWN BUSINESS DIRECTORY. 243

Dye Woods and Dye Stuffs
ARNOLD HOFFMAN & CO INC 55-61 Canal Providence
—see page 12

Electric Water Supply Systems
BROWNELL & HINMAN 17 Lincoln av Riverside—see page 4

Embalmers
BERNS CO 301 Pearl Providence—see page 15

Expressing
BROWN'S MOTOR EXPRESS 65 Broad Providence—see page 11
WHEATON'S EXPRESS 288 Bullocks Point av Riverside—see page 10

Farmers' Supplies
PINO WILLIS S 41 Washington Providence—see page 12

Farming Implements
BARRETT W E CO Canal and Waterman Prov—see opp page 77

Fertilizers
BARRETT W E CO Canal and Waterman Prov—see opp page 77
MANCHESTER & HUDSON CO 55 Point Providence—see page 28
RIVERSIDE HAY & GRAIN CO 288 Bullocks Point av Riverside—see page 10

Fire Clay and Sand
GOFF JAMES C CO 31 to 49 Point Providence—see head lines
MANCHESTER & HUDSON CO 55 Point Providence—see page 28

Floor Coverings
BARRETT CO (THE) 35 Wendell Boston Mass—see back cover

WHITTEMORE & COLBURN
PRINTERS   15 Pine St., PROV.

JAMES C. GOFF CO. Sole Agents for   **ATLAS**
31 to 49 POINT ST.   **Portland Cement**
Providence, R. I.

OUT-OF-TOWN BUSINESS DIRECTORY.

Foresters
EVERETT C J INC 86 Weybosset Providence—see opp page 45

Funeral Directors
BERNS CO 301 Pearl Providence—see page 15

Furniture Movers
BROWN'S MOTOR EXPRESS 65 Broad Providence—see page 11
WHEATON'S EXPRESS 288 Bullocks Point av Riverside—see page 10

Garden Tools
PINO WILLIS S 41 Washington Providence—see page 12

Gas and Water Pipe Fitters
MEREWETHER & DUNN 31 Turner av Riverside—see foot lines

Gents' Furnishings
BROWN E S CO 166-188 N Main Fall River Mass—see opp page 92

Granite Cutters and Dealers
KIMBALL & COMBE CO 96 Westminster Providence—see page 2
RICHARDS JOHN R (J Cravin mgr) 977 N Main Providence—see opp inside back cover

Grocers (Wholesale)
ALLEN SLADE & CO INC 18 to 26 Third Fall River Mass—see page 13

Hair, Plaster, etc.
GOFF JAMES C CO 31 to 49 Point Providence—see head lines
MANCHESTER & HUDSON CO 55 Point Providence—see page 28

Hay and Grain
RIVERSIDE HAY & GRAIN CO 288 Bullocks Point av Riverside—see page 10

Heating
BROWNELL & HINMAN 17 Lincoln av Riverside—see page 4

RALPH C. WATROUS CO.
Real Estate Auctioneers
437 INDUSTRIAL TRUST BUILDING

OUT-OF-TOWN BUSINESS DIRECTORY.

Hydraulic Engineers
JACKSON WALTER H CO 435 Industrial Trust bldg Providence—see head lines
JAGER CHARLES J CO 33 Canal Providence—see head lines

Insulating Papers
BARRETT CO (THE) 35 Wendell Boston Mass—see back cover

Insurance Agents
COOKE HENRY W CO 15 Westminster Providence—see front cover
LEACH ALBERT E 1205 Union Trust bldg Providence—see front cover
PENN MUTUAL LIFE INS CO 17 Exchange Providence—see opp page 44
WATSON E L & CO 205 Industrial Trust bldg Providence—see front cover

Insurance Company
PENN MUTUAL LIFE INS CO 17 Exchange Providence—see opp page 44

Irrigation Systems
JACKSON WALTER H CO 435 Industrial Trust bldg Providence—see head lines
JAGER CHARLES J CO 33 Canal Providence—see head lines

Ladies' and Children's Wear
BROWN E S CO 166-188 N Main Fall River Mass—see opp page 92

Ladies' Shoes
BROWN E S CO 166-188 N Main Fall River Mass—see opp page 92

Laundries
BUTMAN & TUCKER CO 140 Pine Providence—see page 3
LOUTTIT HOME HAND LAUNDRY CO 307 Broad Providence—see page 13

Blackstone Canal Nat'l Bank | **BEST FACILITIES**
20 MARKET SQ., PROVIDENCE | **Prompt Attention**

WARREN MONUMENTAL WORKS
Cor. Railroad Avenue and Croade Streets, Warren, R. I.

RIVERSIDE WET WASH LAUNDRY 16 First East Providence—see page 11
SAM-O-SET LAUNDRY INC 802 Union Trust bldg Providence—see page 14
WHAT CHEER LAUNDRY 36 Burgess Providence—see opp page 44

Lawyer

ARMINGTON ARTHUR A 530 Industrial Trust bldg Providence—see outside front cover

Life Insurance Agents

LEACH ALBERT E 1205 Union Trust bldg Providence—see front cover
PENN MUTUAL LIFE INS CO 17 Exchange Providence —see opp page 44

Loose Leaf Forms and Devices

LOOSE LEAF MFG CO 257 West Exchange Providence —see page 2

Lumber Dealers

HAWKINS LUMBER CO 1 Washington av East Providence—see page 11

Marble Workers

KIMBALL & COMBE CO 96 Westminster Providence— see page 2
RICHARDS JOHN R (J Cravin mgr) 977 N Main Providence—see opp inside back cover

Marine and Stationery Boilers

PROVIDENCE BOILER CO cor Dyer and Ship Providence—see page 10

Masons' Materials

GOFF JAMES C CO 31 to 49 Point Providence—see head lines
MANCHESTER & HUDSON CO 55 Point Providence— see page 28

Mercantile Agency

WESTERN MERCANTILE CORP 420 Grosvenor bldg Providence—see head lines

Millinery Goods

BROWN E S CO 166-188 N Main Fall River Mass—see opp page 92

NATIONAL EXCHANGE BANK One of the Oldest and Strongest Banks
63 Westminster St., Providence   In Rhode Island

OUT-OF-TOWN BUSINESS DIRECTORY.   247

Monuments and Monumental Works
KIMBALL & COMBE CO 96 Westminster Providence—see page 2
RICHARDS JOHN R (J Cravin mgr) 977 N Main Providence—see opp inside back cover

Mortgage Brokers
COOKE HENRY W CO 15 Westminster Providence—see front cover

Newspaper
PROVIDENCE JOURNAL CO Westminster and Eddy sts Providence—see opp page 76

Notary Public
BERNS CO 301 Pearl Providence—see page 15

Oil and Gasoline Engines
JACKSON WALTER H CO 435 Industrial Trust bldg Providence—see head lines
JAGER CHARLES J CO 33 Canal Providence—see head lines

Paint Manufacturers
BARRETT CO (THE) 35 Wendell Boston Mass—see back cover

Painters' Supplies
JOHNSON OLIVER & CO INC 18-24 Custom House Providence—see page 12

Patent Attorney
ARMINGTON ARTHUR A 530 Industrial Trust bldg Providence—see outside front cover

Paving Materials
BARRETT CO (THE) 35 Wendell Boston Mass—see back cover

Photographers
YE ROSE STUDIO 385 Westminster Providence—see opp page 93

Merewether & Dunn
Plumbing and Heating Contractors
31 TURNER AVENUE,   RIVERSIDE, R. I.

Gasoline Engines — Established 1876 — Automatic Pressure Systems
Pumps — Wind Mills — Tanks, Towers — Irrigation — Spray Goods
CHARLES J. JAGER CO.
33 Canal St., Providence, R. I.
Electric Pumps — Well Supplies — Repairs And Accessories

Picture Frames
CLARK WALTER B 131 Washington Providence—see page 15

Pitch (Coal Tar)
BARRETT CO (THE) 35 Wendell Boston Mass—see back cover

Plumbers
BROWNELL & HINMAN 17 Lincoln av Riverside—see page 4
MEREWETHER & DUNN 31 Turner av Riverside—see foot lines

Poultry and Animal Remedies
RIVERSIDE HAY & GRAIN CO 288 Bullocks Point av Riverside—see page 10

Poultry Supplies
BARRETT W E CO Canal and Waterman Prov—see opp page 77

Power Pumps
JACKSON WALTER H CO 435 Industrial Trust bldg Providence—see head lines
JAGER CHARLES J CO 33 Canal Providence—see head lines

Printers
LOOSE LEAF MFG CO 257 West Exchange Providence —see page 2
VANCE ALBERT M CO 30 Warren East Providence— see page 15

Real Estate Agents
COOKE HENRY W CO 15 Westminster Providence— see front cover
KEHOE JOHN L 217 Grosvenor bldg Providence—see foot lines
WATROUS RALPH C CO 437 Industrial Trust bldg Providence—see head lines

Refrigerators
BELL WM G CO (THE) 44-54 Commercial Boston—see opp page 70

Road Preservatives
BARRETT CO (THE) 35 Wendell Boston Mass—see back cover

OUR CREDIT REPORTS TELL—Whom to trust; whom not to trust; who pay promptly; who pay slowly; who never pay their bills except under pressure.   Telephone Union 1526
Western Mercantile Corporation, Providence, R. I.

OUT-OF-TOWN BUSINESS DIRECTORY.   249

Roof Connections
BARRETT CO (THE) 35 Wendell Boston Mass—see back cover

Roofing and Paving Materials
BARRETT CO (THE) 35 Wendell Boston Mass—see back cover
HAWKINS LUMBER CO 1 Washington av East Providence—see page 11

Rubber Clothing
HOPE RUBBER CO 93-97 Westminster Providence—see page opp Barrington Directory

Rubber Goods Manufacturers
HOPE RUBBER CO 93-97 Westminster Providence—see page opp Barrington Directory

Rubber Hose
HOPE RUBBER CO 93-97 Westminster Providence—see page opp Barrington Directory

Rubber Stamps, Stencils and Seals
WHITE A A CO 114 Westminster Providence—see page 15

Rug and Mat Manufacturers
RHODE ISLAND RUG WORKS 678 Westminster Providence—see page 28

Rugs and Mats
BARRETT CO (THE) 35 Wendell Boston Mass—see back cover

School
CHILDS BUSINESS COLLEGE 290 Westminster Providence—see page 28

Seeds
BARRETT W E CO Canal and Waterman Prov—see opp page 77
PINO WILLIS S 41 Washington Providence—see page 12

R. I. RUG WORKS
Rugs Woven from old and new carpets.   Telephones { 2203 / 2204
678 WESTMINSTER ST.,   PROVIDENCE

Shingles
BARRETT CO (THE) 35 Wendell Boston Mass—see back cover
HAWKINS LUMBER CO 1 Washington av East Providence—see page 11

Shingle Stain
BARRETT CO (THE) 35 Wendell Boston Mass—see back cover

Shoe Mfrs Goods—Fillers
BARRETT CO (THE) 35 Wendell Boston Mass—see back cover

Slate Dealers
BARRETT CO (THE) 35 Wendell Boston Mass—see back cover

Steam, Gas and Water Pipe Fitters
MEREWETHER & DUNN 31 Turner av Riverside—see foot lines

Surveyor
LATHAM JOSEPH A 87 Weybosset Providence—see insert opp Barrington Directory

Tanks and Smokestacks
PROVIDENCE BOILER CO cor Dyer and Ship Providence—see page 10

Tar Manufacturers
BARRETT CO (THE) 35 Wendell Boston Mass—see back cover

Tin, Sheet Iron and Copper Workers
BROWNELL & HINMAN 17 Lincoln av Riverside—see page 4
MEREWETHER & DUNN 31 Turner av Riverside—see foot lines

Title Guarantee Co
TITLE GUARANTEE CO OF R I 66 S Main Providence—see page 13

Tops, Dust and Slip Covers
WEBSTER & CO 270 Pearl Providence—see page 15

| Water Supply Outfits House Pumps | Walter H. Jackson Co. 435 Industrial Trust Building Providence, - R. I. | "Dodd" System Lightning PROTECTION |

OUT-OF-TOWN BUSINESS DIRECTORY. 251

Transportation Line
DYER TRANSPORTATION LINE 185 S Water Providence—see page 11

Trucking
BROWN'S MOTOR EXPRESS 65 Broad Providence—see page 11
WHEATON'S EXPRESS 288 Bullocks Point av Riverside—see page 10

Typewriters
NEILAN TYPEWRITER EXCHANGE 43 Weybosset Providence—see back cover

Typewriters to Let
NEILAN TYPEWRITER EXCHANGE 43 Weybosset Providence—see back cover

Typewriting and Shorthand
CHILDS BUSINESS COLLEGE 290 Westminster Providence—see page 28

Undertakers
BERNS CO 301 Pearl Providence—see page 15

Water Supply Systems
JACKSON WALTER H CO 435 Industrial Trust bldg Providence—see head lines
JAGER CHARLES J CO 33 Canal Providence—see head lines

Waterproofing Materials
BARRETT CO (THE) 35 Wendell Boston Mass—see back cover

Wet Wash Laundry
RIVERSIDE WEST WASH LAUNDRY 16 First East Providence—see page 11

WHITTEMORE & COLBURN
PRINTERS   15 Pine St., PROV.

VALENTINE'S Diamond & Star FIRE BRICK | **JAMES C. GOFF CO.** 31 to 49 POINT ST. Providence, R. I.

252 OUT-OF-TOWN BUSINESS DIRECTORY.

Windmills, Tanks and Towers

JACKSON WALTER H CO 435 Industrial Trust bldg Providence—see head lines

JAGER CHARLES J CO 33 Canal Providence—see head lines

Window Glass

JOHNSON OLIVER & CO INC 18-24 Custom House Providence—see page 12

Wood Preservatives

BARRETT CO (THE) 35 Wendell Boston Mass—see back cover

Yacht Builders

NOCK FREDERIC S ft of Division East Greenwich—see page 3

RALPH C. WATROUS CO.
RESIDENTIAL and INVESTMENT PROPERTY
Of All Kinds For Sale
487 Industrial Trust Building

BRISTOL TOWN OFFICERS.

1917.

MODERATOR—George U. Arnold.

TOWN CLERK—John M. Coggeshall.

TOWN COUNCIL—Wallis E. Howe, president; John H. Wall, Peter Gasper, Elisha Hibbert, Francis P. McGovern.

PROBATE JUDGE—Edward L. Leahy.

JUSTICES OF THE PEACE—Frank H. Hammill, Philip Brady.

TOWN TREASURER AND COLLECTOR OF TAXES—Winthrop G. Thurston.

TOWN SERGEANT—Thomas E. Johnson.

AUCTIONEERS—Clark H. Straight, John Temple Drury, Fred M. Straight, Walter Simpson.

ASSESSORS OF TAXES—Clark H. Straight, 1918; Robert Newbold, 1919; Philip Brady, 1920.

CORDERS AND SURVEYORS OF WOOD—Oliver L. Mason, Thomas J. Connery, Algernon L. Johnston.

SURVEYOR OF HIGHWAYS—Luke H. Callan.

DOG CONSTABLE—Philip T. Morris.

POLICE CONSTABLES—Thomas Dwyer, Henry Serbst, James W. Goff, Hugh Kelly, James Holmes, John M. Gallagher.

POLICE OFFICERS—Chief, Thomas Dwyer; Captain, James W. Goff.

SEALER OF WEIGHTS AND MEASURES—Frank C. Child.

HEALTH OFFICER—Henry L. Teller, M.D.

CORONER—George U. Arnold.

OVERSEER OF THE POOR—DeWitt E. Bolster.

SUPERINTENDENT OF SCHOOLS—Thomas H. De Coudres.

HARBOR MASTER—Samuel C. Wardwell.

SENATOR—William L. Connery.

REPRESENTATIVES—Frank H Hammill, 1st district; William H. Thayer, 2d district.

Blackstone Canal Nat'l Bank | **BEST FACILITIES**
20 MARKET SQ., PROVIDENCE | **Prompt Attention**

Warren Monumental Works
Cor. Railroad Avenue and Croade Street, Warren, R. I.

MISCELLANEOUS.

BRISTOL HOME FOR AGED WOMEN.

No. 11 Franklin. Pres., Mrs. Evelyn B. Bache; Sec., Miss Florence Nelson; Treas., Mrs. Martha A. Johnson; Matron, Mrs. Annie W. Tirrell; Managers, Mrs. Sarah E. Spooner, Mrs. C. J. Hasbrouck, Mrs. Charlotte Corthell, Miss Hattie Peckham, Mrs. Hezekiah W. Church, Mrs. George U. Arnold, Miss Lavina Farrally, Mrs. George F. Stanton, Mrs. Charles Church, Mrs. J. Young.

BENJAMIN CHURCH HOME FOR AGED MEN.

1010 Hope street. Charles O. Coggeshall, keeper. Trustees, Samuel C. Dimond, Charles F. Dimond, Francis Moore Dimond.

SOLDIERS' HOME.

Off Metacom avenue, near Chestnut. Commander, Capt. Benjamin L. Hall; Adjt., James B. Hathaway.

CHILDREN'S HOME.

Established 1867. 48 Union street. Meets the second Tuesday afternoon of each month at 3 o'clock. Sec., Mrs. Evelyn B. Bache, 86 State; Treas., Mrs. Edward H. Tingley; Matron, Mrs. Theresa Hay.

BRISTOL EXCHANGE FOR WOMAN'S WORK.

No. 331 Hope street. Pres., Mrs. W. F. Williams; Sec., Mrs. A. E. Macdougall; Treas., Miss Nellie N. Read; Board of Directors, Mrs. W. Fred Williams, Mrs. Annie E. Macdougall, Mrs. I. N. Brownell, Mrs. S. A. H. DeWolf, Miss Annie Fitch, Miss Sarah Peck, Miss Anna B. Manchester, Miss Madeline M. Wyatt, Miss Harriet P. Wardwell, Miss Elizabeth Wardwell, Mrs. Harold DeWolf, Mrs. N. G. Herreshoff.

NEWSPAPER.

BRISTOL PHOENIX (THE) SEMI-WEEKLY—No. 547 Hope street. Editors and props., Farrally Bros. Published every Tuesday and Friday. Terms, $2.00 per annum in advance; $1.00 for six months; two cents per single copy.

BRISTOL CHURCHES.

FIRST BAPTIST CHURCH—Sunday services, 10.30 A. M., 7.30 P. M. Sunday School, 12 M.; Treas., George U. Arnold; Supt., Fred F. Hodgson. Weekday service, Friday evenings, 7.30 P. M.

FIRST CONGREGATIONAL CHURCH—Rev. John E. Whitley, pastor; residence, 35 Church. Treas., P. Skinner, Jr.

MISCELLANEOUS. 255

Sunday services, 10.30 A. M., 7.30 P. M. Sunday School, 12 M.; Supt., Robert Munro. Weekday services, Friday evening, 7.30 P. M.

JEWISH SYNAGOGUE—16 Richmond street. Meets Friday evenings.

PENTECOSTAL CHURCH OF THE NAZARENE, OF BRISTOL—Rev. Mary A. Constance and Rev. Annie S. Allen, pastors; residence, 154 Wood street. Sunday service, 10.30 A. M.; Revival service, 7 P. M.; Sunday School, 12 M.; Supt., Ralph Morgan. Weekday services, Thursday evening at 7.30.

ST. ELIZABETH'S ROMAN CATHOLIC CHURCH—Rev. Antonio Rebello, pastor; residence, 577 Wood street. Sunday services, masses, 8.30, 10.30 A. M. Sunday School, 2 .00 P. M. Benediction, 7.30 P. M.

ST. MARY'S ROMAN CATHOLIC CHURCH—Rev. Thomas J. Gillan, pastor; residence, 330 Wood street. Assistant pastor, Rev. A. L. Cahill. Sunday services, 7.30, 9, 10.30 A. M. Sunday School, 2.30 P. M. Benediction, 7.00 P. M.

ST. MICHAEL'S EPISCOPAL CHURCH—Rector, Rev. George L. Locke, D.D.; Rev. Anson B. Howard, Asst. Sunday services, 10.30 A. M., 7.30 P. M. Sunday School, 12.15 P. M. Supt., Rev. Anson B. Howard.

STATE STREET METHODIST CHURCH—Rev. A. Clark McGilton, pastor; residence, 129 State street. Sunday services, 10.30 A. M.; 7.30 P. M. Sunday School, 12 M ; Supt., Miss Lillian Nicholas. Epworth League, 6.45 P. M. Weekday services, Wednesday evenings at 7.30.

TRINITY EPISCOPAL CHURCH—Rector, vacant. Sunday services, 7.30 and 10.30 A. M., 7.30 P. M. Sunday School, 12 M.; Supt., the Rector.

YOUNG MEN'S CHRISTIAN ASSOCIATION—Pres., John R. Edwards, Rear Admiral, U. S. N. (Ret.); Vice-pres., Alfred M. Merriman, M.D.; Treas., Charles B. Rockwell,; Gen'l Secy., Joseph A. Milligan; Physical Director, Edson W. Forbes.

33 Canal St. **CHARLES J. JAGER CO.** **Providence**
ELECTRIC AND GASOLINE PUMPS AND PRESSURE SYSTEMS
We carry the largest stock of this kind in New England

256   MISCELLANEOUS.

ROGERS FREE LIBRARY, BRISTOL.

Board of Trustees—Rev. George L. Locke, Sec.; C. T. Sherman, Treas.; Ezra Dixon, Joseph F. Farrally, Frank M. Dimond. Librarian, George U. Arnold. Number of volumes, 21,758. The library is free to all dwellers in the town over twelve years of age who apply in due form and who conform to the rules and regulations. The town makes an annual appropriation towards its support, and aid is also received from the State Board of Education. Hours, weekdays, 3 to 6 and 7 to 9 P. M.; Saturdays, 3 to 9.30 P. M.

Bristol Reading Room meets at Club Room, 2 Constitution street. Pres., Dr. Frederick Williams; Vice-Pres., E. A. Barrows; Sec., George E. Leighton.

CEMETERIES.

ANCIENT CEMETERY, BRISTOL—Wood, corner Mt. Hope avenue. First interment in May, 1681.

JUNIPER HILL CEMETERY, BRISTOL—Juniper lane, between Bay View avenue and Malt House lane. Pres., Frederic F. Gladding; Treas., LeB. Bradford; Sec., W. Frederick Williams, M.D.

NORTH BURIAL GROUND, BRISTOL—Warren road, beyond Chestnut street.

ST. MARY'S CATHOLIC CEMETERY, BRISTOL—Chestnut street. Consecrated in September, 1884.

WARREN TOWN OFFICERS.

MODERATOR—Howard K. DeWolf.

TOWN CLERK—Richard S. Smith.

TOWN COUNCIL—Daniel H. Morrissey, Herbert A. Nichols, John Denby, Jeffrey Lajeunesse, George Gregory.

TOWN TREASURER—Charles W. Greene.

COLLECTOR OF TAXES—Michael P. Griffin.

TAX ASSESSORS—John T. Smith, Chairman; Gedeon Laferriere, Hugh H. McCarthy.

OVERSEER OF POOR—Charles H. Bliss.

CHIEF ENGINEER OF FIRE DEPARTMENT—William R. Maxwell.

ASSISTANT ENGINEERS—William B. Child, Joshua Turner, William Monahan, Charles W. Greene, Charles E. Rounds.

LIVE WIRE collectors of BAD BILLS
"No Collection—No Charge"
WESTERN MERCANTILE CORPORATION
420-421 Grosvenor Building. Tel. Union 1526 Providence, R. I.

MISCELLANEOUS. 257

TOWN SERGEANT—George L. Drown.
DOG CONSTABLE—George L. Drown.
FINANCE COMMITTEE—John H. Brown, Henry Deblois, John M. Maloy.
UNDERTAKERS—George M. Wilbur, Oliver Bacon, William J. Smith.
HIGHWAY SURVEYOR—Edward W. Mason.
AUCTIONEERS—Charles H. Sparks, John H. Brown, Joseph Harris, Martin Burke, Dionis E. Vincent.
HEALTH OFFICER—Theodule G. Morisseau, M.D.
SEALER OF WEIGHTS AND MEASURES—Adelard J. Larivee.
MEMBERS OF PERMANENT POLICE FORCE—Robert Walsh, Andre Lemieux, James J. Cronin, Henry F. Hull.
CHIEF OF POLICE—Robert Walsh.
SUPT. OF SCHOOLS—Leroy G. Staples.

WARREN FIRE DEPARTMENT.

NARRAGANSETT STEAMER, No. 3—Foreman, Walter A. Chase; Assistant Foreman, Andrew M. Stevens; Sec. and Treas., John J. Kelley.
MECHANICS' FIRE CO., No. 2—Foreman, William Monahan; Clerk, William F. Ryan.
MASSASOIT HOOK AND LADDER, No. 1—Foreman, Charles H. Sparks; Sec. and Treas., Edward R. Cutler.
ROUGH AND READY HOSE, No. 5, East Warren—Foreman, John Rubery; Sec., Herman Heuberger; Treas., Carl Heuberger.
BURR'S HILL FIRE CO., No. 4, South Warren—Foreman, John P. Brownee; Sec. and Treas., Harry S. Child.
CENTRAL, No. 1—Foreman, James Lonergan.

GEORGE HAIL FREE LIBRARY.

Chartered 1871. South Main, corner Croade. Pres., Rev. Joseph Hutcheson; Vice-Pres., Joseph W. Martin; Sec., Daniel H. Morrissey; Treas., Edward R. Cutler; Standing Committee, Pres. and Vice-Pres., *ex-officio*, Rev. Joseph Hutcheson, chair-

R. I. RUG WORKS
Furniture Repaired and Repolished, Chairs Reseated
678 Westminster Street, Providence. Telephone Union 2202 and also Union 2204

MISCELLANEOUS.

man; George G. Cole, Charles B. Mason, Edwin A. Cady; Librarian, Miss Emilie A. Ide. Asst., L. V. Adams. Library and Reading Room open from 2 to 6 and 6.30 to 8.30 P. M., except Thursday evenings, legal holidays and Sundays.

CHURCHES.

BAPTIST CHURCH IN WARREN—Founded 1764. Corner Main and Miller streets. Pastor, Rev. H. W. Watjen. Sunday School at 12 M.; preaching at 10.30 A. M.; evening service at 7. Supt. of Sunday School, Walter N. Butler; Sec., John B. Batchelor; Treas., Albert Morton; Treas. of Church, Edward R. Cutler; Clerk of Church, Mabel D. Goff.

FIRST METHODIST EPISCOPAL CHURCH—Church street, opposite Common. Pastor, Rev. Francis H. Spear. Rec. Steward and Treas., William B. Child. Services at 10.45 A. M. and 7 P. M. Sunday School, at 12.15 P. M. Epworth League, Tuesday evening at 7.45.

ST. CASIMIR'S (Polish R. C.) CHURCH—80 Child. Rev. Peter Switata, pastor; residence, 82 Child. Masses, 8 A. M. and 10.30 A. M. Sunday School, 2 P. M. Vespers, 3 P. M.

ST. JOHN'S CHURCH (French R. C.)—North Main corner Hope. Pastor, Rev. Elphege Caron. Masses at 7 and 10.30 A. M. Sunday School, 8 P. M. Vespers, 3 P. M.

ST. MARK'S EPISCOPAL CHURCH—Broad, corner Lyndon. Rector, Rev. Louis P. Nissen. Treas., Charles W. Green. Services at 11 A. M. Sunday School at 9.45 A. M. Holy Communion, first Sunday of the month at 11 A. M. and third Sunday of the month at 8 A. M.

ST. MARY'S ROMAN CATHOLIC CHURCH—South Main, corner Luther. Pastor, Rev. Edward J. Colgan. Masses at 9 and 10.30 A. M. Sunday School, 2 P. M. Vespers, 3 P. M. Weekday mass, 7.30 A. M.

NEWSPAPER.

WARREN AND BARRINGTON GAZETTE—State, near Main. Semi-weekly; $1.50 per annum. Warren Printing & Publishing Co., publishers and proprietors.

WALTER H. JACKSON CO. 435 Industrial Trust Building, PROVIDENCE, R. I.
"DELCO" ELECTRIC LIGHTING & PUMPING PLANTS
WINDMILLS, GASOLINE ENGINES AND TRACTORS

CEMETERIES.

NORTH CEMETERY—North Main, near North Water. Treas., John H. Brown; office, 27 North Water.

SOUTH CEMETERY, WARREN—Franklin, near the railroad.

ST. MARY'S CEMETERY, WARREN—Vernon, east of South Cemetery.

ST. JEAN LE BAPTIST CEMETERY, WARREN—Vernon, east of South Cemetery.

BARRINGTON TOWN OFFICERS.

MODERATOR—John F. Richmond.

TOWN CLERK—Frederick P. Church.

SENATOR—Arthur L. Smith.

REPRESENTATIVE—Frederick S. Peck.

TOWN COUNCIL—1. Lewis G. Fisher; 2. Arthur Smith; 3. Charles W. Fiske; 4. Paul A. Colwell; 5. John W. Hanley.

ASSESSORS OF TAXES—Wilbur D. Brown, Henry A. Anthony and Henry A. Martin.

JUSTICE OF THE PEACE—Frederick P. Church, J. Henry Woodard.

TOWN TREASURER—Ebenezer Tiffany.

COLLECTOR OF TAXES—Frederick P. Church.

AUCTIONEERS—Levi Staples, William A. Leonard, Hiram F. Perry and Clinton D. Lewis.

TOWN SERGEANT—Thomas E. Robbins.

OVERSEER OF THE POOR—William S. Martin.

SEALER OF WEIGHTS AND MEASURES—Henry L. Yager.

SCHOOL COMMITTE—Frank H. Elmore, Hubert N. Terrell.

WHITTEMORE & COLBURN
PRINTERS   15 Pine St., PROV.

King's Fibrous Plaster Board & Hard Plaster
JAMES C. GOFF CO.
81 to 49 Point St., Prov., R. I.

MISCELLANEOUS.

CONSTABLES—Frank O. Field, Elmer K. Watson, LeRoy Fales, Reuben A. Gibbs and Thomas E. Robbins.

CHIEF OF POLICE—Thomas E. Robbins.

DOG CONSTABLE—Thomas E. Robbins.

HEALTH OFFICER—Thomas E. Robbins.

BARRINGTON CHURCHES.

BARRINGTON CONGREGATIONAL CHURCH—Rev. Prentice A. Canada, pastor. Sunday services at 10.45 A. M. and 7.30 P. M. Sunday School, 12.15 P. M.

METHODIST EPISCOPAL CHURCH, West Barrington—Sunday services, 10.30 A. M. and 7 P. M. Sunday School, 11.45 A. M.; Supt., R. A. Gibbs.

ST. JOHN'S EPISCOPAL CHURCH, Barrington Center—Rev. William S. Chapin, pastor. Sunday services, 7.45 and 10.45 A. M., 5.15 P. M.

ST. MATTHEW'S CHAPEL, West Barrington—Services the first Sunday of each month, at 9 A. M.; October to May, 4 P. M.; May to October, 5 P. M.

BARRINGTON SCHOOLS.

Chester R. Shaw, Superintendent.

PECK MEMORIAL SCHOOL—County road, next town hall, Barrington. Chester R. Shaw, Principal.

HAMPDEN MEADOWS SCHOOL—New Meadows road.

GEORGE T. BAKER SCHOOL—Lincoln avenue, West Barrington.

NAYATT SCHOOL—Rumstick road, near Nayatt road, Barrington.

BARRINGTON PUBLIC LIBRARY.

Mrs. Emma S. Bradford, Librarian. Trustees, Frank O. Field, William M. Chapin, Ebenezer Tiffany, George T. Baker, Everett L. Spencer. Library open, Tuesday, Thursday and Saturday afternoons and Saturday evenings.

CEMETERIES.

FOREST CHAPEL—Off Nayatt avenue.

THE PRINCESS HILL CEMETERY—County road, east of Town Hall.

TYLER'S CEMETERY—Off County road, Barrington Centre.

Opp. Inside Back Cover

JOHN R. RICHARDS

J. CRAVIN, Manager

Where you get a square deal on ANYTHING in the Monumental line.

THE LARGEST RETAIL WORKS IN NEW ENGLAND

977 North Main St., Providence, R. I.

Telephone 2293 Angell

Providence Pawtucket Cars stop, Cemetery Street

THE W. E. BARRETT CO.
Corner Canal and Waterman Streets
PROVIDENCE, R. I.
1848 — OLDEST SEED STORE IN R. I. — 1918

SEEDS

FARM

SPR   )ES

Large Illustrated Catalog Free to All
Get Your Name On Our Mailing List

TYPEWRITERS

All makes Sold, Rented, Exchanged and Repaired

Typewriter Supplies

AGENTS FOR CORONA TYPEWRITER

Neilan Typewriter Exchange

43 Weybosset Street - - - Providence, R. I.

Telephone Union 1047

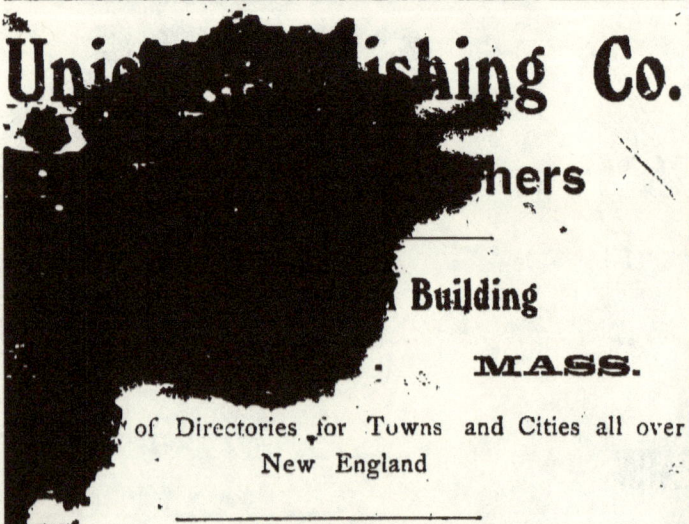

Union Publishing Co.

Publishers

Building

MASS.

of Directories for Towns and Cities all over New England

For RHODE ISLAND as follows:

Bristol, Warren and Barrington Directory
Burrillville and North Smithfield Directory
Cumberland and Lincoln Directory
Jamestown and New Shoreham Directory
North Providence, Johnston and Smithfield Directory
Pawtuxet Valley Directory
Tiverton, Portsmouth and Middletown Directory
Warwick, E. Greenwich and No. Kingstown Directory

www.ingramcontent.com/pod-product-compliance
Lightning Source LLC
Chambersburg PA
CBHW031946230426
43672CB00010B/2063